Compensation of Private Losses

The Evolution of Torts in European Business Law

edited by
Reiner Schulze

sellier.
european law
publishers

ISBN (print) 978-3-86653-175-8
ISBN (eBook) 978-3-86653-934-1

The Deutsche Nationalbibliothek lists this publication in the Deutsche National-bibliografie; detailed bibliographic data are available on the Internet at http://dnb.d-nb.de.

© 2011 by sellier. european law publishers GmbH, Munich.

All rights reserved. No part of this publication may be reproduced, translated, stored in a retrieval system or transmitted, in any form or by any means, electronic, mechanical, photocopying, recording or otherwise, without prior permission of the publisher.

Production: Karina Hack, Munich. Typesetting: fidus Publikations-Service GmbH, Nördlingen. Printing and binding: AZ Druck und Datentechnik, Kempten. Printed on acid-free, non-ageing paper. Printed in Germany.

Foreword

In November 2010, the Round Table "New Challenges in European Private Law" once again brought academics and experts together in Münster at the Centre for European Private Law. This second Round Table concerned the subject of the evolution of torts in European business law, focusing in particular on the questions of compensation of private losses based upon new European legislation and case law in fields such as competition law, capital market law and company law. With this topic the Centre for European Private law continued the debate on the role of business law within European private law, following on, in particular, from the European Law Days 2010 (see Reiner Schulze/Hans Schulte-Nölke (eds) European Private Law – Current Status and Perspectives, 2011). This volume therefore contains the results of the intensive discussions and papers presented over the course of the Round Table.

As in the aforementioned volume, the hard work and efforts of the authors and publishers have once again ensured that the results of the conference have been published within a relatively short period of time. As editor of this volume, I wish to kindly thank all those who assisted in the publication, in particular the laudable support and contribution given by my research assistants *Daniela Schmidt, Jana Pannemann* and *Jonathon Watson*.

Special thanks is owed to Pöllath & Partner, especially *Prof. Dr. Reinhard Pöllath*. Without their generous and kind support it would not have been possible to host the conference or to allow publication of this volume. Furthermore, Reinhard Pöllath's invaluable comments and support during the preparatory stages ensured that this conference approached the issue of torts in European business law.

Münster, March 2011 *Reiner Schulze*

Table of Contents

Foreword   v

Part I
General Aspects of European Tort Law

The Evolution of Torts in European Business Law   3
Reiner Schulze

**The Experiences in National Legal Systems and
the Perspectives of EU Tort Law**   19
Bernhard A. Koch

**General Principles of Tort Law in the
Jurisprudence of the European Court of Justice**   39
Wolfgang Wurmnest / Christian Heinze

Part II
Specific Areas of European Tort Law

Product Liability and the European Tort Landscape   69
Geraint Howells

**Damages for the Infringement of
Intellectual Property Rights under EU Law**   75
Piotr Machnikowski

**The Significance of the Law of Tort with the Example of
the Civil Liability for Erroneous ad hoc Disclosure**   91
Matthias Casper

Table of Contents

Infringement of the Prohibition of
Unfair Commercial Practices and Tort Law 115
Giovanni De Cristofaro

Personenbeförderungs- und Reiserecht 133
Ansgar Staudinger

Part III
Private versus Public Enforcement

Private Losses in European Competition Law:
Public or Private Enforcement? 157
Petra Pohlmann

The Law of Damages and Competition Law:
Bien étonnés de se trouver ensemble? 165
Willem H. van Boom

Private versus Public Enforcement of Laws –
a Law & Economics perspective 179
Lars Klöhn

Part IV
Interaction with Neighbouring Fields

Rechtsvergleichende Beobachtungen zum
Ineinandergreifen von Vertrags- und Deliktsrecht in Europa 201
Christian von Bar

Liability Insurance 213
Helmut Heiss

Part V
Panel Discussion

Statements on the question:
"Are there General Concepts and Principles of Compensation in EU Law?"

Developing General Concepts and Common Principles of EU Tort Law   235
Wolfgang Wurmnest

Why Should One Size Fit All?
A Call for a Differentiated Look on the Renewed European Approach Towards Private Enforcement   237
Konrad Ost, Peter Gussone

Contributors

Christian von Bar, Professor of Civil Law, Comparative Law, European Private and International Private Law, Universität Osnabrück, Germany.

Willem van Boom, Professor of Private Law, Erasmus Universiteit Rotterdam, the Netherlands.

Matthias Casper, Professor of Civil Law, Company Law, Banking Law and Capital Market Law, Westfälische Wilhelms-Universität Münster, Germany.

Giovanni De Cristofaro, Professor of Private Law and Consumer Law, Università di Ferrara, Italy.

Peter Gussone, Dr., European Competition Network (ECN) Coordination at the Bundeskartellamt, Bonn, Germany.

Helmut Heiss, Professor of Private Law, International Private Law and Comparative Law, Universität Zürich, Switzerland.

Christian Heinze, Dr., LL.M. (Cambridge), Max Planck Institute for Comparative and International Private Law, Hamburg, Germany.

Geraint Howells, Professor of Commercial Law, University of Manchester, United Kingdom.

Lars Klöhn, Professor of Civil Law, Commerical Law, Business Law, Comparative Law and Law & Economics, Philipps-Universität Marburg, Germany.

Bernhard A. Koch, Professor of Civil Law and Comparative Law, Universität Innsbruck, Austria.

Piotr Machnikowski, Professor of Civil Law and International Private Law, Uniwersytet Wrocławiu, Poland.

Contributors

Konrad Ost, Dr., LL.M. (Cambridge), Head of the General Policy Division of the Bundeskartellamt, Bonn, Germany.

Petra Pohlmann, Professor of Civil Law, Commercial Law and Civil Procedure, Westfälische Wilhelms-Universität Münster, Germany.

Reiner Schulze, Professor of German and European Civil Law, Westfälische Wilhelms-Universität Münster, Germany.

Ansgar Staudinger, Professor of Civil Law, International Private Law, Procedural Law and Business Law, Universität Bielefeld, Germany.

Wolfgang Wurmnest, Professor of Private Law, Economic Law, Comparative and Private Law, Leibniz Universität Hannover, Germany.

Part I
General Aspects of European Tort Law

The Evolution of Torts in European Business Law

Reiner Schulze

I. Contractual and Non-contractual Liability in European Business Law

In addition to contract law, non-contractual liability is one of the core areas of European private law. Yet it is with good reason that contract law currently stands at the fore of legislative and academic work in this particular field: over past decades, comparative law and research into EU law have suggested common principles and model rules for European contract law, in particular.[1] On this basis, it presently remains to be discussed whether the future EU legislation for this field should be drafted on the basis of a common frame of reference and whether an optional European contract law shall be created via a European regulation.[2]

---

[1] Examples of such common principles and model rules are: *Ole Lando/Hugh Beale* (eds.), Principles of European Contract Law, Parts I and II, The Hague 2000 ("PECL"); *Ole Lando et al.* (eds.), Principles of European Contract Law, Part III, The Hague 2003 ("PECL"); *Giuseppe Gandolfi* (ed.), Code Européen des contracts, Avant-projet, Milano 2002 ("Gandolfi Principles"); *Research Group on the Existing EC Private Law (Acquis Group)* (ed.), Principles of the Existing EC Contract Law ("ACQP") – Contract II, Munich 2009; *Bénédicte Fauvarque-Cosson et al.* (eds.), Principes contractuels communs. Projet de cadre commun de référence, Paris 2008; *Bénédicte Fauvarque-Cosson et al.* (eds.), Terminologie contractuelle commune. Projet de cadre commun de reference, Paris 2008; *Christian von Bar et al.* (eds.), Principles, Definitions and Model Rules of European Private Law, Draft Common Frame of Reference ("DCFR"), Outline Edition, Munich 2009; *Christian von Bar/Eric Clive* (eds.), Principles, Definitions and Model Rules of European Private Law, Draft Common Frame of Reference ("DCFR"), Full Edition, Munich 2009.

[2] Communication from the Commission to the European Parliament and the Council – A more coherent European Contract Law – An action plan, COM(2003) 68 final, O.J. (2003) C 63/27; Green Paper from the Commission on policy options for progress towards a European Contract Law for consumers and businesses,

However, in order to create a stable framework for the development of economic transactions and the development of private autonomy, the European Union also requires the protection of the rights of the individual and of the community. In this respect, the functioning of the Internal Market is not only dependent upon a suitable contract law, but also on legal instruments that secure, with respect to non-contractual liability, the ambit of contracting between private parties. As to contract law, the question is also asked in this regard of whether this can only occur within the national framework or whether legal science – and possibly, in part, the EU institutions – can develop common standards and should promote closer links or even an approximation of laws. This question may have indeed gained greater significance since the Charter of Fundamental Rights became binding law. Its validity underlines, above all, that the protection of an individual's rights and legitimate interests – beyond the development of the Internal Market – is an important matter for the EU as a legal community founded on common values.[3] The Charter of Fundamental Rights therefore increases the necessity to approach the role of non-contractual liability, within the scope of European law, in protecting the individual.

II. Non-contractual Liability in EU Legislation and Jurisprudence

The legislative organs of the EU appear to be thoroughly aware of the growing challenges in this regard. Over past decades, a considerable acquis communautaire has developed in EU secondary law which concerns the non-contractual liability vis-à-vis private persons. In this respect, one can give the examples of product liability[4], non-contractual liability for

---

COM(2010) 348 final, pp. 8 et seq.; Commission Decision of 26 April 2010 setting up the Expert Group on a Common Frame of Reference in the area of European Contract Law, 2010/233/EU, O.J. (2010) L 105/109.

[3] Cf. inter alia *Vasiliki Kosta*, Internal Market Legislation and the Private Law of the Member States – The Impact of Fundamental Rights, (2010) European Review of Contract Law (ERCL), 409 et seq.; *Thorsten Kingreen*, Grundrechtsverband oder Grundrechtsunion? – Zur Entwicklung der subjektiv-öffentlichen Rechte im europäischen Unionsrecht, (2010) Europarecht (EuR), 338 et seq.

[4] Council Directive 85/374/EEC of 25 July 1985 on the approximation of the laws, regulations and administrative provisions of the Member States concerning liability for defective products, O.J. (1985) L 210/29 and Directive 1999/34/EC of

the carriage of passengers and transports (i.a. in air and train travel)[5], the non-contractual liability in competition law (with a basis in the Treaty itself[6]), the liability in capital market law of the issuer or board members[7], the non-contractual liability for an infringement of intellectual property rights[8], non-contractual liability for discriminatory acts[9], infringement of

---

the European Parliament and of the Council of 10 May 1999 amending Council Directive 85/374/EEC on the approximation of the laws, regulations and administrative provisions of the Member States concerning liability for defective products, O.J. (1999) L 141/20.

[5] Regulation (EC) No 261/2004 of the European Parliament and of the Council of 11 February 2004 establishing common rules on compensation and assistance to passengers in the event of denied boarding and of cancellation or long delay of flights, and repealing Regulation, O.J. (2004) L 46/1; Regulation (EC) No 1371/2007 of the European Parliament and of the Council of 23 October 2007 on rail passengers' rights and obligations, O.J. (2007) L 315/14; Regulation (EC) No 392/2009 of the European Parliament and of the Council of 23 April 2009 on the liability of carriers of passengers by sea in the event of accidents, O.J. (2009) L 131/24.

[6] See ECJ, joined cases C-295/04 & C-298/04 *Vincenzo Manfredi and Others v Lloyd and Adriatico Assicurazioni SpA and others*, [2006] ECR I-6619; ECJ, C-453/99 *Courage Ltd v Bernard Crehan* and *Bernard Crehan v Courage Ltd and others*, [2001] ECR I-6297.

[7] In particular, Directive 2003/6/EC of the European Parliament and of the Council of 28 January 2003 on insider dealing and market manipulation (market abuse), O.J. (2003) L 96/16; Commission Directive 2004/72/EC of 29 April 2004 implementing Directive 2003/6/EC of the European Parliament and of the Council as regards accepted market practices, the definition of inside information in relation to derivatives on commodities, the drawing up of lists of insiders, the notification of managers' transactions and the notification of suspicious transactions, O.J. (2004) L 162/70.

[8] Directive 2004/48/EC of the European Parliament and of the Council of 29 April 2004 on the enforcement of intellectual property rights, O.J. (2004) L 157/32; Corrigendum to Directive 2004/48/EC of the European Parliament and of the Council of 29 April 2004 on the enforcement of intellectual property rights, O.J. (2004) L 195/16.

[9] Council Directive 2000/43/EC of 29 June 2000 implementing the principle of equal treatment between persons irrespective of racial or ethnic origin, O.J. (2000) L 180/22; Council Directive 2000/78/EC of 27 November 2000 establishing a general framework for equal treatment in employment and occupation, O.J. (2000) L 303/16; Council Directive 2004/113/EC of 13 December 2004 implementing the principle of equal treatment between men and women in the access to and supply

data protection rights[10] and environmental liability[11]. In addition, one is to also note the extensiveness of the jurisprudence of the European Court of Justice (ECJ) and Court of First Instance based upon Art. 340 par. 2 TFEU (ex. Art. 288 par. 2 EC) and on the liability of the Member States according to EU law.

III. Challenges for Research

1. Research Approaches

Since a number of years, research has focused upon the question of overarching principles for non-contractual liability on European level. However, as was originally the case with contract law, such research into non-contractual liability in European private law was initially primarily based upon comparative studies of national laws.[12] Amongst the many comparative law research projects in this field, one can particularly speak of two important and extensive research projects: the "Principles of European Tort Law" (PETL) drafted by the European Group on Tort Law[13] and the draft of the

---

of goods and services, O.J. (2004) L 373/37; Directive 2006/54/EC of the European Parliament and of the Council of 5 July 2006 on the implementation of the principle of equal opportunities and equal treatment of men and women in matters of employment and occupation (recast), O.J. (2006) L 204/23.

[10] Directive 95/46/EC of the European Parliament and of the Council of 24 October 1995 on the protection of individuals with regard to the processing of personal data and on the free movement of such data, O.J. (1995) L 281/31.

[11] Directive 2004/35/EC of the European Parliament and of the Council of 21 April 2004 on environmental liability with regard to the prevention and remedying of environmental damage; O.J. (2004) L 143/56.

[12] In particular, *Christian von Bar* (ed.), Deliktsrecht in Europa: Systematische Einführungen, Gesetzestexte, Übersetzungen, Köln et al. 1993-1994; *Christian von Bar*, The Common European Law of Torts. Volume I: The Core Areas of Tort Law, its Approximation in Europe, and its Accomodation in the Legal Systems, Oxford 1998; *Christian von Bar*, The Common European Law of Torts. Volume II: Damage and Damages, Liability for and without Personal Misconduct, Causality, and Defences, Oxford 2000; *Reinhard Zimmermann* (ed.), Grundstrukturen des Europäischen Deliktsrechts, Baden-Baden 2003.

[13] *European Group on Tort Law* (ed.), Principles of European Tort Law: Text and Commentary, Wien 2005.

"Non-contractual liability arising out of damage caused to another" in Book VI of the Draft Common Frame of Reference[14] (DCFR) based upon work undertaken by the "Study Group"[15].

In a similar manner as to where contract law is concerned, over past years one can also observe a methodological change for non-contractual liability in European private law.in addition to the comparative studies, an increasing amount of research has been undertaken with regard to the question of European tort law principles or non-contractual liability in existing EU law. Whilst the comparative approach sought "common principles" or "best solutions" on the basis of national laws, the latter research approach is concerned with EU primary and secondary legislation, including the jurisprudence case law of the European Courts (i.e. the "acquis communautaire"), in seeking and determining general principles for European private law. In this respect, the research undertaken by *Wolfgang Wurmnest* on the *"Grundzüge eines europäischen Haftungsrechts"*[16] (The main features of a European liability law) was groundbreaking for tort law: an aspect of the research addressed the individual legal areas of Community law (now Union law) to the extent that an acquis communautaire had developed with relevance for non-contractual liability. Over recent years, further studies have expanded the overview of non-contractual liability in EU law and deepened its relationship to corresponding principles in national laws.[17] With respect to present European law, a further perspective is the comparison of liability principles in EU law with their counterparts in the European Convention

---

[14] DCFR, Full Edition (n. 1).

[15] *Study Group on a European Civil Code* (ed.), Principles of European Law – Non-Contractual Liability Arising out of Damage Caused to Another, Munich 2009.

[16] *Wolfgang Wurmnest*, Grundzüge eines europäischen Haftungsrechts. Eine rechtsver-gleichende Untersuchung des Gemeinschaftsrechts, Tübingen 2003.

[17] For example, *Helmut Koziol/Reiner Schulze* (eds.), Tort Law of the European Community, Wien 2008; including inter alia Aims and Scope *(Denis N. Kelliher)*; Damage *(Antoni Vaquer)*; Causation *(Isabelle C. Durant)*; Fault Liability *(Meinhard Lukas)*; Environmental Liability *(Monika Hinteregger)*; Is European Product Liability Harmonised? *(Geraint Howells)*; Other Strict Liabilities *(Bernhard A. Koch)*; Liability for Others *(Miquel Martín-Casals/Josep Solé Feliu)*; Non-contractual Liability in Damages of Member States for Breach of Community Law *(Robert Rebhahn)*; Community Liability *(Luisa Antoniolli)*; The Nature and Assessment of Damages *(Ken Oliphant)*; Limitations of Liability under EC Tort Law *(Ulrich Magnus)*; Limitation Periods in EC Law *(André Pereira)*; Terminology *(Martin Weitenberg)*; An Overview of Common Elements *(Marc Wissink)* and comparisons of the EU Tort Law with different legal systems and families.

on Human Rights and the corresponding jurisprudence of the European Court of Human Rights.[18] Furthermore, one can also note that the "Acquis Group"[19] is considering succeeding its "Principles of the Existing EC Contract Law"[20] with a similar draft concerning the principles of the existing EU law with respect to non-contractual liability.

These research projects regarding the EU law of non-contractual liability are faced with a number of challenges with respect to their terminology and methodology. These challenges will require in-depth discussion; however, only some of these questions will be briefly outlined in the scope of this paper.

2. Terminology

From the research undertaken thus far, one can note that no uniform terminology exists to describe the particular subject-matter. The term "European tort law" is commonly used;[21] however the adoption of the English terminology does not mean that the English terms "tort" and "tort law" – as developed in the common law tradition – can simply be adopted at European level, too.[22] The term "tort" must rather gain its own "autonomous" meaning when it is used in the European context – a problem that is also faced by a large part of the terminology in European private law (from "reasonable" grounds to "trust").

However, a similar problem is also posed by adopting the term of "delictual liability" ("deliktische Haftung" or "responsabilité délictuelle"), or similar terms (such as "responsabilité civile") from the terminology of civil law jurisdictions. In comparison, the term "non-contractual liability" offers the advantage of referring, to a lesser extent, to one of the larger Western

---

[18] Jan-Thomas Oskierski, Schadensersatz im Europäischen Recht. Eine vergleichende Untersuchung des Acquis Communautaire und der EMRK, Baden-Baden 2010.

[19] Research Group on the Existing EC Private Law (Acquis Group); information about the Acquis Group and the Acquis Principles can be accessed via the Group's homepage: http://www.acquis-group.org.

[20] ACQP (n. 1).

[21] Cf. for example, Principles of European Tort Law (n. 13); Helmut Koziol/Reiner Schulze (n. 17); Martin Immenhauser, Das Dogma von Vertrag und Delikt, Köln 2006, pp. 22 et seq.

[22] Cf. the concerns in DCFR, Full Edition (n. 1), p. 3089 and Christian von Bar, Außervertragliche Haftung für den einen anderem zugefügten Schaden, (2010) ERPL, 205, in particular p. 209.

legal traditions, thereby also appearing relatively "neutral". It does, however, have the disadvantage of only expressing the distinction to contractual liability. It indeed remains undetermined whether (and which) legal fields are incorporated beyond those which usually denote the one tradition as "tort law" and the other as "delictual liability". As an example thereof, one can note the relationship to unjustified enrichment, to benevolent intervention in another's affairs or to the pre-contractual duties. A partial attempt is made by the DCFR to avoid this disadvantage through its description of the subject of its Book VI: "Non-contractual liability arising out of damage caused to another". This denotation offers the advantage that the subject-matter of the book is relatively clearly defined without referring too greatly to individual legal traditions. However, it appears to be so unwieldy that it is not particularly practicable for use in practice or legal education.

3. Acquiring Principles

With respect to the method applied in order to acquire principles of European private law for this field of tort law and non-contractual liability respectively, the aforementioned approaches have been adopted in research: on the one hand the comparison of national laws, on the other hand the analysis of existing EU law. For each of these approaches, the corresponding work on European contract law could serve as a paradigm.[23] Nevertheless, the approaches and experiences from contract law cannot simply be adopted for non-contractual liability. One has to rather bear in mind the idiosyncrasies of this field where each of the approaches are concerned.

a) Common Principles of National Tort Laws?

With respect to the comparison of national laws, this particularly concerns the status of the academic and legislative preparation of a development of common principles. The research into principles of European contract law was able to build upon a relatively long tradition of comparative work already undertaken with the objective of recognising and developing common elements of the national legal traditions. The way was paved in 1936 by *Ernst Rabel* with his work *"Recht des Warenkaufs"*[24] (Law on the sale of

---

[23] See PECL (n. 1); ACQP (n. 1).
[24] *Ernst Rabel*, Das Recht des Warenkaufs. Eine rechtsvergleichende Darstellung, 2 volumes, Tübingen/Berlin 1936 and 1957 (Reprinted in 1964).

goods). The Haag uniform sales law and the Vienna Convention on the International Sale of Goods (CISG) introduced in many European countries common principles, at least for numerous cross-border transactions and often influenced the national legislation on domestic contract law (in new[25] and old[26] EU Member States). Furthermore, the CISG was an important source of inspiration for the European legislation on contract law, in particular for the Consumer Sales Directive 1999/44/EC[27].

In contrast, the drafting of common principles on a comparative basis has not been prepared for the field of non-contractual liability through a similarly strong academic and legislative tradition. Although one can refer here to the economic and social developments, several international conventions and the cross-border circulation of legal perceptions for the emergence of common tendencies and increasing consistency in national laws, there is nevertheless the absence of a common, binding legal text of similar significance as the CISG. It is therefore hardly surprising that the two prominent drafts by international working groups for European principles of non-contractual liability (the Principles of European Tort Law[28] and Book VI of the DCFR[29]) are more greatly distinct from one another than in the field of contract law, e.g. the Principles of European Contract Law

---

[25] Cf. for example, for Lithuania, *Vytautas Mizaras/Vytautas Nekrosius*, Das neue Zivil- und Zivilprozessrecht in Litauen, (2002) Zeitschrift für Europäisches Privatrecht (ZEuP), 466, 467.

[26] Cf. for example the "Schuldrechtsmodernisierung" (Modernisation of the Law of Obligations) in Germany in 2002 the legislation reasoning for the proposal on the modernisation on the law of obligations, BT-Drucksache 14/6040, pp. 86, 89, 92 et seq., 135, 176 et seq., 196, 208 et seq., 217 et seq., 220, 223, 237 et seq., 267 et seq., 284; *Reiner Schulze/Hans Schulte-Nölke*, Schuldrechtsreform und Gemeinschaftsrecht, in: Reiner Schulze/Hans Schulte-Nölke (eds.), Die Schuldrechtsreform vor dem Hintergrund des Gemeinschaftsrechts, Tübingen 2001, pp. 10 et seq; *André Janssen/Reiner Schulze*, Legal Cultures and Legal Transplants in Germany, (2011) ERPL, 225, 240 et seq.

[27] Directive 1999/44/EC of the European Parliament and of the Council of 25 May 1999 on certain aspects of the sale of consumer goods and associated guarantees, O.J. (1999) L 171/12; for the influence of the CISG on this directive see *Dirk Staudenmayer*, Die EG-Richtlinie über den Verbrauchsgüterkauf, (1999) Neue Juristische Wochenschrift (NJW), 2393 et seq.

[28] PETL (n. 13); see on this *Helmut Koziol*, Die "Principles of European Tort Law" der "European Group on Tort Law", (2004) ZEuP, 234 et seq.

[29] DCFR, Full Edition (n. 1); see on this *Christian von Bar*, Non-Contractual Liability Arising out of Damage Caused to Another under the DCFR, (2008) ERA Forum,

(PECL) drafted by the "Lando Commission"[30] and the Books II and III of the DCFR (which do not coincidentally exhibit similarities to the PECL). The distinctions concern, to a great extent, the content of these drafts and, to an even greater extent, the concept and coverage of the drafts as a whole. These drafts on non-contractual liability will therefore be able to claim, to a lesser extent than the aforementioned drafts on European contract law, to consistently represent "common principles" or an "acquis commun"[31] of European private law. Indeed, they do reflect, to a large part, similarities and approximations of national law; however, they often reflect these in different manners and are therefore rather to be understood as an (often controversial) suggestion of the individual groups of authors for – in their view – "best solutions" in the field of non-contractual liability.

b) General Principles of EU-Tort Law?

The research into principles of non-contractual liability on the basis of existing EU law will equally be able to use the experiences from the corresponding work on European contract law, though only under consideration of the peculiarities of its field. Indeed, the objectives correspond to a great extent to those of the drafts on contract law:[32] to be examined is how overarching basic principles and the values underlying the individual Treaty clauses, legal acts and court decisions in the acquis communautaire can be determined in order that they can be used as a guideline for doctrine and also to possibly obtain legislation and jurisprudence with respect to non-contractual liability in EU law. This first requires taking stock of the nu-

---

33 et seq.; *Christian von Bar*, Konturen des Deliktsrechts der Study Group on a European Civil Code – Ein Werkstattbericht, (2001) ZEuP, 515 et seq.

[30] Cf. PECL (n. 1).

[31] Cf. to this term *Nils Jansen/Reinhard Zimmermann*, Grundregeln des bestehenden Gemeinschaftsprivatrechts?, (2007) Juristenzeitung (JZ), 1113, in particular 1118 et seq. (english version: *Nils Jansen/Reinhard Zimmermann*, Restating the Acquis communautaire? A Critical Examination of the "Principles of the Existing EC Contact Law", (2008) Modern Law Review, 505, in particular 516 et seq.); *Fryderyk Zoll*, Die Grundregeln der Acquis-Gruppe im Spannungsverhältnis zwischen acquis commun und acquis communautaire, (2008) Zeitschrift für Gemeinschaftsprivatrecht (GPR), 106, 107 et seq.

[32] *Reiner Schulze*, European Private Law and Existing EC Law, (2005) ERPL, 3 et seq.; *Reiner Schulze*, Gemeinsamer Referenzrahmen und acquis communautaire, (2007) ZEuP, 130 et seq.

merous, unclear individual provisions and court decisions which concern non-contractual liability. However, these provisions and decisions are not only to be viewed as isolated individual acts. The analysis and comparison have to rather stem from the questions concerning the underlying maxims or principles, whether these principles or maxims possibly form a common basis for more legal acts and decisions and whether they thus possibly have general significance for a section or the entire field of non-contractual liability in EU law.[33] The question also has to be approached with regard, inter alia, to many individual provisions and court decisions, which concern, for instance, causation, accountability for acts of third parties (or "vicarious liability"), the scope of damages (also with regard to non-pecuniary damages) or contributory negligence (to give but a few examples).

However, where non-contractual liability is concerned, one will, in each case, have to carefully examine the extent to which such principles can be generalised; these principles, which cover the entirety of this legal field, may possibly play a lesser role than in contract law.[34] The differences between individual "liability regimes"[35] (for instance product liability, liability for infringement of intellectual property rights etc.) could rather require a limitation – with respect to non-contractual liability – of the extent of the principles. Furthermore, it is also to be considered how the relatively extensive jurisprudence of the ECJ on the liability of the Union and the Member States towards private parties relates to other areas of liability. On the one hand, peculiarities may result therefrom that it concerns the liability of the Union and of the Member States. On the other hand the jurisprudence on this liability is concerned with many general questions of liability law (such

---

[33] Cf. *Reiner Schulze/Hans Schulte-Nölke*, Europäisches Vertragsrecht im Gemeinschafts-recht, in: Hans Schulte-Nölke/Reiner Schulze together with Ludovic Bernardeau, European Contract Law in Community Law, Köln 2002, pp. 11 et seq. at p. 15; *Reiner Schulze,* Der Acquis Communautaire und die Entwicklung des europäischen Vertragsrechts, in: Reiner Schulze/Martin Ebers/Hans Christoph Grigoleit (eds.), Informationspflichten und Vertragsschluss im Acquis communautaire, Tübingen 2003, pp. 3, 5 et seq.

[34] For contract law, cf. ACQP (n. 1); DCFR, Full Edition (n. 1), in particular introduction Nr. 57 in DCFR, Outline Edition (n. 1), e.g. *Giovanni De Cristofaro* (ed.), I "principi" del diritto comunitario dei contratti – acquis communautaire e diritto privato europeo, Torino 2009.

[35] See *Wolfgang Wurmnest,* (n. 16), p. 72, 87.

as causation[36], the concept of damage[37], and the nature of damages[38]). With regard to the non-contractual liability of the Union, Art. 340 par. 2 TFEU expressly refers to the general principles common to the laws of the Member States. This also supports the consideration of the general principles of the jurisprudence of the ECJ on the liability of the Union and of the Member States when enquiring about such general principles of non-contractual liability, including damages, in EU law.

4. Non-contractual Liability and Business Law

A crucial task and opportunity for research into non-contractual liability at European level stems from the strong focus of EU policy and legislation on matters of business law. Such matters in this central field of European private law are, for example, competition law (in a narrow sense – as antitrust law) and unfair commercial practices, commercial and company law, capital market law and intellectual property law. These matters are mostly not covered (or only marginally) in the civil codes of the 19th century – such as the French Code civil, the Spanish Código civil or the German BGB with its pandectic background.[39] The same is also true for employment law and consumer law. Both of these legal fields are, to a certain extent, linked with business law as they regulate the legal relationship of business to other participants in legal relations (the employees or consumers). The adoption of such fields in national civil codes is frequently rejected because they are, in comparison to general provisions and doctrines of the civil law, "special fields" of private law or "special private law".[40]

---

[36] Cf. *Isabelle C. Durant*, Causation, in: Helmut Koziol/Reiner Schulze (eds.), (n. 17), pp. 47 et seq., pp. 51 et seq.; in the same volume: *Martin Weitenberg*, Terminology, pp. 309 et seq., pp. 335 et seq.; *Jan-Thomas Oskierski*, (n. 18), p. 41.

[37] Cf. *Antoni Vaquer*, Damage, in: Helmut Koziol/Reiner Schulze (eds.), (n. 17), pp. 23 et seq.

[38] Cf. *Ken Oliphant*, The Nature and Assessment of Damages, in: Helmut Koziol/Reiner Schulze (eds.), (n. 17), pp. 241 et seq.; *Jan-Thomas Oskierski*, (n. 18).

[39] See *Reiner Schulze*, Contours of European Private Law, in: Reiner Schulze/Hans Schulte-Nölke (eds.), European Private Law – Current Status and Perspectives, Munich 2011, p. 3, in particular pp. 6 et seq.

[40] With respect to the discussion on this issues *Hans-Wolfgang Micklitz*, in: Münchner Kommentar zum Bürgerlichen Gesetzbuch, volume I, 5th edition, München 2006, Vorbemerkung §§ 13, 14, Rn. 15 et seq.; *Karsten Schmidt*, Die Zukunft der

With regard to "unity of private law", the question is however to be asked of how such special fields and traditional matters of civil law – such as contract law or the non-contractual liability (or tort law) – are to be jointly administered in an overarching perspective. For the European private law, such an overarching perspective can not unilaterally emanate from the traditional matters and principles of the "pure" civil codes of the 19th century. One has to rather consider the experiences of a growing number of European countries that, since this time, have integrated a large part of these special fields into their civil codes – for example the Netherlands and (with respect to civil and business law) Italy. For the present development of EU private law one has to also consider that the aforementioned field of business law, as well as employment law and consumer law, are not marginal areas. Intensive research is therefore required for the extent to which the emerging new concepts, legal institutions and principles can have general significance for private law.

With respect to contract law, the recently published "Acquis Principles"[41] are also based upon the examination of numerous legal fields that, in following the traditional separation in several national civil codes, are not to be assigned to civil law, but rather to business law and consumer law. For example, it is shown in this research that, in the acquis communitaire, traditional matters of civil law are linked with matters and instruments of business law e.g. to e-commerce[42] or payment services[43]. Above all, they have shown that provisions from EU legal acts, which were only passed for a specific field, can be based upon principles that are of wider-reaching significance. Thus, several provisions of the Consumer Sales Directive[44] are based upon principles that can be significant for core matters of contract law, such as fulfilment of obligations and the remedies for non-performance, and not

---

Kodifikationsidee, Heidelberg 1985, pp. 11 et seq.; *Babara Dauner-Lieb*, Verbraucherschutz durch Ausbildung eines Sonderprivatrechts für Verbraucher, Berlin 1983.

[41] ACQP (n. 1).

[42] Directive 2000/31/EC of the European Parliament and of the Council of 8 June 2000 on certain legal aspects of information society services, in particular electronic commerce, in the Internal Market (Directive on electronic commerce), O.J. (2000) L 178/1.

[43] Directive 2007/64/EC of the European Parliament and of the Council of 13 November 2007 on payment services in the internal market amending Directives 97/7/EC, 2002/65/EC, 2005/60/EC and 2006/48/EC and repealing Directive 97/5/EC, O.J. (2007) L 319/1.

[44] Directive 1999/44/EC (n. 27).

just for consumer law.[45] This is not surprising given that these principles of EU consumer contract law have their origins in the CISG, i.e. from a law primarily conceived for transactions between businesses. During the transposition of the Consumer Sales Directive within the framework of the *"Schuldrechtsmodernisierung"*[46] (Modernisation of the Law of Obligations) these principles even became, in part, a basis of general contract law and the law of obligations in Germany.

Similarly, a further matter which will have to be examined for non-contractual liability is the extent to which concepts, institutions and principles can be recognised within the "special fields" – and particularly in the various aspects of business law – and which are of general importance for many of these fields and possibly for extra-contractual liability as a whole. The evolution of torts (or of non-contractual liability) is, in this respect, not to be viewed as a "pure civil law" matter, independent from business law and other "special fields" of European private law. The evolution rather covers many areas of European private law including matters of business law. In accordance with the aforementioned approach in the research on Principles of the Existing EU Law[47], of moving from specific to general, one should therefore not neglect the (often quite broad) acquis communautaire in the various aspects of business law when attempting to ascertain basic tenets for non-contractual liability and torts, respectively, in European private law.

IV. Compensation of Private Losses

The inclusion of business law in the research into European tort law can arise through the closer examination of the acquis communautaire; however by examining specific aspects, or legal matters, including all the various areas of the EU law concerned with non-contractual liability. In doing so, such a cross-sectional study allows for an overview of the legislation, jurisprudence and doctrine of EU law to be obtained which goes beyond the boundaries of the individual policies and sections. It can therefore contribute to the recognition of overarching tasks, tendencies in development and potential common tenets and legal principles in many aspects of private law.

---

[45] See, for the generalisation of these provisions of the directives the comments to Art. 7:101 et seq. and Art. 8:101 et seq. ACQP (n. 1), pp. 339 et seq., 401 et seq.
[46] Supra n. 26.
[47] *Reiner Schulze/Hans Schulte-Nölke*, (n. 33).

The following contributions to this volume attempt to obtain such a cross-sectional overview with respect to several questions concerning the compensation of private losses, focussing primarily on business law[48]. The contributions to this volume consider methodological starting points of general significance for European tort law.[49] The main parts are, however, devoted to the compensation of private losses in specific areas of European tort law. This volume focuses on a number of different aspects, including intellectual property rights[50], capital market law[51], unfair commercial practices[52] and transport and travel law[53]. Furthermore, the relationship between the law of damages and competition law has particularly become of relevance through recent ECJ jurisprudence[54]. The development of the compensation of private losses in this field requires a general enquiry into the significance of private enforcement and public enforcement therein.[55] Alongside these disciplines of business law, product liability has been included a complementary element of European private law.[56] Moreover, the following repeats two statements on the general concepts and principles of

---

[48] The participating academics met at a "Round Table" held in November 2010 at the Centre for European Private Law, Münster.

[49] Bernhard A. Koch, The Experiences in National Legal Systems and the Perspectives of EU Tort Law, in this volume; *Wolfgang Wurmnest/Christian Heinze*, General Principles of Tort Law in the Jurisprudence of the European Court of Justice, in this volume.

[50] *Piotr Machnikowski*, Damages for the Infringement of Intellectual Property Rights under EU Law, in this volume.

[51] *Matthias Casper*, The Significance of the Law of Tort with the Example of the Civil Liability for Erroneous ad hoc Disclosure, in this volume.

[52] *Giovanni De Cristofaro*, Infringement of the Prohibition of Unfair Commercial Practices and Tort Law, in this volume.

[53] *Ansgar Staudinger*, Personenbeförderungs- und Reiserecht, in this volume.

[54] Supra n. 6.

[55] *Petra Pohlmann*, Private Losses in European Competition Law: Public or Private Enforcement?, in this volume; *Willem van Boom*, The Law of Damages and Competition Law: Bien étonnés de se trouver ensemble?, in this volume; *Lars Klöhn*, Private versus Public Enforcement of Laws – a Law & Economics Perspective, in this volume.

[56] *Geraint Howells*, Product Liability and the European Tort Landscape, in this volume.

compensation in EU private law and on private enforcement, which arose out of the intense discussions over the course of the conference.[57] Particular attention is also to be given to the interaction of European tort law with neighbouring fields, namely contract law. With regard to business law and also to consumer law, it is especially insurance law[58] which extends across the fields of contract and torts. Comparative law observations regarding the interaction between contract and tort law in Europe[59] belong to the essential academic bases for developing proposals as to how the relationship between these two fields is to be determined for both the present and future EU law.

However, at present the distinctions between the laws in the Member States appear to lead to the conclusion that hardly any general statements can be made for the jurisdictions of all EU Member States on the interaction between contract and tort.[60] This analysis may indeed be considered a disappointment or rather as a challenge to strengthen the exchange of experiences and motivations and the efforts towards an approximation between the national laws. With regard to the supranational law, it underlines the need to carefully analyse which approaches are developing in the acquis communautaire itself that concern the interaction between tort law and contract law (also under consideration of European Private International law, in particular Art. 2 par. 2 Rome II Regulation). This analysis will possibly be able to give inspiration to the future development of national laws.

Beyond those matters which are covered in this volume, the question on the relationship between tort law and contract law also directs one's attention to ever-expanding fields of EU private law, such as anti-discrimination law and the many pre-contractual information duties. The provisions and legal principles of such fields greatly affect the conclusion and the content of contracts. However, they are not bound by the requirement of a contractual agreement between the parties; in this respect they must also be considered

---

[57] *Wolfgang Wurmnest*, Developing general concepts and common principles of EU Tort Law, in this volume; *Konrad Ost/Peter Gussone*, Why should one size fit all? A call for a differentiated look on the renewed European approach towards Private Enforcement, in this volume.

[58] *Helmut Heiss*, Insurance Law, in this volume.

[59] *Christian von Bar*, Rechtsvergleichende Beobachtungen zum Ineinandergreifen von Vertrags- und Deliktsrecht in Europa, in this volume; *Christian von Bar/Ulrich Drobnig*, The Interaction of Contract Law and Tort and Property Law in Europe – A Comparative Study, Munich 2004.

[60] Cf. *Christian von Bar*, Rechtsvergleichende Beobachtungen zum Ineinandergreifen von Vertrags- und Deliktsrecht in Europa, chapter VIII., in this volume.

within the context of non-contractual liability. Many questions arise which correspond to those of the area of non-contractual liability covered by this volume and which also correspond to the area of contractual liability. These questions are not limited to concept, scope and limitations of the compensation of private losses. They rather cover, for example, issues from the concept of damage to the matters of attribution and causation of damage and vicarious liability, to the types and extent of damages to the matter of the compensation of immaterial losses and disgorgement of profits. Where the further research into European private law is concerned, the extending fields "between" tort law and contract law may particularly contribute to consider the question whether there are some common principles which cover both contractual as well as non contractual liability.

The Experiences in National Legal Systems and the Perspectives of EU Tort Law[*]

Bernhard A. Koch

I. Introduction

Since other contributions to this volume will address quite a range of specific areas where tort law already did play a significant role in business in the past or may do so in the future, the following overview will focus less on these special topics individually, but rather aim at sketching out the overall perspective and add a few more general remarks for setting the scene.

While the title of this paper may raise certain expectations, it is important to note upfront that this brief outline will of course not offer a full-fledged analysis of what has happened before the courts of the EU jurisdictions, not even in the recent past. However, it builds upon extensive research collected (and accessible) elsewhere.[1]

Instead, the following will first briefly touch upon the theoretical foundations of the general topic, with an eye to how law in general interferes with market behaviour, and what role tort law can play in this context. Its preventive effect is of course of prime interest here.

Furthermore, a few of the classic elements of a tort claim have been selected in order to look at their specific relevance in the business context. After summarizing trends that seem to have shaped the development in the past, a short list of actual sightings of where tort law seems to play a

---

[*] This paper is based upon a presentation given at the "Round Table – Challenges in European Private Law" conference held in Münster, Germany, on 25 November 2010. Both style and format of an oral presentation have been mostly maintained for this written version, subject to certain additions and references in the footnotes.

[1] In particular, the most significant tort law developments of the past decade in most European jurisdictions, not only in the field of business law, are presented in the "Tort and Insurance Law Yearbook" series edited by Helmut Koziol and Barbara Steininger. The jurisprudence reported in these volumes as well as others is also accessible via the Eurotort database (http://www.eurotort.org).

19

more active role in the business arena will be given, with just one particular industry as a slightly more detailed example.

The focus will be on tort law proper and therefore neither extend to developments in procedural law nor to the insurance practice, even though both would be of significant importance here for obvious reasons.

The European perspective on these items will be given throughout by references to the relevant proposals of the two main competing drafts of European tort law, the "Principles of European Tort Law" (PETL) of the European Group on Tort Law[2] and the "Principles of European Law on Non-Contractual Liability Arising out of Damage Caused to Another" (PEL Liab. Dam.) prepared by the Study Group on a European Civil Code[3]. Both of them in their own way show the potential of harmonization in the field of tort law and thereby build upon common grounds determined by way of extensive comparative research.[4]

---

[2] *European Group on Tort Law,* Principles of European Tort Law, 2005 (cited in the following as "PETL Commentary"). The text of the Principles as well as translations thereof are available on the Group's website at http://www.egtl.org/Principles. The PETL are presented in an overview, e.g., by *Bernhard A. Koch,* The "European Group on Tort Law" and its "Principles of European Tort Law", (2005) 53 American Journal of Comparative Law 189; *id.,* Principles of European Tort Law, (2009) 20 King's Law Journal (KLJ) 203 ff.

[3] *Christian von Bar,* Principles of European Law on Non-Contractual Liability Arising out of Damage Caused to Another, 2009 (cited in the following as "PEL/*von Bar,* Liab. Dam."). The PEL Liab. Dam. were essentially taken over as Book VI of the DCFR, subject to slight modifications due to the latter's much broader scope. See, e.g., *John Blackie,* The Provisions for 'Non-contractual Liability Arising out of Damage Caused to Another' in the Draft Common Frame of Reference, (2009) 20 KLJ 215 ff.

[4] The European Group on Tort Law has published a series called "Principles of European Tort Law" on the most fundamental aspects of tort law: Helmut Koziol (ed.), Unification of Tort Law: Wrongfulness, 1998; Jaap Spier (ed.), Unification of Tort Law: Causation, 2000; Ulrich Magnus (ed.), Unification of Tort Law: Damages, 2001; Bernhard A. Koch/Helmut Koziol (eds.), Unification of Tort Law: Strict Liability, 2002; Jaap Spier (ed.), Unification of Tort Law: Liability for Damage Caused by Others, 2003; Ulrich Magnus/Miquel Martín-Casals (eds.), Unification of Tort Law: Contributory Negligence, 2004; W.V. Horton Rogers (ed.), Unification of Tort Law: Multiple Tortfeasors, 2004; Pierre Widmer (ed.), Unification of Tort Law: Fault, 2005.

The book publication of the PEL Liab. Dam. contains extensive comparative references in the "Notes" section to each Article. Furthermore, they build upon the

II. Theoretical foundations

1. Steering market behaviour in general

When thinking about the law steering market behaviour in general, torts is certainly not the first body of law that comes to one's mind. Administrative law seems to play the predominant role here instead. More generally speaking, we are primarily looking at rules prescribing or prohibiting specific behaviour, defining thresholds for permissible conduct. Criminal law contributes to demarcate its rough edges. While penal law does not define legitimate behaviour actively, but like tort law rather provides for sanctions instead if certain limits of acceptable conduct are exceeded, these limits nevertheless tend to be defined much more specifically, as guaranteed by Art. 7 ECHR.

The extent to which such rules are actually employed in any given legal system depends inter alia upon its overall willingness to regulate, and in our context upon its position regarding the dichotomy of free market access on the one hand and state control on the other. Some systems are more proactive inasmuch as they try to define proper market participation ex ante, whereas others tend to follow the *laissez faire* principle more often and only provide for backup solutions in case things go wrong this way. European legal systems more or less tend to be counted towards the first group, with U.S. jurisdictions typically seen as the role models of the second type.[5] The low level of products liability litigation in Europe as compared to the U.S. is often cited as one example thereof – EU law is already so concerned with product safety, recall duties and other ex ante provisions that there seem to be fewer court cases where product liability is contested.[6]

---

preceding research of their prime drafter, *Christian von Bar*, in particular his two volumes on "The Common European Law of Torts" (english translation published 1998 and 2000 respectively).

[5] Cf., e.g., *Ulrich Magnus*, Why is U.S. Tort Law so Different?, (2010) Journal of European Tort Law (JETL) 102, 121.

[6] While this does not necessarily mean that European products are per se much safer than those placed on the U.S. market, the existing products liability rules coupled with rather rigid ex ante provisions defining what can be expected from a product may deter court litigation and induce insurers to settle at an earlier stage. Cf. the second Report from the Commission on the Application of Directive 85/374 on Liability for Defective Products, COM(2000) 893 final, 31.1.2001, 10: "The number of product liability cases seems to be relatively low ... This situation results from the existence of a high safety level ensured by a strict regulatory framework, ...

The question whether there is any role left for tort law to influence businesses depends upon the efficiency of these ex ante approaches. If administrative law rules are implemented and executed properly, businesses already have ample incentives to behave well on the market, and there is simply no room left for other areas of the law to step in. There is no comparative form of "law-abiding".

However, even in a system where the law provides for an all-encompassing set of rules and regulations determining entrepreneurial behaviour upfront, starting from concessions to safety provisions to licensing of new products etc., which in theory should suffice to steer the market, there still may be weak spots which call for a backup set of rules such as the ones tort law could offer. Just think of flaws in the enforcement of the administrative regime – controlling bodies may be overburdened with work, court dockets may be overloaded or access too costly. The rules themselves may be coupled with imperfect sanctions, which tends to affect smaller offences more than the more serious ones. Take the example of road traffic – a high percentage of drivers exceeds lower speed limits in particular.[7] They tend to drive faster than permitted as long as (a) the likelihood to be caught is low and (b) the fine to be paid is too low in absolute figures. The same applies to market behaviour, where the situation is complicated by the fact that the measure of proper behaviour is not equally clear as a speed limit.

Furthermore, states more and more seem to be willing to shift at least some of their traditional duties towards their citizens. Private enforcement is getting more popular as it seems, so far particularly in the area of competition law.

So despite a significant importance of other areas of the law which at least historically tended to leave little or nothing for tort law to do in the area of market control, opportunities for the law of delict to step in and assume at least some tasks are apparently on the rise.

Industry is said to take into account these safety features in design, production, labelling and post-marketing systems and uses extensively good practice standards. The replies confirm that the Directive on Product Liability has a deterrent effect on manufacturers and suppliers and gives them a strong incentive, alongside the obligations under the afore-mentioned safety regulations, to improve the safety level."

[7] Cf. http://www.parkline.at/studien/Verk.-Studie-Tempobolzerl.pdf.

2. Prevention as a goal of tort law

Since tort law by definition always comes to late inasmuch as it primarily aims at compensating harm already incurred, we can only consider indirect effects of tort law that may have the potential to leave an impact upon the conduct of market participants. The key question therefore is whether tort law indeed has a preventive effect, and whether that effect can be used proactively with the ultimate goal to influence market behaviour.[8]

From a law and economics perspective, this is not even considered to be a question, but rather a matter of course. While I personally have serious doubts about the actual impact of the fear of possible liability upon one's conduct, if considered at all by the actor, I nevertheless concede that it may play a role in business,[9] since entrepreneurs at least in theory are expected to consider all costs and benefits of their activities ex ante, and I can well imagine that they do, the more risky they perceive their own products or services to be. Liability insurance not only buffers the preventive effect, but at least ideally via its costs tends to leave a mark on the way business is conducted, particularly the more premia are adjusted to the individual risk.[10]

---

[8] Though with a certain bias coming from the author's law and economics background, the most fundamental analysis of this question in recent years is given by *Gerhard Wagner*, Prävention und Verhaltenssteuerung durch Privatrecht – Anmaßung oder legitime Aufgabe?, Archiv für die civilistische Praxis 206, 2006, 355, in particular 451 ff.

[9] Similarly *Willem van Boom*, Compensating and preventing damage: is there any future left for tort law? in: Festskrift till Bill W. Dufwa – Essays on Tort, Insurance Law and Society in Honour of Bill W. Dufwa, vol. I, 2006, pp. 287, 288 ff.: "To conclude, I would speculate that tort law has little grasp on preventing either incidental negligence or intentional wrongdoing by private individuals. Instinctively, I would assume that the tort law incentive has more impact on the 'corporate tortfeasor': businesses and institutions that are being held liable for not preventing certain accidents." (289).

[10] On the two prime ways to address the moral hazard problem – monitoring the insured with adjustment of premia on the one hand and partial exposure of the insured to the risk via deductibles or caps – see e.g. *Michael Faure*, The View from Law and Economics, in: Gerhard Wagner (ed.), Tort Law and Liability Insurance, 2006, pp. 239, 265 ff. The "economic virtues of liability insurance" are listed by *Gerhard Wagner*, Tort law and liability insurance, in: Michael Faure (ed.), Tort Law and Economics, 2009, pp. 377, 393 ff.

III. Tort law participating in market regulation

1. Elements of a tort claim in the business context

Among the core elements of a tort claim, there are a few distinct facets of liability law that may be of particular significance in the business context. Whether or not these specialties are recognized in a legal system is at least one indicator of how specifically it addresses market behaviour. Let us look at some examples.

a) Damage

When we start with the notion of damage, there are two variations which are of interest here. It is not self-evident, for example, that businesses are recognized as protected interests in themselves.

aa) The right to carry on an established trade or business

As well known, a right to carry on an established trade or business was confirmed in Germany shortly after the BGB came into force, if not earlier,[11] despite the fact that § 823 BGB does not mention it expressly. France and the Netherlands, for example, essentially come to the same result, though addressing the matter from the conduct side and not with a first eye to the harmed interest.[12] It is fair to say that enterprises as such are protected under all European tort laws, though the scope of protection varies, as does the range of interferences that are specifically addressed.

While the cases falling under these theories are somewhat diffuse, to say the least, they nevertheless show that unlawfully messing with someone's business may be sanctioned, thereby laying down the outer battle-lines for the market game.

Of the two drafts of European tort law, only the Study Group's proposal expressly addresses the loss upon unlawful impairment of business in its

---

[11] *Gerhard Wagner*, in: Münchener Kommentar zum BGB, 5th ed. 2009, § 823 no. 187 f.

[12] See the comparative overview of the way European jurisdictions handle "delicts concerning the protection of a business" given by *Christian von Bar*, The Common European Law of Torts, vol. I, 1998, pp. 60 ff. (on France and the Netherlands 66 f.).

Art. 2:208 par. 1 PEL Liab. Dam.[13] The PETL do not list specific injuries as such, but merely give guidance as to the range of possibly protected interests (Art. 2:102 PETL). However, this does not mean that they rule out the right to enterprise, of course.

bb) Personality rights of enterprises

The second type of losses that applies to businesses specifically is that enterprises are increasingly deemed to have personality rights of their own which may be violated. This is expanding the scope of protection for businesses even one step further. A follow-up question thereto is whether violations of such personality rights can also trigger compensable non-pecuniary losses.

Just to illustrate this development, a sample case from Spain: In 1990, a Spanish magazine published a report saying that FedEx would buy the Spanish company Aerpons. This was simply untrue. Aerpons not only recovered compensation for its economic losses, but also 10 million pesetas (the equivalent of about €60,000 at the time) for its non-pecuniary loss suffered because of the degrading use of its logo in an illustration accompanying the article.[14]

Similarly, in *Jameel*, the House of Lords ruled that a trading company which itself conducts no business but which has a trading reputation within England and Wales should be entitled to recover general damages for libel without pleading special damage. The defendants had denied this by arguing that if a company is defamed its directors and individuals were free to sue as personal plaintiffs. Lord Bingham expressed sincere "doubt if this is always so, although in some cases it will be. But, to the extent that it is so, I question whether the possibility of a claim by the company will add significantly to the chilling effect of a claim by the individuals."[15]

---

[13] It reads as follows: "Loss caused to a person as a result of an unlawful impairment of that person's exercise of a profession or conduct of a trade is legally relevant damage."

[14] *Tribunal Supremo* 20.2.2002, 127/2002, http://sentencias.juridicas.com/docs/00120659.html; see María Paz García Rubio/Javier Lete, Spain, in: Helmut Koziol/Barbara Steininger (eds.), European Tort Law 2002, 2003, pp. 380, 386-387.

[15] *House of Lords* 11.10.2006, *Jameel and others v. Wall Street Journal Europe Sprl*, [2006] United Kingdom House of Lords (UKHL) 44 (at no. 21); see *Ken Oliphant*, England and Wales, in: Helmut Koziol/Barbara Steininger (eds.), European Tort Law 2006, 2007, pp. 153, 167-169.

The Austrian Supreme Court equally has no problems to award compensation for non-pecuniary losses to corporations and other legal entities, as exemplified by the *Dorotheum* case, where this pawnbroker, auctioneer and arts dealer was awarded around 3.600 € for the insult experienced by defamatory statements made by the defendant competitor.[16]

On the other hand, while companies may have corporate personality rights in Germany whose infringement may trigger other remedies,[17] they cannot recover immaterial losses because they are unable to experience satisfaction, as the BGH ruled already 30 years ago.[18]

The Study Group's Principles expressly recognize injury to a company's reputation as legally relevant damage (by not limiting the "person" in Art. 2:203 par. 2 PEL Liab. Dam.[19] to a "natural" person as in the previous paragraph[20]), whereas all other personality rights shall fall under the general clause of Art. 2:101[21], thereby depending inter alia upon the fundamental rights recognized in the respective jurisdiction.[22]

Corporate personality rights also fall under the general rule of the PETL, whose Art. 10:301 does not require that the victim needs to be a natural person.[23]

---

[16] *Oberster Gerichtshof* (OGH) 6.11.1990, 4 Ob 135/90, Juristische Blätter (JBl) 1991, 58.

[17] *Bundesgerichtshof* (BGH) 11.3.2008 VI ZR 7/07 Neue Juristische Wochenschrift (NJW) 2008, 439 ("Gen-Milch", injunctive relief denied on other grounds).

[18] BGH 8.7.1980 VI ZR 177/78 Entscheidungen des Bundesgerichtshofs in Zivilsachen (BGHZ) 78, 24 ("Medizin-Syndikat I").

[19] This provision reads: "Loss caused to a person as a result of injury to that person's reputation and the injury as such are also legally relevant damage if national law so provides."

[20] Art. 2.203 par. 1 PEL Liab. Dam. reads: "Loss caused to a *natural* person as a result of infringement of his or her right to respect for his or her dignity, such as the rights to liberty and privacy, and the injury as such are legally relevant damage." (emphasis added).

[21] According to Art. 2:101 par. 3 PEL Liab. Dam., a loss may be deemed "legally relevant" and therefore compensable if due regard is being had "to the ground of accountability, to the nature and proximity of the damage or impending damage, to the reasonable expectations of the person who suffers or would suffer the damage, and to considerations of public policy".

[22] PEL/*von Bar*, Liab. Dam. (n. 3) Chapter 2, Art. 2:203, Comments, C, no. 14.

[23] Art. 10:301 par. 1 PETL reads in relevant part: "(1) Considering the scope of its protection (Article 2:102), the violation of an interest may justify compensation of non-pecuniary damage …" See also *Ulrich Magnus* in PETL Commentary (n. 2),

b) From vicarious to enterprise liability

The way vicarious liability is applied in practice may be decisive for the likelihood of businesses to be held liable, and consequently also for the degree of a possible preventive effect of such a threat. Austrian law traditionally is very restrictive in this context,[24] and in the current heated debate about a possible reform of the law of torts in Austria, where almost everything is in dispute,[25] the one thing the two rival groups fully agree is that a reform in this specific area (within the meaning of an expansion of vicarious liability beyond its present restrictions) is a must.

If we look at the various options for holding an employer liable for his employees, there is a sliding scale from a theory of personal misconduct of the employer to be proven by the victim to a presumption of the former's fault as codified, for example, in § 831 BGB, moving on to "direct" liability of the employer for the misconduct of his employees, as is probably the majority opinion or at least major trend in Europe at present, and finally to a full-fledged enterprise liability where there is no element of reproach against the employee anymore, but rather a sense of risk inherent in the enterprise as such.[26] In some way, the original starting point thereby comes back inasmuch as the theory of liability is focussing again directly on the employer, with the ultimate trigger remaining the same throughout, of course – the deep pocket argument that tips the scales in all these scenarios.

Art. 10:301 no. 7: "We do not attempt to lay down a rigid list of qualifying interests. However, we do specifically refer to personal injury ... because it is so widely accepted that these are the prime areas in which awards for non-pecuniary loss are made. That is not to say that such an award is automatically barred in any other case."

[24] *Helmut Koziol/Klaus Vogel,* Liability for Damage Caused by Others under Austrian Law, in: Jaap Spier (ed.), Unification of Tort Law: Liability for Damage Caused by Others, 2003, pp. 11 ff.

[25] The two competing drafts are presented by (and their text can be found in the respective annex to) *Barbara Steininger,* Austria, in: Helmut Koziol/Barbara Steininger (eds.), European Tort Law 2007, 2008, pp. 134, 158 ff. (revised draft of the Working Group installed by the Ministry of Justice); and to *Barbara Steininger,* Austria, in: Helmut Koziol/Barbara Steininger (eds.), European Tort Law 2008, 2009, pp. 108, 138 ff. (alternative draft by the opponents of the original draft).

[26] On this development, see also *Gerhard Wagner,* Grundstrukturen des Europäischen Deliktsrechts, in: Reinhard Zimmermann (ed.), Grundstrukturen des Europäischen Deliktsrechts, 2003, pp. 189, 290-305.

The two European drafts both of course have rules on vicarious liability that hold the employer liable without his personal fault for misconduct of his employee and thereby endorse the third theory just mentioned.[27]

The PETL add to this by offering a rule on "enterprise liability"[28], however, this is not entirely of the kind just mentioned. Instead, it is a combination of the second and the last theory – it offers the enterpreneur to escape liability upon proof that he has met a high objective standard of conduct, so in essence, it is a qualified liability for fault with a reversal of the burden of proving it. The focus, however, is on the enterprise as such, thereby trying to address in particular scenarios where neither "classic" vicarious liability nor strict liability can be established: Despite the belief that the wrong originated in the enterprise, it may often be difficult to prove whether it was human misconduct that triggered the loss or the malfunctioning of some technical equipment, even if the employer were strictly liable for the latter as its keeper. Flaws in the organisation are at the core of this concept,[29] but are not the only cases it seeks to encompass, as indicated.

c) Punitive damages

Finally, when looking at the remedies available for victims of a tortious conduct, the question whether or not punitive damages are available in a legal system is an important indicator of how seriously it takes the idea of prevention by tort law.

Most European jurisdictions show at least some punitive elements in their laws of delict, as a recent comparative study on the topic shows.[30] However, only few of them acknowledge this openly, the remaining ones emphatically deny it and are therefore experts at repression.

---

[27] Art. 6:102 PETL, Art. 3:201 PEL Liab. Dam.

[28] Art. 4:202 PETL reads:
"(1) A person pursuing a lasting enterprise for economic or professional purposes who uses auxiliaries or technical equipment is liable for any harm caused by a defect of such enterprise or of its output unless he proves that he has conformed to the required standard of conduct.
(2) 'Defect' is any deviation from standards that are reasonably to be expected from the enterprise or from its products or services."

[29] Cf. *Bernhard A. Koch* in: PETL Commentary (n. 2), Art. 4:202 no. 5.

[30] *Helmut Koziol/Vanessa Wilcox* (eds.), Punitive Damages: Common Law and Civil Law Perspective, 2009.

The common law jurisdictions belong to the former category, even though exemplary damages are awarded under very restrictive conditions. Despite efforts by the English Law Commission[31] towards expanding the range defined by *Rookes v. Barnard*[32], the Department for Constitutional Affairs only a few years ago expressly ruled out legislative steps in that direction.[33]

In Germany (as well as elsewhere), penal aspects sneak in through the backdoor of immaterial losses: Since these are per definition not accurately measurable in monetary terms, judges tend to use their discretion to be more generous to victims of highly reproachable conduct.[34] Furthermore, they (ab)use such remedies to sanction conduct whose consequences leave no or little actual loss with the victim, but considerable profits with the tortfeasor. *The Princess of Monaco* cases belong to this group.[35] Another

---

[31] *Law Commission for England and Wales*, Aggravated, Exemplary and Restitutionary Damages, Law Com. No. 247, 1997 (http://www.lawcom.gov.uk/docs/lc247.pdf), 4-5.

[32] *Rookes v Barnard*, [1964] 1 All England Law Reports (All ER) 367.

[33] *Department for Constitutional Affairs*, The Law on Damages, Consultation Paper CP 9/07, 2007 (http://www.justice.gov.uk/consultations/docs/cp0907.pdf) 77: "It remains the Government's view that the availability of exemplary damages in civil proceedings should not be extended beyond the limited instances in which they are currently available under the common law, namely in the case of oppressive, arbitrary or unconstitutional action by a public servant and where the tortfeasor's conduct was calculated to make a profit which might well exceed the compensation payable to the claimant."

[34] See only BGH 6.7.1955 BGHZ 18, 149, 157, 159: "Der Grad des Verschuldens ist nicht nur ... im Hinblick auf die Reaktion zu berücksichtigen, die er beim Verletzten ausübt ... [G]anz abgesehen von der Reaktion des Verletzten kann es der Billigkeit und dem Genugtuungsgedanken entsprechen, wenn im Einzelfall Vorsatz und grobe Fahrlässigkeit bei der Festsetzung der Entschädigung aus § 847 BGB zu Ungunsten des Schädigers, besonders leichte Fahrlässigkeit dagegen zu seinen Gunsten berücksichtigt wird. Es wäre nicht zu verstehen, wenn dem Tatrichter nicht die Befugnis zustände, das Schmerzensgeld für die Folgen eines Verbrechens höher festzusetzen als für die äußerlich gleichen Folgen eines Fehlverhaltens im Verkehr, wie es jedem unterlaufen kann."

[35] See, e.g., BGH 15.11.1994 BGHZ 128, 1: "Der Fall ist dadurch gekennzeichnet, daß die Beklagte unter vorsätzlichem Rechtsbruch die Persönlichkeit der Klägerin als Mittel zur Auflagensteigerung und damit zur Verfolgung eigener kommerzieller Interessen eingesetzt hat. Ohne eine für die Beklagte fühlbare Geldentschädigung wäre die Klägerin einer solchen rücksichtslosen Zwangskommerzialisierung ihrer

specific set of cases recognized not only in Germany, but even legislated in France,[36] concern insurance companies which settle claims too late or otherwise unsatisfactorily. The award for non-pecuniary losses to the beneficiaries are subsequently increased for this very reason, not because the beneficiaries actually suffer more.[37]

Even though the Commission tried to label punitive damages as violating some imaginary European *ordre public* not so long ago,[38] they are still being considered today as possible additions to European tort law regimes. Apart from an Estonian draft law,[39] the most recent step ahead was taken

---

[36] Persönlichkeit weitgehend schutzlos ausgeliefert; Verurteilungen zu Widerruf und Richtigstellung erreichen ... nur einen unzureichenden Schutz der Klägerin. Eine Verurteilung zur Geldentschädigung ist aber nur dann geeignet, den aus dem Persönlichkeitsrecht heraus gebotenen Präventionszweck zu erreichen, wenn die Entschädigung der Höhe nach ein Gegenstück auch dazu bildet, daß hier die Persönlichkeitsrechte zur Gewinnerzielung verletzt worden sind."

[36] Art. L. 211-13 *Code des assurances*. See also Art. L. 1142-14 *Code de la santé publique*: If the liability insurer of a health care professional or institution made a "manifestly insufficient" ("manifestement insuffisante") offer to an injured patient, the insurer has to pay an extra 15 % of the ultimate damages award as a penalty to the state compensation fund ONIAM.

[37] Cf. *Oberlandesgericht* (OLG) Frankfurt 22.9.1993, Deutsches Autorecht (DAR) 1994, 21: "Gerade wegen der schweren Verletzung des Klägers ... ist die verzögerliche Schadensregulierung durch die Beklagte zu 2), die auch bis heute nicht einmal die Beträge in vollem Umfang gezahlt hat, die sie selbst für gerechtfertigt hält, unverständlich und grob pflichtwidrig. Da dies den schwerverletzten Kläger auch in erheblicher Weise treffen mußte, hat das Landgericht in Übereinstimmung mit der Rechtsprechung ... zu Recht eine Erhöhung des Schmerzensgeldbetrages im Rahmen der Genugtuungsfunktion vorgenommen. Selbst wenn man also aufgrund der Ausgleichsfunktion des Schmerzensgeldes einen etwas niedrigeren Betrag ansetzen wollte, müßte das Schmerzensgeld wegen der verzögerlichen Zahlung durch die Beklagte zu 2) um jedenfalls 30.000 DM erhöht werden."

[38] Art. 24 of the Proposal for a Regulation of the European Parliament and the Council on the Law Applicable to Non-Contractual Obligations ("Rome II"), 22.7.2003, COM(2003) 427 final.

[39] *Janno Lahe/Irene Kull*, Estonia, in: Helmut Koziol/Barbara Steininger (eds.), European Tort Law 2009, 2010, pp. 169 ff. (no. 53). See also the recent amendments to the Law of Obligations Act introduced by the end of 2010, in particular the additions to § 134, according to which the gravity of the violation is one determinant of the extent of compensation for non-pecuniary loss.

in the French Senate, which in the 2010 draft tort reform act[40] suggested a modified version of the more far-reaching proposal in the *Catala* project.[41] Germany as well had its share of discussion on the topic after the 2006 Juristentag, following *Gerhard Wagner's* seminal study on "new perspectives" in the law of torts.[42] His proposal was far more refined than what the debate seemed to believe – after all, he did not suggest to increase compensatory damages with the aim to punish, but rather to deter. He consequently also pleaded in favour of "preventive damages" in cases where tort (or any other area of the) law and the way it is being enforced does not sufficiently satisfy the need for the prevention of harm. He thinks this is the case (inter alia) when someone makes a profit by abusing someone else's right, and even after compensating the latter in full still retains a certain portion of these profits, which would run afoul of the principle that "a tort must not pay".

Despite significant differences in other aspects, the two drafts of European tort law are in full accord on this point: Both rule out punitive damages as desirable for the law of torts and insist that a victim should not be overcompensated beyond reparation of the harm actually suffered. This is

---

[40] *Proposition de loi portant réforme de la responsabilité civile*, n° 657 (2009-2010), http://www.senat.fr/leg/ppl09-657.html. Its Art. 1386-25 foresees punitive damages in cases of wilful infliction of harm, but only if it has led to an enrichment of the tortfeasor which remains even after he has paid full compensation The punitive award must not exceed double of the compensatory award and need not necessarily be paid to the victim exclusively, but may also go in part into a compensation fund installed for this "or similar" losses (alternatively to the state).

[41] Art. 1371 of the Catala draft (English translation by *Alain Levasseur* available at http://www.henricapitant.org/sites/default/files/Traduction_definitive_Alain_Levasseur.pdf) reads: "One whose fault is manifestly premeditated, particularly a fault whose purpose is monetary gain, may be ordered to pay punitive damages besides compensatory damages. The judge may direct a part of such damages to the public treasury. The judge must provide specific reasons for ordering such punitive damages and must clearly distinguish their amount from that of other damages awarded to the victim. Punitive damages may not be the subject of a contract of insurance."

[42] *Gerhard Wagner*, Neue Perspektiven im Schadenersatzrecht – Kommerzialisierung, Strafschadensersatz, Kollektivschäden, Gutachten für den 66. Deutschen Juristentag, in: Verhandlungen des 66. Deutschen Juristentages Stuttgart 2006, 2006, I, sec. A, pp. 68 ff.

Bernhard A. Koch

not addressed expressly in the black letter rules, but spelled out in the respective commentary thereto.[43]

The Study Group's proposal nevertheless addresses the specific problem of the cases mentioned where the tortfeasor would still retain at least part of his profit despite paying full compensation. As an alternative to compensation of the loss suffered, Art. 6:101 para. (4) allows the victim to claim "recovery from the person accountable … of any advantage obtained by the latter in connection with causing the damage", but "only where this is reasonable".[44] This renders the need to siphon off this profit via punitive damages moot.[45]

---

[43] As stated by *Helmut Koziol* in PETL Commentary (n. 2), Art. 1:101 no. 2, "the principles of tort law are no basis for punitive damages or other payments which are not in correspondence with harm suffered by the victim". See also PEL/*von Bar*, Liab. Dam. (n. 3) Chapter 6, Art. 6:101, Comments, C, no. 8: "The punishment of wrongdoers is a question for criminal law, not private law. Under these model rules, punitive damages are not available. They are not consistent with the principle of reparation."

[44] In the DCFR, where this paragraph was included as Art. VI-6:101 para. 4, it actually duplicates a corresponding provision in the proposed rules on unjust enrichment, which goes farther, however, inasmuch as it also encompasses cases where the victim has suffered no loss at all because she did not want to exploit her interests herself anyhow: Art. VII-4:101 DCFR attributes an enrichment to another's disadvantage "in particular where … (c) the enriched person uses that other's asset, especially where the enriched person infringes the disadvantaged person's rights or legally protected interests …". This duplicity of norms is explained primarily by the need to warn potential wrongdoers "that there is no profit to be made from a civil wrong": PEL/*von Bar*, Liab. Dam. (n. 3) Chapter 6, Art. 6:101, Comments, F, no. 16. One may wonder, however, whether this message has not already been conveyed by Art. VII-4:101 DCFR itself. The fact that a person unjustifiedly enriched but still acting in good faith may have the defence of disenrichment (Art. VII-6:101 DCFR) does not seem to trigger an urgent need either to implant a rule with "an unjustified enrichment 'varnish'" into the provisions on tort law.

[45] Needless to say, *Gerhard Wagner* is quite fond of this particular proposal: *Gerhard Wagner*, The Law of Torts in the DCFR, in: Gerhard Wagner (ed.), The Common Frame of Reference: A View from Law & Economics, 2009, pp. 225, 266.

2. Trends shaping the development

When looking back at these and other developments of the past, one can identify three general themes which seem to have driven these trends.

First of all, the type of injury was and still is important. Bodily integrity is undeniably still at the top of the list of protected interests in all legal systems,[46] so it came as no surprise that the first cases shifting the perspective from individual to corporate liability concerned personal injuries, from slips on vegetable leaves in stores to the first product liability cases. The reluctance of some legal systems to compensate pure economic losses[47] also delayed the development of actionable torts in the business arena.

The second layer concerns the range of protection granted by the legal system. Actions arising out of a legal relationship such as a contract were the model for quasi-contractual claims, which were just invented to overcome the formal restrictions of some legal systems and still benefit from the same degree of protection.[48] Claims by the public at large arising out of delicts in the classic sense could only develop later, sometimes via statutory intervention.

And thirdly, the underlying policy of granting a claim seems to have been decisive for the development of actions against businesses. While consumer protection is certainly not an ancient *topos*, it nevertheless turned out to be an important driver also for the advance of business tort litigation.

---

[46] Cf. Art. 2:102 para. 2 PETL: "(2) Life, bodily or mental integrity, human dignity and liberty enjoy the most extensive protection."

[47] "Pure economic loss probably is one of the main problems in expanding tort law": W.V. Horton Rogers/Jaap Spier/Geneviève Viney, Preliminary Observations, in J. Spier (ed.), The Limits of Liability – Keeping the Floodgates Shut, 1996, p. 1, 8. See also the contributions to Willem van Boom/Helmut Koziol/Christian A. Witting (eds.), Pure Economic Loss, 2004.

[48] Cf. *Christian von Bar/Ulrich Drobnig*, Study on Property Law and Non-contractual Liability Law as they relate to Contract Law, 2002 (http://ec.europa.eu/consumers/cons_int/safe_shop/fair_bus_pract/cont_law/study.pdf), p. 436 (no. 709). On the contract-tort-divide see also *Christian von Bar*, Rechtsvergleichende Beobachtungen zum Ineinandergreifen von Vertrags- und Deliktsrecht in Europa, in this volume.

3. Actual sightings of tort law affecting the market

If we look at the kinds of areas where these trends have led to specific tort causes of action, we see liability for unsafe business premises at the beginning, probably around the same time as liability for work-related accidents and diseases took off. IP-related claims were introduced with legislation in this field,[49] as were the first sightings of private torts arising out of competition law.[50] Product liability is historically the first area where harmonization was at least attempted in Europe,[51] whereas efforts to establish a parallel regime governing liability for services were unsuccessful so far.[52] While environmental liability equally failed on the European level, leaving just the name, but not its substance behind,[53] there was nevertheless quite some national legislation triggered by (or – as in Germany – preceding) the Directive which goes beyond its implementation and foresees individual

---

[49] See *Piotr Machnikowski,* Damages for the Infringement of Intellectual Property Rights under EU Law, in this volume.

[50] On this question, see the contributions by *Willem van Boom,* The Law of Damages and Competition Law: Bien étonnés de se trouver ensemble?, in this volume; and *Petra Pohlmann,* Private Losses in European Competition Law: Public or Private Enforcement?, in this volume.

[51] See *Geraint Howells,* Product Liability and the European Tort Landscape, in this volume.

[52] Proposal for a Council Directive on the Liability of Suppliers of Services, COM(1990) 482 final, O.J. 1991 C 12/8. The Commission officially withdrew the draft on 24 June 1994: COM(1994) 260 final.

[53] Directive 2004/35/CE of the European Parliament and of the Council of 21 April 2004 on environmental liability with regard to the prevention and remedying of environmental damage, O.J. 2004 L 143/56. On the problematic use of tort law language stemming from the original draft in the ultimate outcome, which is primarily an administrative compensation regime, see e.g. *Bernhard A. Koch,* Damage Caused by GMOs: Comparative Analysis, in: id. (ed.), Damage Caused by Genetically Modified Organisms. Comparative Survey of Redress Options for Harm to Persons, Property or the Environment, 2010, pp. 882, 912 ff.

[54] *Koch* (n. 53) 917 ff.

[55] The efforts by the EU Commission can be seen at http://ec.europa.eu/internal_market/auditing/liability/index_en.htm, including links to the text of and the preparatory works for the Commission Recommendation of 5 June 2008 concerning

causes of action.[54] Current items on debate include auditors liability[55] and other efforts to spread individual losses incurred on the capital market.[56]

While most of these areas will be addressed by further contributions to this volume in the following, let me just focus on one rather peculiar area, and this is liability for genetically modified organisms in agriculture.[57] As it turns out, this is a perfect sandbox for showing how tort law is actually used (or its potential deliberately ignored) in order to control market behaviour.

The Austrian[58] and German statutory solutions to address harm caused by GMOs, for example, were designed specifically with the legislator's intent to deter farmers from considering that technology.[59] Since EU law prevented these jurisdictions from introducing a full ban of GM farming, the response was sought in the law of delict, combined with elements of the law of nuisance and therefore with ample possibilities for opponents to seek injunctions against allegedly harmful business conduct. Austria in particular imposed a very strict liability regime which between the lines reads: "Don't even think about it!"[60]

---

the limitation of the civil liability of statutory auditors and audit firms, O.J. 2008 L 162/39. See also *W.V. Horton Rogers*, Auditors' Liability, in: van Boom/Koziol/Witting (n. 47) p. 93 ff.

[56] See, e.g., *Susanne Kalss*, The Liability of Banks, in: van Boom/Koziol/Witting (n. 47) pp. 77 ff.; *id.*, Recent developments in liability for nondisclosure of capital market information, (2007) 27 International Review of Law and Economics 70 ff.; *Paul Davies*, Liability for misstatements to the market, (2010) Capital Markets Law Journal 443 ff.

[57] On this topic, see the contributions to Bernhard A. Koch (ed.), Economic Loss Caused by Genetically Modified Organisms. Liability and Redress for the Adventitious Presence of GMOs in Non-GM Crops, 2008 (in the following: Koch, Economic Loss); and id. (ed.), Damage Caused by Genetically Modified Organisms. Comparative Survey of Redress Options for Harm to Persons, Property or the Environment, 2010 (in the following: Koch, Damage).

[58] *Manuela Weissenbacher*, Damage Caused by GMOs under Austrian Law, in: Koch, Damage (n. 57) pp. 2 ff.

[59] *Jörg Fedtke*, Damage Caused by GMOs under German Law, in: Koch, Damage (n. 57) pp. 212 ff., in particular 222 ff.

[60] Cf. *Bernhard A. Koch*, Comparative Report, in: Koch, Economic Loss (n. 57) pp. 585, 590 f.

Conversely, states which see this technology more favourably have introduced state-supported fund solutions with the specific goal to circumvent the potential (and indeed actual) deterrent effect even classic tort law without the extremities of the Austrian or German kind had on the market.[61] After all, no European insurer was willing to underwrite the potential liability risks of GM farming, particularly due to the lack of experience and therefore data to calculate the premia.[62] By deliberate state intervention specifically sidestepping the tort law problems, cultivation could start, which in turn generates the missing data such as how far GM pollen is blown in a specific environment, thereby causing admixture with non-GM material and consequently potential market losses, whose likelihood and possible extent are crucial determinants of insurance premia.

IV. Outlook

In this brief introductory overview, it was only possible to sketch out a few general trends and to hint at some particulars. The further contributions in the following will be much more detailed and provide more substantiated insight into several specific areas only touched upon here so far.

As a bottom line, I think it is fair to say already at this point, however, that the potential of tort law to influence market behaviour is being used more and more often throughout Europe, and that the national legal systems seem to be getting bolder both when it comes to applying existing rules as well as in introducing new approaches to the law of delict. Important developments in the laws of civil procedure such as the introduction of class actions and similar alleviations of multi-party lawsuits serve as additional accelerators which could not be addressed in the framework of this short introduction.

The two projects on European tort law do not approach the matter in the same way, as could be seen. The PEL Liab. Dam. go into more detail, which is also due to the different approach taken by this project from the start, envisaging at least as one option to serve as a model code. The PETL,

---

[61] Cf., e.g., the Danish model presented by *Vibe Ulfbeck,* Economic Loss Caused by GMOs in Denmark, in: Koch, Economic Loss (n. 57) pp. 145 ff.

[62] *Ina Ebert/Christian Lahnstein,* GMO Liability: Options for Insurers, in: Koch, Economic Loss (n. 57) pp. 577 ff.; *Thomas K. Epprecht,* Did Biotechnology Regulation Come to a Conclusion? An Insurers' Perspective, in: Koch, Damage (n. 57) pp. 813 ff.

on the other hand, were designed to outline indeed just principles rather than rules, though the former had to be expressed in the style of the latter.[63] The value judgments underlying both projects do not seem to be far apart, however, and the two drafts at least when it comes to their outcome are certainly not incompatible.[64]

---

[63] But see *Reinhard Zimmermann*, Principles of European Contract Law and Principles of European Tort Law: Comparison and Points of Contact, in: Helmut Koziol/ Barbara Steininger (ed.), European Tort Law 2003, 2004, pp. 2, 9 ff. on the "understatement" by using the term "principles" in both the PECL and the PETL.

[64] See also *Blackie* (2009) 20 KLJ 234 ff.

General Principles of Tort Law in the Jurisprudence of the European Court of Justice

Wolfgang Wurmnest
Christian Heinze

I. Introduction

"Indeed it is a vain thing to imagine a right without a remedy, for want of right and want of remedy are reciprocal".[1] This dictum by *Chief Justice Holt* is a subtle paraphrase for the "principle that injury to individual rights gives rise to a cause of action",[2] a principle well-established in modern private law.[3] In the private law of the European Union (EU), however, no such general reciprocity of right and remedy may be found. Rather, in its enforcement and remedial dimension, EU legislation often proves to be incomplete, restricting itself to establishing primary rights and duties, while questions of remedies and enforcement are left to the law of the Member States. Such division between European rights and national remedies creates a risk of ineffective or discriminatory enforcement by Member States, a risk which has been countered by the European Court of Justice (ECJ) requiring the Member States to ensure effective and non-discriminatory (equivalent) enforcement of rights which derive from EU law.[4] But it is not only the European Court, it is also the European legislator who is increasingly turning an eye to the question of remedies, going beyond the ritual incantation of effective, proportionate and dissuasive remedies by prescribing specific sanctions in directives and regulations.[5] Against this backdrop, this paper

---

[1] *Ashby v. White*, 92 Eng. Rep. 126, 135 (1703) (KB).
[2] *Arwed Blomeyer*, Types of Relief Available (Judicial Remedies), in: Mauro Cappelletti (ed.), International Encyclopedia of Comparative Law, Volume XVI: Civil Procedure, 1982, para. 51.
[3] *Blomeyer* (n. 2), para. 51.
[4] European Court of Justice (ECJ) 16.12.1976, Case 33/76 (*Rewe-Zentralfinanz eG and Rewe-Zentral AG/Landwirtschaftskammer für das Saarland*), [1976] ECR 1989 para. 5.
[5] For an example Art. 17 of Directive 2004/25/EC of the European Parliament and of the Council of 21 april 2004 on takeover bids, OJ 2004 L 142/12; for further discussion of EU secondary law below II.3.

will try to distil some overarching tort law principles from the case law of the ECJ – without expounding too much on special torts, as there will be various papers on different business torts later on. This paper is, therefore, structured as follows:

The first part (II.) gives an overview of the different facets of EU tort law in order to disclose the legal foundations from which general principles may be inferred. "General principles" in this context do not refer to general principles of Union law of a fundamental (often constitutional) character such as the principle of proportionality, the rights of defence, or, more generally, the existence of fundamental rights and the rule of law.[6] These fundamental principles do not only serve interpretative and gap-filling functions, they also enjoy the status of primary law against which the legality of directives or regulations can be controlled.[7] Instead, this paper focuses on general principles of a private law nature which may be helpful for the sake of coherent interpretation of EU private law, without necessarily having the nature of primary law.[8] The second part (III.) will highlight some contours of an emerging judge-made European tort law. It will focus on two general aspects, namely the function(s) of tort law and compensation for non-material loss. As the present state of European tort law is far from being satisfactory, the third and final part (IV.) will turn to proposals for the way forward towards a more consistent tort law on the European level. Outside the scope of this paper will be the rules of the Draft Common Frame of Reference and of the Principles of European Tort Law, as there are

---

[6] On these principles *Takis Tridimas*, The General Principles of EC law, 2nd edition, 2005; *Hanns Peter Nehl*, Principles of Administrative Procedure in EC Law, 1999, pp. 19 ff.; for further examples Advocate General *Trstenjak* 30.6.2009, Case C-101/08 *(Audiolux SA e.a./Groupe Bruxelles Lambert SA (GBL) and Others and Bertelsmann AG and Others)*, [2008] ECR I-9823 paras. 71 ff.; for the different levels of abstraction *Axel Metzger*, Extra legem – intra ius: Allgemeine Rechtsgrundsätze im Europäischen Privatrecht, 2009, p. 545.

[7] For the functions of general principles of EU law *Koen Lenaerts/Jose A. Gutiérrez-Fons*, The Constitutional Allocation of Powers and General Principles of EU Law, (2010) 47 Common Market Law Review (CMLR) 1629, 1629.

[8] For the distinction between "General Principles of Union law" and "General Principles of European Private Law" *Jürgen Basedow*, The Court of Justice and Private Law: Vacillations, General Principles and the Architecture of the European Judiciary, (2010) 18 European Review of Private Law (ERPL) 443, 462; *Idem*, Mangold, Audiolux und die allgemeinen Grundsätze des europäischen Privatrechts, in: Stefan Grundmann et al. (eds.), Festschrift für Klaus Hopt, 2010, pp. 27, 41 ff.

specific papers on both projects.[9] Likewise, the European Convention on Human Rights and its impact on tort law will be left out of the paper due to space constraints.[10]

II. The different facets of EU tort law

In the absence of any overarching codification at the European level, EU tort law presents itself in different facets, each of which may potentially serve as a basis to infer common principles of EU tort law.

1. Liability of public authorities

In the beginning, Art. 340(2) TFEU deserves to be mentioned. Under this provision, the Union can be held liable to "make good any damage caused by its institutions or by its servants in the performance of their duties", "in accordance with the general principles common to the laws of the Member States". Naming a tort law regime applying to public law bodies as a source of EU private law may come as a surprise. In many, though not all national legal systems public and private liability law are separate.[11] However, on the level of European law, the foundations of the liability of the Union were developed to a large extent on the basis of general principles of private law common to the Member States. For example, Advocate General *Capotorti* emphasized in *Ireks-Arkady*, a case concerning the liability of the Union for the enactment of a discriminatory refund system in the agricultural sector, that his remarks "are not limited to the field of private law, but apply also to the liability of public authorities, and more especially to the non-contractual

---

[9] See the papers by *Christian von Bar* and *Bernhard A. Koch* in this book; see also *Christian von Bar*, Außervertragliche Haftung für den Einem Anderen zugefügten Schaden, (2010) 18 ERPL 205 ff.

[10] On the ECHR case law in this field *Gerhard Dannemann*, Schadensersatz bei Verletzung der Europäischen Menschenrechtskonvention: Eine rechtsvergleichende Untersuchung zur Haftung nach Art. 50 EMRK, pp. 79 ff.; *Jan-Thomas Oskierski*, Schadensersatz im Europäischen Recht: Eine vergleichende Untersuchung des Acquis Communautaire und der EMRK, 2010, pp. 57 ff.

[11] *Cees van Dam*, European Tort Law, 2006, pp. 472, 474 ff. with the examples of France, Germany and UK.

liability of the Community".[12] Such private law principles applied by the ECJ when interpreting Art. 340 TFEU are, for example, the duty of the victim to mitigate the loss[13] or the distinction between *lucrum cessans* and *damnum emergens*.[14]

Closely related to the liability of the EU under Art. 340(2) TFEU is the non-contractual liability of the Member States for breach of EU law. This remedy has been shaped by the ECJ in a strand of cases subsequent to the *Francovich* judgment.[15] Over time, the ECJ has streamlined the liability of the Union and the liability of the Member States in many respects, a process that can be characterized as a form of judicial amendment of the European Treaties which was necessary to close gaps in the protection of Union rights conferred upon individuals. If, for example, a Member State had not transposed a directive into national law individuals could not rely on rights granted to them in this directive – unless its provisions were directly applicable, which will normally not be the case in disputes between private parties.[16] Similar gaps of judicial protection occurred with regard to infringements of primary law: In *Brasserie du Pêcheur* the ECJ therefore emphasized that the protection of the rights which individuals derive from Union law, in principle, "cannot vary depending on whether a national authority or a Union authority is responsible for the damage".[17] Therefore,

---

[12] Advocate General *Capotorti* 12.9.1979, Case 238/78 *(Ireks-Arkady/Council and Commission)*, [1979] ECR 2976, 2999.

[13] ECJ 19.5.1992, Joined cases C-104/89 and C-37/90 *(Mulder/Commission)*, [1992] ECR I-3061 para. 33.

[14] ECJ 3.2.1994, Case C-308/87 *(Grifoni/European Atomic Energy Community)*, [1994] ECR I-341 paras. 10 ff. ("expenditure caused by the accident") and paras. 20 ff. ("loss of earnings"). For further examples *Wolfgang Wurmnest*, Grundzüge eines europäischen Haftungsrechts: Eine rechtsvergleichende Untersuchung des Gemeinschaftsrechts, 2003, pp. 272 ff.; *Vaquer*, in: Helmut Koziol/Reiner Schulze (eds.), Tort Law of the European Community, 2008, pp. 23, 32 ff.; *Oskierski* (n. 10) pp. 176 ff.

[15] ECJ 19.11.1991, Joined cases C-6/90 and C-9/90 *(Francovich/Italian Republic)*, [1991] ECR I-5357; ECJ 25.11.2010, Case C-429/09 *(Fuß/Stadt Halle)*, paras. 45 ff. (not yet reported).

[16] In practice, the lack of direct effect between private parties is mitigated by a broad understanding of the principle that national law must be interpreted in conformity with EU law, ECJ 4.7.2006, Case C-212/04 *(Adeneler/ELOG)*, [2004] ECR I-6057 para. 111.

[17] ECJ 5.3.1996, Joined cases C-46/93 and C-48/93 *(Brasserie du pêcheur/Germany and The Queen/Secretary of State for Transport ex parte: Factortame)*, [1996] ECR I-1029 para. 42.

the requirements for liability of a public authority are similar under both systems, unless there is a special justification for a different regime.[18] However, it deserves to be mentioned that, even if the right to reparation under *Francovich* flows directly from EU law, reparation is made on the basis of the national rules on liability, provided that the conditions for reparation laid down by national law are not less favourable than those relating to similar domestic claims and are not so "framed as to make it, in practice, impossible or excessively difficult to obtain reparation".[19]

2. The principles of effectiveness and equivalence

While the liability of public authorities for breach of Union law is firmly established, it is less certain whether and under which conditions a comparable form of horizontal liability between private parties for breach of EU law exists, as proposed by Advocate General *van Gerven* in his opinion in *Banks*.[20] Such a form of horizontal liability has been confirmed by the ECJ for the infringement of EU competition rules (Art. 101, 102 TFEU)[21] and for the enforcement of EU regulations between private parties.[22] It is yet unclear how far horizontal liability may be extended to other areas, such as the market freedoms or fundamental rights. In any event, it may be safely said that the second pillar on which the case law of the ECJ in tort

---

[18] ECJ, *Brasserie du pêcheur/Germany and The Queen/Secretary of State for Transport ex parte: Factortame* (n. 17) para. 42 (The "conditions under which the State may incur liability for damage caused to individuals by a breach of Community law cannot, in the absence of particular justification, differ from those governing the liability of the Community in like circumstances").

[19] ECJ 30.9.2003, Case C-224/01 *(Köbler/Republik Österreich)*, [2003] ECR I-10239 para. 58; ECJ 26.1.2010, Case C-118/08 *(Transportes Urbanos y Servicios Generales SAL/Administración del Estado)*, para. 31 (not yet reported).

[20] Advocate General *van Gerven* 27.10.1993, Case C-128/92 *(H. J. Banks & Co. Ltd/ British Coal Corporation)*, [1994] ECR I-1209 paras. 36ff.; *Norbert Reich*, Rights without duties? Reflections on the state of liability law in the multilevel governance system of the Community: Is there a need for a more coherent approach in European Private Law?, EUI Working Paper Law 2009/10, pp. 9ff.; contra *Angela Ward*, Judicial Review and the Rights of Private Parties in EU law, 2nd edition, 2007, p. 251 f.

[21] ECJ 20.9.2001, Case C-453/99 *(Courage/Crehan)*, [2001] ECR I-6297 para. 26.

[22] ECJ 17.9.2002, Case C-253/00 *(Muñoz and Superior Fruiticola SA/Frumar Ltd and Redbridge Produce Marketing Ltd)*, [2002] ECR I-7289 para. 30.

law matters rests today are the principles of effectiveness and equivalence[23] which apply both to public and to private law remedies.[24] These principles imply essentially two consequences for national tort law: National tort law remedies for safeguarding individual rights under EU law (both primary and secondary law) must be no less favourable than those governing similar domestic actions (principle of equivalence) and must not render practically impossible or excessively difficult the exercise of rights conferred by Union law (principle of effectiveness).[25]

Even if the principles of effectiveness and equivalence do not lead to a harmonisation of tort law at the European level, but leave it to the "domestic legal system of each Member State to set the criteria for determining the extent of the damages, provided that the principles of equivalence and effectiveness are observed",[26] both principles may be a powerful tool for imposing European standards on national tort regimes.[27] For example, the

---

[23] These principles are referred to here in their implications for tort law. Another facet of the effectiveness principle is the right to an effective remedy for violation of rights guaranteed by the law of the EU, which is left out for the purposes of this paper as it impacts (mainly) on procedural remedies. The principle of effectiveness has also implications outside the law of remedies, e.g. for interpretation of EU law or the doctrine of direct effect, *Christian Heinze*, Effektivitätsgrundsatz, in: Jürgen Basedow/Klaus Hopt/Reinhard Zimmermann (eds.), Handwörterbuch des Europäischen Privatrechts, Band I, 2009, pp. 337 ff.

[24] For the application of these principles in private law see n. 21 and n. 22.

[25] ECJ, *Fuß/Stadt Halle* (n. 15), para. 62.

[26] ECJ 13.7.2006, Joined cases C-295/04 to C-298/04 *(Manfredi/Lloyd Adriatico)*, [2006] ECR I-6619, para. 92; *Norbert Reich*, Horizontal liability in EC law: Hybridization of remedies for compensation in case of breaches of EC rights, (2007) 44 CMLR 705, 709 ("hybridization of remedies"); *Christian Heinze*, Europäisches Primärrecht und Zivilprozess, Europarecht (EuR) 2008, 654, 688 ("Rahmensetzung").

[27] For a more thorough assessment *Evelyn Ellis*, EU Anti-Discrimination Law, 2005, pp. 77 ff. (for the impact on anti-discrimination law); *Renato Nazzini*, Potency and Act of the Principle of Effectiveness: The Development of Competition Law Remedies and Procedures in Community Law, in: Catherine Barnard/Okeoghene Odudu (eds.), The Outer Limits of EU Law, 2009, pp. 401 ff. (for the impact on private enforcement of competition law); *Ansgar Ohly*, Three principles of European IP enforcement law: Effectiveness, proportionality, dissuasiveness, in: Josef Drexl et al. (eds.), Technology and Competition: Contributions in Honour of Hanns Ullrich, 2009, pp. 257, 271 ff. (for the impact on the enforcement of intellectual property).

ECJ has scrutinised national rules of prescription under which the limitation period begins to run from the day on which the illegal practice was adopted under the doctrine of effectiveness, as such rules could make it practically impossible to exercise the right to seek compensation for the harm caused by that practice.[28]

At first sight, it may be tempting to regard the principles of effectiveness and equivalence as an element of EU primary law, as they are based on the Member States' cooperation obligations under Art. 4(3) TEU and Art. 19(1)3 TEU. However, a closer look reveals that the ECJ will assess the effectiveness of national (tort law) remedies "by reference to the role of that provision in the procedure, its progress and its special features, viewed as a whole".[29] In order to judge the effectiveness of a national tort law remedy, the ECJ will thus consider the specific legal environment in which the remedy is employed, in particular the wording, the general context and the aim of the substantive right the remedy seeks to enforce. As a result, the effectiveness in a given case will to a large extent depend on the aims and functions of the substantive right in question, which may be a right guaranteed either in primary (for example Art. 101 TFEU) or secondary law (directive or regulation). For these reasons most of the rules developed by the ECJ on the basis of the principle of effectiveness should be characterized as a form of hybrid between primary and secondary law, finding their legal justification in the duty of cooperation under the Treaty, but being defined in their specific contours by the substantive law in question which will (in most private law cases) have the nature of secondary law. As a result, the European legislator may, possibly subject to an undeniable core of effectiveness of substantive rights based on primary law, deviate from ECJ case law by legislative action as much as the legislator could abolish the substantive law itself. A good example of the hybrid nature of the principle of effectiveness can be seen in the field of anti-discrimination law: After the ECJ had defined certain minimum standards of effectiveness for enforcing the right against

---

[28] ECJ, *Manfredi/Lloyd Adriatico* (n. 26) para. 78. For a more general analysis of national limitation periods ECJ 16.7.2009, Case C-69/08 *(Raffaello Visciano/Istituto nazionale della previdenza sociale)*, [2009] ECR I-6741 paras. 43 ff.; for further references Advocate General *Trstenjak* 2.4.2009, Case C-69/08 *(Raffaello Visciano/ Istituto nazionale della previdenza sociale)*, [2009] ECR I-6741 paras. 87 ff.

[29] ECJ 14.12.1995, Case C-312/93 *(Peterbroeck/Belgian State)*, [1995] ECR I-4599 para. 14; ECR 4.12.2003, Case C-63/01 *(Evans/The Secretary of State for the Environment, Transport and the Regions and The Motor Insurers' Bureau)*, [2003] ECR I-14447 para. 46.

discrimination on grounds of sex, the European legislator adopted these standards in secondary legislation, however only in directives concerning discrimination on grounds of sex, not discrimination on other grounds.[30]

3. The growing body of secondary law

The third source of EU tort law which needs to be mentioned is a growing body of secondary law. Over the years, the European legislature has enacted various directives and regulations containing rules on tort or damages

---

[30] See recital 33 of Directive 2006/54/EC of the European Parliament and of the Council of 5 July 2006 on the implementation of the principle of equal opportunities and equal treatment of men and women in matters of employment and occupation (recast), OJ 2006 L 204/23.

[31] Council Directive 85/374/EEC of 25 July 1985 on the approximation of the laws, regulations and administrative provisions of the Member States concerning liability for defective products, OJ 1985 L 210/29.

[32] Art. 13 (see also Art. 7(4), 9(7)) of Directive 2004/48/EC of the European Parliament and of the Council of 29 April 2004 on the enforcement of intellectual property rights, OJ 2004 L 157/45, corrigendum in OJ 2004 L 195/16; Art. 94(2) of Council Regulation (EC) No 2100/94 of 27 July 1994 on Community plant variety rights, OJ 1994 L 227/1. See also Art. 9 of the (draft) Anti-Counterfeiting Trade Agreement, http://trade.ec.europa.eu/doclib/docs/2010/december/tradoc_147079.pdf and Art. 41 of the Draft Agreement on the European and Community Patents Court and Draft Statute, Council Document No 7928/09 of 23.3.2009. For the evaluation of Art. 13 of Directive 2004/48/EC Report from the Commission to the European Parliament, the Council, the European Social and Economic Committee and the Committee of the Regions: Application of Directive 2004/48/EC of the European Parliament and the Council of 29 April 2004 on the enforcement of intellectual property rights, COM(2010) 779 final, p. 8.

law, ranging from product liability[31] via intellectual property[32] and anti-discrimination law[33] to travel[34] and transportation[35] law. Other examples

---

[33] Art. 8(2) of Council Directive 2004/113/EC of 13 December 2004 implementing the principle of equal treatment between men and women in the access to and supply of goods and services, OJ 2004 L 373/37; Art. 18 of Directive 2006/54 (above n. 30); Art. 10 of Directive 2010/41/EU of the European Parliament and of the Council of 7 July 2010 on the application of the principle of equal treatment between men and women engaged in an activity in a self-employed capacity and repealing Council Directive 86/613/EEC, OJ 2010 L 180/1. For a less specific guarantee of remedies Art. 15 of Council Directive 2000/43/EC of 29 June 2000 implementing the principle of equal treatment between persons irrespective of racial or ethnic origin, OJ 2000 L 180/22; Art. 17 of Council Directive 2000/78/EC of 27 November 2000 establishing a general framework for equal treatment in employment and occupation, OJ 2000 L 303/16.

[34] Art. 5 of Council Directive 90/314/EEC of 13 June 1990 on package travel, package holidays and package tours, OJ 1990 L 158/59.

[35] See, for example, Art. 7 of Regulation (EC) No 261/2004 of the European Parliament and of the Council of 11 February 2004 establishing common rules on compensation and assistance to passengers in the event of denied boarding and of cancellation or long delay of flights, and repealing Regulation (EEC) No 295/91, OJ 2004 L 46/1; Council Regulation (EC) No 2027/97 of 9 October 1997 on air carrier liability in the event of accidents, OJ 1997 L 285/1, as amended by Regulation (EC) No 889/2002 of the European Parliament and of the Council of 13 May 2002 amending Council Regulation (EC) No 2027/97 on air carrier liability in the event of accidents; OJ 2002 L 140/2. The latter regulations refer largely (Art. 3) to the Montreal Convention, for EU approval of this Convention Council Decision 2001/539/EC of 5 April 2001 on the conclusion by the European Community of the Convention for the Unification of Certain Rules for International Carriage by Air (the Montreal Convention), OJ 2001 L 194/38. An analysis of tort claims under EU transport law can be found in the paper by *Ansgar Staudinger* in this book.

include data protection,[36] public procurement,[37] environmental liability,[38] and capital market regulation.[39]

While the diversity of these measures is impressive, all European instruments share certain characteristic features which are clearly distinct from national tort law: First and foremost, EU legislation in the field of tort law

---

[36] Art. 23 of Directive 95/46/EC of the European Parliament and of the Council of 24 October 1995 on the protection of individuals with regard to the processing of personal data and on the free movement of such data, OJ 1995 L 281/31. In the E-Commerce Directive, there is a rather general reference to "measures", Art. 18 and recital 52 of Directive 2000/31/EC of the European Parliament and of the Council of 8 June 2000 on certain legal aspects of information society services, in particular electronic commerce, in the Internal Market ('Directive on electronic commerce'), OJ 2000 L 178/1. However, this directive includes important privileges for liability for "mere conduit", "caching" and "hosting" (Art. 12-15). For the special field of electronic signatures Art. 6 of Directive 1999/93/EC of the European Parliament and of the Council of 13 December 1999 on a Community framework for electronic signatures, OJ 2000 L 13/12.

[37] Art. 2(1)(c) of Directive 2007/66/EC of the European Parliament and of the Council of 11 December 2007 amending Council Directives 89/665/EEC and 92/13/EEC with regard to improving the effectiveness of review procedures concerning the award of public contracts, OJ 2007 L 335/31.

[38] Directive 2004/35/EC of the European Parliament and of the Council of 21 April 2004 on environmental liability with regard to the prevention and remedying of environmental damage, OJ 2004 L 143/56 (which does not give private parties a right of compensation as a consequence of environmental damage, Art 1(3)).

[39] Art. 6 of Directive 2003/71/EC of the European Parliament and of the Council of 4 November 2003 on the prospectus to be published when securities are offered to the public or admitted to trading and amending Directive 2001/34/EC, OJ 2003 L 345/64, as amended by Directive 2010/73/EU of the European Parliament and of the Council of 24 November 2010 amending Directives 2003/71/EC on the prospectus to be published when securities are offered to the public or admitted to trading and 2004/109/EC on the harmonisation of transparency requirements in relation to information about issuers whose securities are admitted to trading on a regulated market, OJ 2010 L 327/1; Art. 7 of Directive 2004/109/EC of the European Parliament and of the Council of 15 December 2004 on the harmonisation of transparency requirements in relation to information about issuers whose securities are admitted to trading on a regulated market and amending Directive 2001/34/EC, OJ 2004 L 390/38. As to the impact of these provisions *Alexander Hellgardt*, Kapitalmarktdeliktsrecht, 2008, p. 7; see also the paper by *Matthias Casper* in this book.

(and private law in general) is driven largely by the implementation of certain Union policies, in particular the functioning of the Internal Market.[40] As a result, EU legislation appears to be fragmentary and unsystematic, at least judged against the standards of modern national codifications.[41] As a further consequence of this policy-driven legislation, EU tort law lacks a general set of tort law rules as it is found in national codifications, for example in §§ 823 ff. BGB and Art. 1382 ff. Code Civil. Instead, we find an abundance of special torts, in particular economic torts, which characterize European tort law as a sort of fragmentary *Sonderdeliktsrecht*.

4. Principles common to the law of the Member States

Finally, it may be discussed whether principles common to the national law of the Member States may also serve as a source of EU tort law.[42] As pointed out above, "general principles common to the laws of the Member States" are explicitly mentioned in the text of Art. 340(2) TFEU. Therefore, it does not come as a surprise that there are references to common principles of national law in the ECJ's jurisprudence on that liability regime.[43] In a similar manner, principles common to the national law of the Member States are being referred to in the jurisprudence on liability of the Member States for breach of EU law under the *Francovich* doctrine.[44] However, it has been doubted whether the reference to common principles in Art. 340(2) TFEU has indeed led to comparative law analysis influencing the case law of the ECJ in this field or whether it has rather been a normative approach which has guided the ECJ.[45] Beyond the liability of public bodies, comparative law analysis may also become relevant in the assessment under the principle of

---

[40] *Basedow,* (2010) 18 ERPL 443, 451.
[41] *Helmut Koziol/Reiner Schulze,* Conclusio, in: Helmut Koziol/Reiner Schulze (eds.), Tort Law of the European Community, 2008, pp. 589, 590 ff.
[42] For the role of internal and external principles of EU private law *Metzger* (n. 6) p. 555.
[43] ECJ, *Mulder/Council of the European Communities and Commission* (n. 13) para. 33.
[44] ECJ, *Brasserie du pêcheur/Germany and The Queen/Secretary of State for Transport ex parte: Factortame* (n. 17) para. 85; ECJ 24.3.2009, Case C-445/06 *(Danske Slagterier/Bundesrepublik Deutschland),* [2009] ECR I-2119 para. 61; ECJ, *Fuß/Stadt Halle* (n. 15) para. 76.
[45] *Sebastian Martens,* Rechtsvergleichung und grenzüberwindende Jurisprudenz im Gemeinschaftsrecht, in: Christoph Busch et al. (eds.), Europäische Methodik: Konvergenz und Diskrepanz europäischen und nationalen Privatrechts, 2010, pp. 27,

effectiveness whether a specific rule of national law limiting the effectiveness of EU law is consistent with European standards. For example, the ECJ has repeatedly accepted the principle of *res judicata* as a limit for the principle of effectiveness, pointing to the importance of *res judicata* "both for the Community legal order and for the national legal systems".[46] Occasionally, there is reference to national law being made also in cases concerning EU secondary law, albeit mostly in the opinion of the advocates general,[47] less so in the reasoning of the Luxembourg court.[48]

All in all, it may be summarised that comparative analysis, at least comparative analysis being made explicit in the reasoning of the decision, seems to be less important than other methods of interpretation of EU law.[49] Possible reasons are manifold: On the one hand, it becomes more and more difficult to deduce common principles from the national laws, on the necessary level of specificity, in a Union with more than 27 private law jurisdictions. In addition, even in cases where the analysis of national law tends towards a certain solution, it may be that the EU instrument in question pursues specific European policies, which are not necessarily the same as those furthered by national law.[50] Finally, the more mature the legal order of the European Union becomes, the more inclined will both the Union's court and the Union's legislator be to follow concepts which have already

---

40; *Götz Schulze*, in: Martin Gebauer/Thomas Wiedmann, Zivilrecht unter europäischem Einfluss, 2nd edition, 2010, chapter 18 para. 12.

[46] ECJ 6.10.2009, Case C-40/08 *(Asturcom Telecomunicaciones SL/Rodríguez Nogueira)*, [2009] ECR I-9579 para. 35 (further references in para. 36).

[47] For an example Advocate General *Tizzano* 20.9.2001, Case C-168/00 *(Leitner/TUI Deutschland GmbH & Co. KG)*, [2002] ECR I-2631 paras. 39 ff.

[48] For an example ECJ, *Evans/The Secretary of State for the Environment, Transport and the Regions and The Motor Insurers' Bureau* (n. 29) paras. 75, 78, where the view of "most of the Member States" was brought forward as an argument for qualifying the reimbursement of legal costs as procedural and thus being, in general, outside the scope of a right to compensation under the Directive.

[49] *Burkhard Hess*, Methoden der Rechtsfindung im Europäischen Zivilprozessrecht, Praxis des Internationalen Privat- und Verfahrensrechts (IPRax) 2006, 348, 352 ff. (for the Brussels Regulation); an important role for principles common to the law of the Member States is advocated by *Martens* (n. 45) pp. 32, 39.

[50] One may only think of the objective of market integration beyond national borders, which is a clear priority of EU legislation, while being less relevant for national legislators. For an interesting example rejecting comparative analysis Advocate General *Alber* 24.10.2002, *Evans/The Secretary of State for the Environment, Transport and the Regions and The Motor Insurers' Bureau* (n. 29) para. 35.

been developed in other areas of EU law, instead of undergoing the difficult task of a comparative analysis of dozens of national laws.[51] For all these reasons, principles common to the national law of the Member States will not be analyzed further in this paper, while it shall not be denied that such principles may play a role, in particular between the lines of EU legislation or jurisprudence.

5. Noble isolation?

Our brief *tour d'horizon* has shown that EU tort law presents itself as a complex synthesis of both primary and secondary law, stretching over a broad range of very different areas of substantive law. This begs the question whether it is at all meaningful to draw broader principles from these – at first sight: disparate – sources, or whether each regime flourishes in noble isolation.

In this context, three issues have to be distinguished. The first point is whether it is meaningful to infer overarching principles from (at least) some of the liability regimes for (at least) some aspects of tort law. The second issue is whether the ECJ has already started to connect the different regimes, while a third question may be whether the current approach found in ECJ jurisprudence gives sufficient guidance to national courts. The first two issues will be addressed in the following comments. The third issue – which essentially concerns the quality of the case law – will be dealt with in the last part of the paper (below IV.).

With respect to the first issue, it does indeed appear meaningful to infer overarching principles from (at least) some of the liability regimes for (at least) some aspects of tort law. In this context, it is important to note that EU law has grown considerably over the last years. Whereas fifteen years ago, EU tort law was primarily seen as a justifiably neglected area of "consumer tort law" not worth considering when elaborating comparative principles of European tort law,[52] the European legislator has since that time enacted a number of other instruments, mostly in the field of business law.[53] More

---

[51] See *Metzger* (n. 6) p. 556 (predicting a relative decline of external principles the more mature EU private law becomes).

[52] *Nils Jansen*, Book review of van Dam, European Tort Law, (2010) 73 The Rabel Journal of Comparative and International Private Law (RabelsZ) 205. The most comprehensive treatise on a common European tort law therefore addressed EU law therefore very briefly only, see *Christian von Bar,* The Common Tort European Law of Torts, Volume I, 1998, pp. 400 ff.

[53] For examples above n. 32, 33, 35, 37, 39.

importantly, there is also a much richer body of case law than fifteen years ago. Formulating common principles for at least some areas of EU tort law is meaningful to the extent that such principles can enhance the consistency of the case law and provide guidance for national courts in applying EU law to issues not yet decided by the ECJ. More importantly, it seems – *faute de mieux* – the best means available to ensure a truly autonomous interpretation of EU law: As national courts and private litigants will not always be willing to wait for the outcome of a preliminary reference to the Court of Justice, using existing ECJ case law and EU secondary law in one area to interpret EU law in another (comparable) field may be the best a national court can do to ensure a truly autonomous interpretation of European law. Necessarily, this does not mean that the different functions and settings of the different regimes do not have to be taken into account.[54] For example, it goes without saying that the liability of the Union under Art. 340(2) TFEU will be structured in a way that the work of public institutions is not severely hampered by the threat of actions for damages,[55] while the participants of a hard-core cartel might expect less understanding for their activities. However, these differences do not mean that the case law on Art. 340(2) TFEU and the liability of the Member States for breach of EU law should or even could be disregarded when the ECJ is asked to interpret tort law in other areas.[56]

It is neither possible nor intended in this paper to come up with a complete elaboration of European principles. However, and this leads to the second point identified above, this paper wants to draw attention to the fact that the Court of Justice has already – sometimes reluctantly and not in a very systematic or coherent manner – begun to connect the different liability regimes when deciding a given case. An example is the *Manfredi* judgment.[57] This case concerned a claim for damages brought by consum-

---

[54] This point is emphasised by *Wurmnest* (n. 14) p. 91; *Friedrich Wenzel Bulst*, Zum Manfredi-Urteil des EuGH, Zeitschrift für Europäisches Privatrecht (ZEuP) 2008, 178, 189 f.; *Oskierski* (n. 10) pp. 62 ff.

[55] See for example *Court of First Instance (CFI)* 9.9.2008, Case T-212/03 *(MyTravel Group plc/Commission)*, [2008] ECR II-1967 para. 42.

[56] *Walter Van Gerven*, The Emergence of a Common European Law in the Area of Tort Law: The EU Contribution, in: Duncan Fairgrieve/Mats Andenas/John Bell (eds.), Tort Liability of Public Authorities in Comparative Perspective, 2002, pp. 125, 142 f. ("ECJ will … draw inspiration from its earlier case law concerning liability of Community institutions and of Member States"); see also *Wurmnest* (n. 14) pp. 87 ff.; *Oskierski* (n. 10) pp. 62 ff.; *Bulst*, ZEuP 2008, 178, 190.

[57] ECJ, *Manfredi/Lloyd Adriatico* (n. 26).

ers against a price fixing cartel for a violation of Art. 101 TFEU. The Court ruled that the compensation to be paid by the cartelist to the consumer for breach of the EU competition rules must include actual loss *(damnum emergens)*, loss of future profits *(lucrum cessans)* and interest, while national courts were permitted to take "steps to ensure that the protection of the rights guaranteed by Community law does not entail the unjust enrichment of those who enjoy them".[58] These results were inferred by the Court, *inter alia*, with reference to the *Francovich* case law on liability of the Member States, the *Marshall* decision on compensation for discrimination on grounds of sex and the *Ireks-Arkady* judgment on Art. 340(2) TFEU.[59]

Necessarily, such "judge-made" harmonization will never become as coherent and complete as a body of national tort law. The reasons for this are simple: As the EU has no general tort law but only a number of specific instruments which establish special (mostly economic) torts, one has to be careful to infer common rules from a basis which is limited in scope and specific in nature. Moreover, the Court has to decide on the basis of the legislation as it stands and can only partly iron out potential deficiencies of legislative drafting.

III. Emerging principles

The following part of this paper will focus on two rather general examples of emerging principles of European tort law. It will address the functions of tort law and the recoverability of non-pecuniary loss, leaving more specific questions of tort law to the later papers to follow.

1. Functions

a) (Full) Compensation

As under national law,[60] the primary function of EU tort law is to compensate the injured person for the loss suffered, as far as this can be achieved by means of damages. This function has been confirmed by the ECJ for the

---

[58] ECJ, *Manfredi/Lloyd Adriatico* (n. 26) paras. 94, 100.
[59] ECJ, *Manfredi/Lloyd Adriatico* (n. 26) paras. 94, 96, 97.
[60] For the importance of compensation as primary function of tort law *Ulrich Magnus*, Comparative Report on the Law of Damages, in: Ulrich Magnus (ed.), Unifica-

liability of the Union under Art. 340(2) TFEU,[61] as well as for the liability of the Member States for breach of EU law.[62] The aim of full compensation has also been upheld in secondary law, for example in insurance law[63] and in the directive on the enforcement of intellectual property rights (hereafter: IP Enforcement Directive).[64] Under this directive, damages shall be awarded "appropriate to the actual prejudice suffered ... as a result of the infringement" (Art. 13(1) IP Enforcement Directive), "with a view to compensating for the prejudice suffered as a result of an infringement" (recital 26 IP Enforcement Directive). The purpose of compensation can also be found in anti-discrimination law, where EU directives – modelled on earlier case law[65] – require the Member States "to ensure real and effective com-

---

tion of tort Law: Damages, 2001, p. 185; *Nils Jansen*, Die Struktur des Haftungsrechts, 2002, pp. 373 ff.

[61] ECJ 7.10.1982, Case 131/81 *(Berti/Commission)*, [1982] ECR 3493 para. 24; ECJ 8.10.1986, Joined cases 169/83 and 136/84 *(Leussink/Commission)*, [1986] ECR 2801 para. 13 ("full compensation for the injury suffered"); ECJ, *Grifoni/European Atomic Energy Community* (n. 14) para. 40 ("compensation for loss is intended so far as possible to provide restitution for the victim"); ECJ, *Mulder/Council of the European Communities and Commission* (n. 13) para. 34 ("compensation payable by the Community should correspond to the damage which it caused"); ECJ 9.9.1999, Case C-257/98 P *(Lucaccioni/Commission)*, [1999] ECR I-5251 para. 28 ("an official who has suffered harm following a fault committed by an institution must receive full, but not double, compensation"); ECJ 21.2.2008, Case C-348/06 P *(Commission/Girardot)*, [2008] ECR I-833 para. 76 ("ensure that the individual damage actually suffered by the party concerned because of the particular unlawful acts ... is fully compensated").

[62] ECJ, *Brasserie du pêcheur/Germany and The Queen/Secretary of State for Transport ex parte: Factortame* (n. 17) para. 82 ("Reparation for loss or damage caused to individuals as a result of breaches of Community law must be commensurate with the loss or damage sustained"); ECJ 10.7.1997, Joined cases C-94/95 and C-95/95 *(Bonifaci/INPS)*, [1997] ECR I-3969 paras. 48, 53.

[63] ECJ, *Evans/The Secretary of State for the Environment, Transport and the Regions and The Motor Insurers' Bureau* (n. 29) para. 67 ("compensation for loss is intended so far as possible to provide restitution", citing Grifoni, n. 14 above, para. 69: "guarantee the victims of damage or injury caused by unidentified or insufficiently insured vehicles the adequate compensation which that directive seeks to provide").

[64] Above n. 32.

[65] ECJ 10.4.1984, Case 14/83 *(von Colson und Kamann/Land Nordrhein-Westfalen)*, [1984] ECR 1891 para. 23; ECJ 10.4.1984, Case 79/83 *(Harz/Deutsche Tradax GmbH)*, [1984] ECR 1921 para. 28 ("compensation must in any event be adequate

pensation or reparation ... for the loss or damage sustained by a person as a result of discrimination on grounds of sex" (Art. 10 Directive 2010/41; Art. 18 Directive 2006/54).[66] Adequate compensation means in principle full compensation and usually includes the payment of interest, as the ECJ has recently reiterated in the *Manfredi* case.[67] A certain exception to the principle of full compensation could be seen, at least at first sight, in the Product Liability Directive. Art. 9(b) of this directive excludes compensation for damaged objects below 500 Euros to be recovered under the directive. Yet, this does not mean that the principle of full compensation is unknown to product liability law. In *Veedfald*, the ECJ has confirmed that "save for non-material damage whose reparation is governed solely by national law, full and proper compensation for persons injured by a defective product must be available".[68] Therefore, the exclusion in Art. 9(b) Product Liability Directive has to be seen as an exception to the general rule, an exception introduced as a political compromise between those states that wanted to keep damages to objects outsides the directive's scope and those who wanted to have such pecuniary losses inside its scope.[69]

---

in relation to the damage sustained and must therefore amount to more than purely nominal compensation"); ECJ 2.8.1993, Case C-271/91 *(Marshall/Southampton and South-West Hampshire Area Health Authority)*, [1993] ECR I-4367 para. 34 ("compensation must be full and may not be limited a priori in terms of its amount"); ECJ 22.4.1997, C-180/95 *(Draehmpaehl/Urania Immobilienservice OHG)*, [1997] ECR I-2195, paras. 39 f.

[66] The provisions for discrimination for other grounds than sex are less explicit, see Art. 15 Directive 2000/43; Art. 17 of Directive 2000/78 ("The sanctions, which may comprise the payment of compensation to the victim, must be effective, proportionate and dissuasive").

[67] ECJ, *Manfredi/Lloyd Adriatico* (n. 26) paras. 94, 100; see also ECJ, *Marshall/Southampton and South-West Hampshire Area Health Authority* (n. 55), para. 31; for a similar result ECJ, *Evans/The Secretary of State for the Environment, Transport and the Regions and The Motor Insurers' Bureau* (n. 29) para. 70 ("In that connection, the Member States are free, in order to compensate for the loss suffered by victims as a result of the effluxion of time, to choose between awarding interest or paying compensation in the form of aggregate sums which take account of the effluxion of time"). However, *Evans* did not concern a damages claim, but a claim under compulsory insurance.

[68] ECJ 10.5.2001, Case C-203/99 *(Veedfald/Århus Amtskommune)*, [2001] ECR I-3569 para. 27.

[69] Hans Claudius Taschner/Erwin Frietsch, Produkthaftungsgesetz und EG-Produkthaftungsrichtlinier, Kommentar, 2nd edition, 1990, § 11 ProdHaftG paras. 4 f.; see

In addition, it should be emphasized that Art. 13 Product Liability Directive does not exclude national tort claims based on fault or contractual actions for damages, which may compensate for the sum of 500 Euro not recoverable under the directive.

b) Beyond compensation

Compensation is, however, not the only function of EU tort law. A closer look at the legal sources reveals that, at least in certain contexts, EU tort law also serves the goal of prevention.[70] The element of prevention has been recognized explicitly in the field of anti-discrimination law, where the ECJ requires Member States to ensure that compensation, if chosen as a remedy for infringement, must not only "guarantee real and effective judicial protection", but also "have a real deterrent effect on the employer and must in any event be adequate in relation to the damage sustained".[71] Also with regard to enforcement of EU competition rules, the ECJ has acknowledged in the *Courage* case that actions for damages serve preventive purposes as a functioning system of private enforcement "strengthens the working of the Community competition rules and discourages agreements or practices, which are frequently covert, which are liable to restrict or distort competition."[72] From that point of view, actions for damages in the national

---

also Gert Brüggemeier, Haftungsrecht: Struktur, Prinzipien, Schutzbereich, 2006, p. 440.

[70] For an extensive analysis *Gerhard Wagner,* Prävention und Verhaltenssteuerung durch Privatrecht – Anmaßung oder legitime Aufgabe?, Archiv für die civilistische Praxis (AcP) 2010, 352, 389 ff.; see also *Norbert Reich,* Horizontal liability in secondary EC law: Also a critique of ECJ case law on remedies for compensation in product liability, non-discrimination, and intellectual property law, in: Mads Andenas et al. (eds.), Liber Amicorum Guido Alpa: Private Law Beyond the National Systems, 2007, pp. 846, 867.

[71] ECJ, *Draehmpaehl/Urania Immobilienservice OHG* (n. 65) para. 25; ECJ, *von Colson und Kamann/Land Nordrhein-Westfalen* (n. 65) para 23.

[72] ECJ, *Courage/Crehan* (n. 21) para. 27. This implies that the European legislator requires a functioning enforcement system having a preventive effect, see *Jürgen Basedow,* Perspektiven des Kartellprivatrechts, Zeitschrift für Wettbewerbsrecht (ZWeR) 2006, 294, 296; *Wolfgang Wurmnest,* Schadensersatz wegen Verletzung des EU-Kartellrechts – Grundfragen und Entwicklungslinien, in: Oliver Remien (ed.), Schadensersatz im europäischen Privat- und Wirtschaftsrecht, Tübingen (forthcoming 2011); for a more general view on the relevance of prevention in

courts can make "a significant contribution to the maintenance of effective competition in the Community".[73]

An element of prevention may further be recognized in provisions which establish a right to "standardized" damages. An example for this can be found in Regulation 261/2004 on compensation and assistance to passengers in the event of denied boarding and of cancellation or long delay of flights.[74] Art. 7 of this regulation gives passengers a right to compensation amounting to 250, 400 or 600 Euro, depending on the distance of the flight, irrespective of individual loss. The purpose of such "standardized" damages is not only to repair damage consisting in a loss of time,[75] but also to create an incentive for the operating carrier to perform better and to prevent them from cancelling flights.[76]

Another example for a broader understanding of tort law may be identified in Art. 13 IP Enforcement Directive. While the initial proposal for double royalties[77] was not taken up in the final text of the directive,[78] the final text of the directive still provides in Art. 13(1)(a) for "damages appropriate

---

EU competition law enforcement *Ackermann*, Prävention als Paradigma: Zur Verteidigung eines effektiven kartellrechtlichen Sanktionssystems, ZWeR 2010, 329 ff.

[73] ECJ, *Courage/Crehan* (n. 21) para. 27.
[74] Above n. 35.
[75] ECJ 19.11.2009, Joined cases C-402/07 and C-432/07 *(Sturgeon/Condor Flugdienst GmbH)*, paras. 51 f. (not yet reported); for the distinction between "standardised" damages and individual damages for delayed flights ECJ 10.1.2006, Case C-344/04 *(The Queen, on the application of International Air Transport Association and European Low Fares Airline Association/Department for Transport)*, [2006] ECR I-403 paras. 43 f.
[76] For the idea of "dissuasion" in the legislative history of the Regulation Advocate General *Sharpston* 2.7.2009, Sturgeon/Condor Flugdienst GmbH (n. 75) paras. 33 f. (not yet reported).
[77] Proposal for a Directive of the European Parliament and of the Council on measures and procedures to ensure the enforcement of intellectual property rights, COM(2003) 46 final, Art. 17(1)(a) ("damages set at double the royalties or fees which would have been due if the infringer had requested authorisation to use the intellectual property right in question"). Multiple royalties are required by Art. 18(2) of Commission Regulation (EC) No 1768/95 of 24 July 1995 implementing rules on the agricultural exemption provided for in Art. 14 (3) of Council Regulation (EC) No 2100/94 on Community plant variety rights, OJ 1995 L 173/14.
[78] Which has not silenced the debate, with some authors arguing in favour of the idea of double royalties, for references *Heinze*, Die Durchsetzung geistigen Eigentums

Wolfgang Wurmnest/Christian Heinze

to the actual prejudice suffered ... as a result of the infringement", which are calculated by taking "into account all appropriate aspects, such as the negative economic consequences, including lost profits, which the injured party has suffered, any unfair profits made by the infringer and, in appropriate cases, elements other than economic factors, such as the moral prejudice caused to the rightholder by the infringement". In particular the reference to "unfair profits made by the infringer" opens the door for a broader perspective on the law of damages,[79] as skimming off the wrongdoers profits is traditionally not regarded as a remedy of tort law.[80] Such a broader approach may also find support in recital 17 IP Enforcement Directive, which allows "to take due account of the specific characteristics of that case, including the specific features of each intellectual property right and, where appropriate, the intentional or unintentional character of the infringement".[81]

In sum, there is a tendency in some areas of EU tort law, namely in the field of market regulation (competition, intellectual property, transport law), but also in anti-discrimination law, to broaden our perspective on tort law beyond compensation (at least in its traditional understanding) to include the idea of prevention. However, it is yet unclear whether this holds true for all fields of European tort law. Further, it is uncertain how the idea of prevention relates to the traditional goal of (full) compensation and how it may be translated into the assessment of damages in an individual case.[82] In this context, it is worth mentioning that EU law allows national courts "to ensure that the protection of the rights guaranteed by Union law does not entail the unjust enrichment of those who enjoy them",[83] a statement

---

in Europa – Zur Umsetzung der Richtlinie 2004/48/EG in Deutschland, England und Frankreich, ZEuP 2009, 282, 307.

[79] This is underlined by the recent report from the Commission (n. 32), COM(2010) 779 final, p. 8 ("The compensatory and dissuasive effect of damages: ... it could be considered whether the courts should have the power to grant damages commensurate with the infringer's unjust enrichment, even if they exceed the actual damage incurred by the rightholder. Equally, there could be a case for making greater use of the possibility to award damages for other economic consequences and moral damages").

[80] *Helmut Koziol*, Grundfragen des Schadensersatzrechts, 2010, para. 2/45 (Anspruch „im Zwischenbereich von Schadensersatz- und Bereicherungsausgleich").

[81] *Ohly* (n. 27) 273 f.; see also Art. 3(2) IP Enforcement Directive ("effective, proportionate and dissuasive" measures).

[82] For potential consequences for the assessment of damages *Wagner*, AcP 2010, 352, 402 ff., 459 ff.

[83] ECJ, *Manfredi/Lloyd Adriatico* (n. 26) para. 94.

which could be read as *carte blanche* for national rules not only preventing punitive, but also any form of supra-compensatory damages (while probably not being meant as such). In turn, recital 32 Rome II Regulation[84] makes clear that only "non-compensatory exemplary or punitive damages *of an excessive nature*" (i.e. not all forms of supra-compensatory damages)[85] may be regarded as being contrary to the public policy of the forum. As final example for a sceptical approach towards punitive damages it is worth quoting again the IP Enforcement Directive: According to its recital 26, this directive does not aim "to introduce an obligation to provide for punitive damages".[86]

2. Non-material loss

As a second overarching concept of European tort law, compensation for non-material loss may be mentioned. Whereas Art. 9 Product Liability Directive excludes claims for non-material loss from its scope,[87] other EU instruments and the jurisprudence of the Luxembourg court have stressed the importance of compensation for this type of damage.[88]

To begin with, compensation for non-material loss has played an important role in liability under Art. 340(2) TFEU: Many cases decided under this provision concerned compensation for non-material loss, especially if one takes the case law into account in which the administrative personnel claimed damages from the Union.[89] Examples include compensation for pain and suffering as a result of a violation of bodily health,[90] but also

---

[84] Regulation (EC) No 864/2007 of the European Parliament and of the Council of 11 July 2007 on the law applicable to non-contractual obligations (Rome II), OJ 2007 L 199/40.
[85] *Ackermann*, ZWeR 2010, 329, 350.
[86] A specific reference to "deterrent sanctions" can be found in ECJ 26.4.2007, Case C-348/04 *(Boehringer Ingelheim KG/Swingward and Dowelhurst)*, [2007] ECR I-3391 para. 64. Today, this situation would be governed by Art. 13 of the IP enforcement Directive.
[87] ECJ, *Veedfald/Århus Amtskommune* (n. 68) para. 27.
[88] *Reich* (n. 70) 866; *Oskierski* (n. 10) 255 ff.
[89] For further discussion see *Wurmnest* (n. 14) 289 ff.; *Oskierski* (n. 10) 255 ff.
[90] ECJ, *Grifoni/European Atomic Energy Community* (n. 14) para. 37 ("physical or mental suffering"); ECJ, *Leussink/Commission* (n. 61) para. 18 (non-economic consequences as far as family and social relationships are considered as "non-material damage giving rise to entitlement to compensation").

compensation for an infringement of reputation.[91] A right to compensation for non-material damage (in this case for pain and suffering and loss of enjoyment of the holidays) has also been recognized under the Package Travel Directive.[92] Further examples for compensation of non-material loss may be found in transport law, where the ECJ has developed a distinction between "individual" non-material damage (to be compensated under the Montreal Convention)[93] and another form of (apparently) non-material damage "constituted by the inconvenience that delay in the carriage of passengers by air causes"[94] (to be compensated under Regulation 261/2004). Non-material loss may also be seen as an element of "real and effective compensation" under anti-discrimination law, and even the infringement of intellectual property rights may lead to non-material losses which have to be included in the court's assessment of damages (Art. 13(1)(a) IP Enforcement Directive).[95] As a result, it may be concluded that European law shows a trend towards compensation for non-material loss, even if the ECJ did not seize the chance to elevate this idea into the rank of a general principle of Union private law in the *Leitner* case.

IV. The way forward

Even though the ECJ deserves applause for any step towards a more coherent and systematic understanding of European tort law, the present state of the evolving judge-made law is far from being satisfactory. The last part of this paper therefore highlights apparent deficiencies in the case law and discusses possible means of weeding them out in the near future.

---

[91] CFI 9.7.1999, Case T-231/97 *(New Europe Consulting and Brown/Commission)*, [1999] ECR II-2403 paras. 53 f.
[92] ECJ 12.3.2002, Case C-168/00 *(Leitner/TUI Deutschland)*, [2002] ECR I-2631 para. 23.
[93] ECJ 6.5.2010, Case C-63/09 *(Walz/Clickair SA)*, para. 29 (not yet reported) (interpreting the Montreal Convention).
[94] ECJ, *The Queen, on the application of International Air Transport Association and European Low Fares Airline Association/Department for Transport* (n. 75) paras. 43, 45.
[95] However, the division line between material and non-material loss is disputed in case of infringement of intellectual property rights, *Heinze*, ZEuP 2009, 282, 308.

1. More courage

A first deficiency is the undue caution and self-restraint of the European judges when handling private law cases.[96] Instead of developing broader principles of tort law, the judges in Luxembourg often stick narrowly to the EU instrument which has to be interpreted in the case at hand. A good example is the *Simone Leitner* case relating to non-material loss under the Package Travel Directive.[97] Whereas Advocate General *Tizzano* had analyzed this matter from a broad perspective, taking into account not only the Package Travel Directive, but also other directives as well as the case law on the Union's non-contractual liability under Art. 340(2) TFEU,[98] the ECJ proved much less courageous: Although confirming *Tizzano*'s view that the Directive also covers non-pecuniary losses, the judges based their reasoning solely on arguments that directly flow from the wording and context of the Directive.[99]

Another worrying trend in the case law of the ECJ is the tendency, at least in certain cases, to avoid difficult issues by giving open or evasive answers in response to the national reference or, even more problematic, to delegate the decision back to the national courts and legislators.[100] A particular prominent example of this trend can be found in intellectual property law: When asked by a Spanish court whether EU law must be interpreted as requiring Member States to lay down an obligation to communicate personal data in the context of civil proceedings under Art. 8 IP Enforcement Directive, in order to ensure effective protection of copyright, the ECJ referred this question back to national law. The court concluded that Member States have to "take care to rely on an interpretation" of the relevant EU law "which allows a fair balance to be struck between the various fundamental rights protected

---

[96] This critique has been expounded for European private law in general by *Basedow*, (2010) 18 ERPL 443, 466; see also *Walter van Gerven*, The ECJ Case Law as a Means of Unification of Private Law?, in Arthur Hartkamp et al. (eds.), Towards a European Civil Code, 3rd edition, 2004, pp. 101, 103 (noting that whereas the ECJ's interpretation of Treaty provisions is "frequently bold, or even audacious", its interpretation of specific directive provisions is often of a rather "textual nature").
[97] Above n. 34.
[98] Advocate General *Tizzano*, *Leitner/TUI Deutschland* (n. 47) paras. 27 ff.
[99] ECJ, *Leitner/TUI Deutschland* (n. 92) paras. 19 ff.
[100] *Basedow*, (2010) 18 ERPL 443, 455 ff. (with the example of review of standard contract terms).

by the Community legal order".[101] How this balance could be achieved was not revealed by the oracle of Luxembourg, a balance between, *nota bene*, conflicting EU directives (protection of intellectual property vs. data protection). Undoubtedly, the answer is not obvious, but it can hardly be the purpose of EU harmonization both of intellectual property enforcement and data protection that the ECJ, when asked how these two fields interact, tells the national courts to find a "fair balance", whatever this means. Other cases such as *Manfredi*[102] or *Evans*[103] – where the ECJ refers to earlier case law in neighbouring areas in order to support his reasoning in the case at hand – show that the Court can do better than this. Instead of limiting its reasoning to what is absolutely necessary to answer the questions of the national court, or even avoiding a clear answer altogether, the ECJ should give more guidance and inspiration to national courts on how to interpret and understand EU law in a truly autonomous manner. By formulating broader principles which go beyond a specific instrument wherever this is possible, the court could bridge gaps in European legislation, enhance the consistency between different EU instruments and make the interpretation of EU law more foreseeable, as a result reached under one instrument could be applied in analogous cases where the question has not been decided yet.

2. More private law expertise

A second, probably related shortcoming of the case law is that the European judges often address private law issues from a constitutional perspective. This can be explained by the fact that the ECJ has usually propounded general principles of Union law in a public law context.[104] In addition, it seems that most judges and advocates general in Luxembourg have a public law background, which is unsurprising as EU law is a subject which is traditionally regarded as part of this field of law. Consequently, the case law on private law principles hinges very much on such constitutional concepts. The consistency of European tort law and Union private law in general could be enhanced if the judges relied more strongly on private law reasoning.

---

[101] ECJ 29.1.2008, Case C-275/06 (*Promusicae/Telefónica de España SAU*), [2008] ECR I-271 para. 70.

[102] ECJ, *Manfredi/Lloyd Adriatico* (n. 26) paras. 94 ff.

[103] ECJ, *Evans/The Secretary of State for the Environment, Transport and the Regions and The Motor Insurers' Bureau* (n. 29) paras. 67 f.

[104] *Reiner Schulze*, Allgemeine Rechtsgrundsätze und europäisches Privatrecht, ZEuP 1993, 442, 456 f.

An example shall prove this point. In *von Colson and Kamann*, one of the leading cases on EU anti-discrimination law, the ECJ ruled that the German transposition did not comply with the principle of effectiveness.[105] The German legislator had limited the right to claim damages in cases of sex-based employment discrimination to the so-called *Vertrauensschaden*, i.e. to losses actually occurred through reliance on an expectation. In cases in which an employer discriminated against applicants seeking an employment relationship, the rejected applicants could generally only claim costs associated with their application, such as the postage for their application package. The Court concluded that such nominal compensation is not an adequate sanction for the protection of Community rights. To reach this result, the court focused on the Member States' duty to guarantee "real and effective judicial protection".[106] In other words, the decision was essentially grounded on the argument that the minimal level of compensation contemplated by German law cannot be judged an effective sanction because it violates the right of access to justice. This is, of course, a valid argument. But for the national judge dealing with private law issues, it would have been more useful to solve the case on the basis of private law theory, thus addressing the question of how the principle of full compensation is to be vindicated in discrimination cases.

3. More sector-specific rules

Finally, it may be regretted that the ECJ does not try to identify commonalities at least within a specific sector, which would allow a limited generalization of solutions which have been pronounced for a specific instrument. For the guidance of national courts, it would make sense if the ECJ tried to shape such sector-specific rules or "sub-rules" which could apply for a specific group of torts, such as competition delicts, or a specific area with common features, while not necessarily being suitable of rising to the full dignity of a general principle of European tort law. A simple example may serve as an illustration: In anti-discrimination law, the ECJ has ruled in *Dekker* that a claim for damages cannot be made contingent upon the condition of fault *(Verschulden)*.[107] This decision was based essentially on two justifications: First, the court pointed out that the instrument does not mention

---

[105] ECJ, *von Colson und Kamann/Land Nordrhein-Westfalen* (n. 65) para. 24.
[106] ECJ, *von Colson und Kamann/Land Nordrhein-Westfalen* (n. 65) para. 23.
[107] ECJ 8.11.1990, Case C-177/88 *(Dekker/Stichting Vormingcentrum voor Jong Volwassenen)*, [1990] ECR I-3941 para. 24.

fault as a condition for liability.[108] More interestingly, the court added that if the employer's liability was made subject to proof of fault, the practical effect of the principles of "real and effective protection" would be weakened considerably.[109] Just recently, the ECJ was faced with a similar question in *Strabag*[110] in the field of public procurement. The Court held that Directive 89/665[111] precludes national legislation which makes the claim for damages conditional on the infringement being culpable. Again, the court referred to the guarantee of "effective judicial remedies" for which the requirement of fault might prove too high a hurdle to obtain compensation.[112] In particular, the court pointed to the potential excuse of legal error. Both the guarantee of effective judicial remedies and the potential excuse of legal error are no speciality of anti-discrimination or public procurement law, but may be equally relevant for other torts. Nevertheless, the ECJ has limited his reasoning in both cases to the directive in question. In *Strabag*, the court did not even refer to *Dekker*, even though there were apparent similarities in the reasoning in both cases.

As a result of this insular approach, it remains unclear whether strict liability may also apply, for example, to other business torts which are influenced by European law, such as damages claims for breach of EU competition rules.[113] While it may be true that fault liability and strict liability tend to converge in general tort law,[114] the element of fault can still be relevant in complex matters, where a defendant might argue that the legal error it is

---

[108] ECJ, *Dekker/Stichting Vormingscentrum voor Jong Volwassenen* (n. 107) para. 22.

[109] ECJ, *Dekker/Stichting Vormingscentrum voor Jong Volwassenen* (n. 107) para. 24.

[110] ECJ 30.9.2010, Case C-314/09 *(Stadt Graz/Strabag)* (not yet reported).

[111] Council Directive 89/665/EEC of 21 December 1989 on the coordination of the laws, regulations and administrative provisions relating to the application of review procedures to the award of public supply and public works contracts, OJ 1989 L 395/33. Now amended by Directive 2007/66/EC of the European Parliament and of the Council of 11 December 2007 amending Council Directives 89/665/EEC and 92/13/EEC with regard to improving the effectiveness of review procedures concerning the award of public contracts, OJ 2007 L 335/31.

[112] ECJ, *Stadt Graz/Strabag* (n. 110) paras. 41, 43.

[113] For the relevance of fault in competition law *Ashurst*, Study on the conditions of claims for damages in case of infringement of EC competition rules, 2004, http://ec.europa.eu/competition/antitrust/actionsdamages/comparative_report_clean_en.pdf, p. 50 ff. For a general analysis of fault in EU tort law *Meinhard Lukas*, in: Helmut Koziol/Reiner Schulze (eds.), Tort Law of the European Community, 2008, pp. 81 ff.

[114] *Jansen* (n. 60) 433 ff.

alleged to have made is excusable.[115] It has to be noted that even though the ECJ has now decided two cases concerning the enforcement of EU competition law by private plaintiffs,[116] the Court has stuck narrowly to the preliminary questions and has not addressed the issue of fault. Consequently, it is disputed whether liability for breach of the EU competition rules is fault-based.[117] In *Strabag*, the ECJ would have had the chance to clarify the relevance of fault for at least a certain group of torts. For example, the Court could have clarified that an infringement of European competition law, both under Art. 101 and 102 TFEU and under public procurement law, constitutes such a serious threat for the goal of undistorted competition that it needs to be sanctioned under a regime of strict liability. Alternatively, the Luxembourg judges could have explained to us that it is the effectiveness of European law that triggers, absent a legislative provision to the contrary (as in the IP Enforcement Directive), a regime of strict liability for any infringement of European law. This explanation would have tied together the strict liability regimes under *Dekker* and *Strabag*. The ECJ, however, did not say anything in this regard, nor did it give any alternative explanation for the similarities found in the two judgments. The Court just confirmed strict liability for yet another field, as if similar questions may not and will not come up in a whole number of other areas. A broader perspective in *Strabag* would have contributed to the enhancement of legal certainty. More importantly, it would have deepened our understanding of European law of (competition) torts.

V. Conclusion

1. The elaboration of overarching principles of EU tort law may be helpful both for ensuring a genuinely uniform and autonomous interpretation

---

[115] An explicit concern in ECJ, *Stadt Graz/Strabag* (n. 110) para. 41.

[116] ECJ, *Courage/Crehan* (n. 21); ECJ, *Manfredi/Lloyd Adriatico* (n. 26).

[117] See *Walter van Gerven*, Private Enforcement of EC Competition Rules in the ECJ – Courage v. Crehan and the Way Ahead, in Jürgen Basedow (ed.), Private Enforcement of EC Competition Law, 2007, pp. 19, 28; *Gerhard Wagner*, AcP 2006, 352, 420 (both arguing for "strict" liability); but see *Tobias Lettl*, Der Schadensersatzanspruch gemäß § 823 Abs. 2 BGB i.V. mit Art. 81 Abs. 1 EG, ZHR 167 (2003), 473, 485; *Ernst-Joachim Mestmäcker/Heike Schweitzer*, Europäisches Wettbewerbsrecht, 2nd edition, 2004, p. 525 (both claiming that liability for breach of the EU competition rules is fault-based).

of the European instruments in tort law and for the sake of coherence of Union law.
2. Over the last decades the ECJ has started to elaborate such principles by deciding cases, *inter alia*, with reference to case law which has been issued in respect of other liability regimes. However, in other cases, in particular in secondary law, the Court has been much more reluctant to do so.
3. As examples for common principles of EU tort law we may identify the principle of full compensation, a trend towards prevention as an additional goal of tort law and the recoverability of non-material loss.
4. To guide national courts, more coherent and specific principles of EU tort law should be formulated by the ECJ. The judges should therefore analyze cases from a broader perspective, shift their focus from the prevailing constitutional perspective to private law theory and try, where it is not possible to identify a general principle, to devise at least sub-rules or sector-specific rules that may apply to a certain group of torts in Union law.

Part II
Specific Areas of European Tort Law

Product Liability and the European Tort Landscape

Geraint Howells

Product liability is the grandfather of European torts, with the Directive having been adopted in 1985 after a decade or so of discussion.[1] It was a very brave venture into the area of tort law as it proclaimed a regime of liability without fault[2] and certainly introduced a form of strict liability. Just how strict that regime is, is still much debated.

I. The Product Liability Directive

Many contours of this strict product liability regime remain uncertain and basic questions relating to the role of risk: benefit or consumer expectations in the defectiveness standard or the relationship with regulatory standards or approval remain insufficiently unexplored. This contrasts with the very prompt and thorough revision of the product safety directive carried out by DG SANCO.[3] However, product liability has remained largely dormant – apart from one small amendment bringing primary agricultural produce firmly within its scope – in DG Internal Market where it was introduced by its father Dr. Taschner. It would have been natural to have brought it together with other consumer protection directives that were later under the control of DG SANCO or have transferred it more recently along with the consumer contract law directives to DG Civil Justice in the recent reforms as part of the civil law reform process. However, it remains in splendid isolation. Probably a reason, apart from apathy, as to why the European legislation has not been developed is because the fragile balance between producer and injured party struck by the Directive has to-date not provoked a major high profile catastrophe on the scale of thalidomide. The closest scares have been in relation to contaminated blood and usually the dilemmas have

---

[1] Directive 85/374/EEC: OJ 1985 L 210/29.
[2] Rectials 2 and 3.
[3] Directive 2001/95/EC: OJ 1995 L11/4.

69

been resolved by courts or special ad hoc political solutions. However, not rocking the boat is not a good reason for inactivity and potential problems may well go unnoticed as the issue is low down the list of concerns of the consumer movement and handled on a day to day basis by lawyers that are less concerned with the development of the law than with the specific cases they are handling.

II. Discussion of ECJ decisions

What is clear from the jurisprudence of the European Court of Justice (ECJ) is that general product liability regimes are viewed as distinct from both sector specific regimes (such as the German pharmaceutical liability regime) and contractual and non-contractual liability (warranty law and fault). Whilst Art. 13 of the Directive allows Member States the freedom to maintain both these latter forms of liability, the ECJ has made it clear that "Article 13 of the Directive cannot be interpreted as giving the Member States the possibility of maintaining a general system of product liability different from that provided for in the Directive."[4] However, whether this distinction can be maintained with rigour is hard to determine given that the borderline is hard to discern between strict liability regimes of general application and the application of traditional contract and fault liability. This is evidenced by the French development of a regime of strict liability based on the civil code and Danish attempts to circumvent the ECJ's ruling that it could not impose strict liability on suppliers[5] by imposing liability for fault where fault is given an extended meaning.

There are, however, limits to the extent of this maximal harmonisation: the ECJ in *Moteurs Leroy Somer v Dalkia*[6] held that as damage to business property was outside the scope of the Directive it could not be used as a reason to prevent the application of stricter forms of liability under French law. This underlines that when one considers the impact of torts on liability for business damages business property is not covered by the European strict product liability regime, but producers remain liable for any damage caused by business products and of course liability for personal injury and death is a major concern for manufacturers. This *Somer* decision might

---

[4] *Commission v France* Case C-52/00, [2002] ECR I-3827.
[5] *Skov v Bilka Lauprisvarenhus A/S,* Case C-402/03, [2006] 2 CMLR 16; *Commission v Denmark,* Case 327/05, [2007] ECR I-93.
[6] Case C-285/08, [2009] ECR I-4733.

also be significant for the debate on the scope of the consumer acquis as it might suggest any attempt to create a European maximal harmonised level of consumer protection would simply leave to national law any situations not covered by the European definition of consumer. Thus one might even see in areas of maximal harmonisation consumers seeking to disclaim their consumer status in order to benefit from more protective national law rules. Arguably the ECJ might suggest the consumer protection standard should impliedly be the limit on protection in all transactions, but that seems problematic as the EU might not even have competence in other fields.

When the ECJ has grappled with substantive product liability principles it has usually been fairly welcoming of the strict liability principle and been prepared to underline the strict nature of the liability regime and its protective aspirations. Thus in *Veedfald v Århus Amtskommune*[7] there was said to be a supply when a patient had to bring himself within the sphere of control of the hospital that produced the product; the fact that patients did not pay the hospital directly did not detract from the economic and business character of the operation and so prevented the hospital invoking a special defence for non-economic actors; and the damage to the kidney caused by the defective perfusion liquid had to be viewed as damage, although the ECJ ducked having to decide if it was personal injury or property damage by leaving that tricky matter to the national courts. Equally in *O'Byrne v Sanofi Pasteur MSD*[8] and the follow on case of *Aventis Pastuer v OB*,[9] the ECJ, whilst showing a change of tone between the two decisions on whether national courts should have procedural autonomy to substitute defendants beyond the ten year long stop, nevertheless showed a clear desire that the companies should not be able to hide behind supplies within a corporate group to escape liability at least where the supplier had failed to disclose it was not the producer of the product manufactured by its parent company.

In the most important decision by the ECJ to-date on the Directive and its strict liability regime the ECJ showed that it was not unsympathetic to the need to confine the development risks defence in order to respect the strict liability nature of the Directive. In *Commission v United Kingdom*[10] Advocate-General *Tesauro*, with whom the Court agreed equated the state of scientific knowledge not with "the views expressed by the majority of learned opinion" (the negligence approach) "but with the most advanced level of research which has been carried out at a given time." However, fore-

---

[7] Case C-200/13, [2001] ECR I-3596.
[8] Case C-127/04, [2006] ECR I-1313.
[9] Case C-358/08: OJ 2010 C 24/11.
[10] Case C-300/95, [1997] ECR I-2649.

seeability issues were promoted by reference to the need for the knowledge to be accessible, despite this criterion not being obvious from the Directive's wording. Moreover, the lack of appreciation of the context of products liability litigation is demonstrated by the ECJ's view that the Commission should have waited for the case law to demonstrate whether the United Kingdom had improperly implemented the Directive. In the United Kingdom there is simply not enough litigation before the courts to allow the principles to be regularly tested. Development risks cases are even rarer and the costs of litigating such issues only encourage the parties to negotiate in the shadow of the law. This is perhaps another example of the ECJ not being attuned to the context of private law litigation.

The Product Liability Directive cannot claim to be the forerunner for a paradigm shift from fault to strict liability in European tort law more generally. It is largely isolated to its own particular context – something which it symptomatic of many areas of tort law and may hinder the development of overarching principles. The extent to which it really marks a shift from fault liability is still unclear both on the face of the Directive due to the circularity and opaqueness of the definition of defect and in the utterances of the ECJ as the *Commission v United Kingdom*[11] case illustrates. Neither has it added to our knowledge of damages as the *Veedfald*[12] decision essentially left the characterisation of the damage to the national courts and the Directive expressly leaves non-pecuniary damage to national law. Furthermore the Directive does not touch on causation although this is a key aspect of many product liability claims. The fact causation is written on the face of the Directive might arguably suggest the concept must be given an independent European meaning in this context, but such a radical intrusion on national law seems to be hard to infer from the mere fact it is said to be a condition of liability without more.

III. Outlook

The European Commission seems about to embark on a consultation exercise on product liability. One hopes this will produce some outcomes that improve our understanding of the contours of European product liability. Whether that will assist in our general understanding of European tort law depends upon the extent to which product liability is viewed as a

---

[11] See n. 10.
[12] See n. 7.

having sectoral characteristics. My view is probably that it is a very specific response to the risks created by the consumer society, although one that is yet to be properly and fully worked out. However, from an internal market perspective the impact of the laws requires not only the harmonisation of the substantive rules but also creating a more level playing field as regards damage levels and principles of causation.

Tort law can potentially have a significant impact on business in the internal market and unlike contract, where as between business parties there is a relatively large discretion to modify the rules to suit their preferences, for the most part tort is simply applied with little room to modify its impact. This underlines the importance of the theme of this publication on the need to consider the European dimension of the impact of torts. At the very least common understandings of different liability standards, tests of causation and damage need to be made explicit to understand the variations across Europe and explore the need for convergence.

Damages for the Infringement of Intellectual Property Rights under EU Law

Piotr Machnikowski

I. Introductory remarks

Although European Union law governing liability for the infringement of intellectual property rights does not arouse much interest in researchers working in the area of European tort law, it is nonetheless worthy of attention. Besides the product liability, the liability for infringement of IP rights constitutes an important set of harmonized rules on non-contractual liability for damage.

For a long time European intellectual property law did not regulate in detail sanctions for the infringement of intellectual property rights, especially liability in damages. Directives and regulations dealt with issues such as when the intellectual property right came into being and what its content was but remedies in the case of infringement were left to the Member States. Art. 8 of the Directive 2001/29/EC of the European Parliament and of the Council of 22 May 2001 on the harmonization of certain aspects of copyright and related rights in the information society[1] constitutes good example of this approach:

> Article 8: Sanctions and remedies
> 1. Member States shall provide appropriate sanctions and remedies in respect of infringements of the rights and obligations set out in this Directive and shall take all the measures necessary to ensure that those sanctions and remedies are applied. The sanctions thus provided for shall be effective, proportionate and dissuasive.
> 2. Each Member State shall take the measures necessary to ensure that rightholders whose interests are affected by an infringing activity carried out on its territory can bring an action for damages and/or apply for an injunction and, where appropriate, for the seizure of infringing material as well as of devices, products or components referred to in Article 6(2).

---

[1] O.J. 2001 L 167/10.

3. Member States shall ensure that rightholders are in a position to apply for an injunction against intermediaries whose services are used by a third party to infringe a copyright or related right.

Such a state of affairs was found unsatisfactory in the face of increasing piracy and counterfeiting. Enforcement measures and sanctions provided for by the TRIPs Agreement,[2] international conventions,[3] as well as border measures imposed by the customs authorities according to series of Product Piracy Regulations, were found insufficient. The reaction was the Directive 2004/48/EC of the European Parliament and of the Council of 29 April 2004 on the enforcement of intellectual property rights[4].

II. General overview of the Directive 2004/48/EC

The Directive is a horizontal instrument concerning protection of every kind of intellectual property rights, with the term 'intellectual property right' being understood in a broad sense. Moreover, the Directive applies not only to those IP rights which are provided for by the EU law but also to such rights regulated solely by the Member State's national law. The broad scope of application of the Directive is expressed in Art. 1 and confirmed by recital 13:

Article 1
This Directive concerns the measures, procedures and remedies necessary to ensure the enforcement of intellectual property rights. For the purposes of this Directive, the term "intellectual property rights" includes industrial property rights.

---

[2] The Agreement on Trade-Related Aspects of Intellectual Property, which was concluded in the framework of World Trade Organization and by which all Member States are bound.
[3] In particular, the Paris Convention for the Protection of Industrial Property, the Bern Convention for the Protection of Literary and Artistic Works, and the Rome Convention for the Protection of Performers, Producers of Phonograms and Broadcasting Organisations.
[4] O.J. 2004 L 195/16.

Recital (13)
It is necessary to define the scope of this Directive as widely as possible in order to encompass all the intellectual property rights covered by Community provisions in this field and/or by the national law of the Member State concerned.(...)

The Directive's scope of application was made even clearer by the Commission in a statement published about a year after the Directive was adopted, where the Commission presented a long and non-exhaustive list of IP rights regulated by the Directive[5]:

The Commission considers that at least the following intellectual property rights are covered by the scope of the Directive:

- copyright,
- rights related to copyright,
- sui generis right of a database maker,
- rights of the creator of the topographies of a semiconductor product,
- trademark rights,
- design rights,
- patent rights, including rights derived from supplementary protection certificates,
- geographical indications,
- utility model rights,
- plant variety rights,
- trade names, in so far as these are protected as exclusive property rights in the national law concerned.

It is also worth noting that the Directive, according to its Article 2(1), sets out the minimum standard of protection.

Article 2
(1) Without prejudice to the means which are or may be provided for in Community or national legislation, in so far as those means may be more favourable for rightholders, the measures, procedures and remedies provided for by this Directive shall apply, in accordance with Ar-

---

[5] Statement by the Commission concerning Article 2 of Directive 2004/48/EC of the European Parliament and of the Council on the enforcement of intellectual property rights (2005/295/EC), 13.4.2005, O.J. 2005 L 94/37.

ticle 3, to any infringement of intellectual property rights as provided for by Community law and/or by the national law of the Member State concerned.

The Directive concerns various means of substantive and procedural law, designed to ensure efficient enforcement of intellectual property rights. The means are, in general:

- presenting, obtaining and preserving evidence (Articles 6 and 7)
- right of information (Article 8)
- provisional and precautionary measures (Article 9)
- measures resulting from a decision on the merits of the case, that is corrective measures (Article 10), injunctions (Article 11) and pecuniary compensation as alternative measure (Article 12)
- damages (Article 13)
- legal costs (Article 14)
- publication of judicial decisions (Article 15)

Detailed discussion on the content of the Directive is not the subject of this article, which focuses on the liability for damage. However, a short presentation of the system of sanctions adopted by the Directive seems necessary to fully understand the role that damages play in this system. To some extent this role is special because of the unique economic function of intellectual property law and its remedies.

III. Protection of IP rights – some economic aspects

The role of copyright and patent law is to secure the author or innovator an economic rent and in this way to create conditions for the generation of new knowledge. According to the widely accepted 'incentive theory', in the absence of a system of protection of intellectual property rights, authors and inventors will have a disincentive to invest in their activity and to disclose their works and, as a result, society will fail to achieve the optimal level of creativity and innovation. However, a too strong system of protection may discourage others from building upon existing knowledge or deter the creation of new works that build upon earlier ones. The incentive theory does not apply to trademarks because their economic functions are different. Trademarks lower search costs by allowing buyers to distinguish between products that differ in quality but are difficult to distinguish at the time of purchase. Moreover, protection of trademarks encourages the trademarks owners to maintain the quality of their products and services.[6] For these reasons trademark rights should also be protected.

Most economic analysts of law suggest that the main remedy available in the case of infringement of intellectual property rights should be injunctions. Damages rules play only an auxiliary role, but they are necessary because some infringements go undetected or remain with no sanction for some time, and there is a need for an instrument that would remove the consequences of an infringement. It is argued that the damages rules should preserve both the incentive structure of intellectual property law and the property-like character of IP rights. They should preserve the incentive to create intellectual property by compensating the creator so that he is no worse off as a result of any infringement. They should also deter infringement by rendering it unprofitable – by making the infringer no better off than he would have been had he never used other people's property.[7] The optimal rule is then to award the right holder either his lost profits attributable to the infringement or the infringer's profits resulting from the infringement, whichever is greater. This rule requires, however, further modifications for two reasons. Firstly, the rule which merely renders the infringer no better off as a result of the infringement may be ineffective as a preventive measure as long as there is a possibility that the infringement will remain undetected (and this is often the case). So to achieve an adequate level of deterrence, damages have to be somehow increased or multiplied. Secondly, intellectual property entitlements are not always well defined and in many instances there may be a certain level of doubt as to whether a right exists or whether it was infringed. Therefore, the liability rule should allow for reducing the amount of damages in order to avoid overdeterrence of conduct that may be lawful.[8]

---

[6] See *Roger D. Blair/Thomas F. Cotter*, An Economic Analysis of Damages Rules in Intellectual Property Law, (1998) 39 William and Mary Law Review (WMLR) 1597 ff.; *Robert D. Cooter/Thomas Ulen*, Law and Economics, 2004, pp. 122 ff.; *Hans B. Schäfer/Claus Ott*, The Economic Analysis of Civil Law, 2004, pp. 445 ff.; *Steven Shavell*, Foundations of Economic Analysis of Law, 2004, pp. 137 ff.

[7] See *Blair/Cotter*, (1998) 39 WLMR 1616 ff.; *Roger D. Blair/Thomas F. Cotter*, Intellectual Property: Economic and Legal Dimensions of Rights and Remedies, 2005, p. 40 and the law and economics literature cited therein. See also *William M. Landes/Richard A. Posner*, The Economic Structure of Intellectual Property Law, 2003, pp. 7 ff.

[8] See *Blair/Cotter*, (n. 7), 42 ff.

IV. General obligation – Article 3

Duty to pay compensation as a measure of protection of IP rights plays a double role in the Directive. Firstly, according to Article 13, damages constitute a separate, independent sanction in the case of an infringement of right. Secondly, under Article 12 pecuniary compensation may be awarded as an alternative measure instead of corrective measures and injunctions. This compensation, however, is not called 'damages' by the Directive. Below I will discuss in more details damages governed by Article 13.

At the outset some attention has to be given to the general obligation expressed in Article 3 because this provision, especially its second paragraph, may be important for the proper interpretation of the provisions concerning specific measures.[9]

Article 3: General obligation
1. Member States shall provide for the measures, procedures and remedies necessary to ensure the enforcement of the intellectual property rights covered by this Directive. Those measures, procedures and remedies shall be fair and equitable and shall not be unnecessarily complicated or costly, or entail unreasonable time-limits or unwarranted delays.
2. Those measures, procedures and remedies shall also be effective, proportionate and dissuasive and shall be applied in such a manner as to avoid the creation of barriers to legitimate trade and to provide for safeguards against their abuse.

What is of special interest here is not the general obligation to ensure enforcement of intellectual property rights (which seems to be superfluous in the light of the following, more detailed provisions) but mostly the specific requirements of paragraph (2): effectiveness, proportionality and dissuasion (and I think the conditions set in the last part of the provision – no barriers to legitimate trade and no abuse of remedies – boil down to proportionality again[10]).

---

[9] Cf. *Theo Bodewig/Artur Wandtke*, Die doppelte Lizenzgebühr als Berechnungsmethode im Lichte der Durchsetzungsrichtlinie, Gewerblicher Rechtsschutz und Urheberrecht (GRUR) 2008, 222; *Joachim v. Ungern-Sternberg*, Einwirkung der Durchsetzungsrichtlinie auf das deutsche Schadensersatzrecht, GRUR 2009, 460.

[10] See *Ansgar Ohly*, Three principles of European IP enforcement law: effectiveness, proportionality, dissuasiveness, in: Josef Drexl et al. (eds.), Technology and Competition. Contributions in honour of Hanns Ullrich, 2009, pp. 257 ff.

In my view Article 3(2) may work on two levels: a legislative level and a judiciary level. Undoubtedly the requirements in question are directed primarily to Member States. From this point of view proportionality is the most important of the three. Effectiveness and dissuasion relate to at least how severe the sanctions should be. We can assume that detailed sanctions contained in following provisions of the Directive are effective and dissuasive, and by implementing the minimum standard of the Directive the national legislator provides for effective and dissuasive measures. But proportionality refers to at most how severe the sanctions should be. The requirement of proportionality combined with the minimum harmonization clause creates a new situation. Proportionality of the remedies is the limit of Member States' freedom to decide about adopting more favourable measures of protection. This shows the options granted by the Directive to the Member States in a different light. Provisions declaring that Member States may provide for a certain additional measure of protection – which generally in case of minimum harmonization are pointless – should be treated as a confirmation that the additional measure in question is not disproportionate as such.

As already stated, the requirements of Article 3(2) bind primarily Member States. In my opinion they have to be taken into account also by judicial authorities while deciding individual cases. This view is corroborated by the relevant recital:

Recital (17)
The measures, procedures and remedies provided for in this Directive should be determined in each case in such a manner as to take due account of the specific characteristics of that case, including the specific features of each intellectual property right and, where appropriate, the intentional or unintentional character of the infringement.

Taking account of the specific characteristics of the case seems more possible on the judiciary level than by means of legislation.

V. Rules on damages – Article 13

1. Introduction

The need for more detailed rules on compensation arose not only because there were differences between Member States in this respect. The Commission's Green Paper published in 1998 showed that the amount of damages awarded in most Member States did not compensate for the loss suffered by the injured party.[11] The Industry Report to this Green Paper added that the method of calculating the damages on the basis of a reasonable royalty, used in many countries, did not play a deterrent role at all. So the aim of the Commission was not only to harmonize the national rules on damages but most of all to significantly raise the level of protection by way of introducing a new method of calculating damages.

The initial proposals of the Commission were quite far reaching, because the Commission proposed also damages as a lump sum equal to double the amount of reasonable royalty. This was, however, cancelled in the course of the legislative process. It has been rightly noted that the legislative history of Article 13 shows that there was no agreement between those responsible for drafting and negotiating the Directive as to the general directions and the role that damages should play in the system of protection of intellectual property rights.[12] The point at issue is whether the damages should serve only compensation of the actual loss of the right holder or – and to what extent – the rules on damages should work as a preventive measure. I don't want to suggest that there is a fundamental conflict between compensation and prevention. They are two parts of the mechanism of liability that operate together.[13] The question is in striking the right balance or delimiting the tasks. Whatever the problem is, the final result of the legislative process – the present content of Article 13 – demonstrates that it was not solved clearly and definitively.

Article 13
1. Member States shall ensure that the competent judicial authorities, on application of the injured party, order the infringer who knowingly, or with reasonable grounds to know, engaged in an infringing activity, to pay the rightholder damages appropriate to the actual prejudice suffered by him/her as a result of the infringement.

When the judicial authorities set the damages:

---

[11] See Green Paper of the Commission of the European Communities on 'Combating Counterfeiting and Piracy in the Internal Market' of 15 October 1998, COM(98) 569 final.

[12] See *Michael Walter/Dominik Goebel*, in: *Michael Walter/Silke von Lewinski* (eds.), European Copyright Law: A Commentary, 2010, p. 1307.

[13] See *Bodewig/Wandtke*, (n. 9), 221 ff. See also *Markus Kellner*, 'Tort Law of the European Community': A Plea for an Overarching Pan-European Framework, (2009) 2 European Review of Private Law (ERPL) 138.

(a) they shall take into account all appropriate aspects, such as the negative economic consequences, including lost profits, which the injured party has suffered, any unfair profits made by the infringer and, in appropriate cases, elements other than economic factors, such as the moral prejudice caused to the rightholder by the infringement;
or
(b) as an alternative to (a), they may, in appropriate cases, set the damages as a lump sum on the basis of elements such as at least the amount of royalties or fees which would have been due if the infringer had requested authorisation to use the intellectual property right in question.
2. Where the infringer did not knowingly, or with reasonable grounds know, engage in infringing activity, Member States may lay down that the judicial authorities may order the recovery of profits or the payment of damages, which may be pre-established.

2. Infringement of an intellectual property right and fault

At first we should note that the Directive distinguishes between culpable infringement of right and infringement carried out in good faith. In the former case, the Member States are under obligation to impose rules on damages while in the latter case it is left to their discretion. I will focus first on the culpable violation of IP right, dealt with by Article 13(1).

The basic condition of liability is, of course, violation of the intellectual property right. The second condition is that the infringer acted knowingly, or with reasonable grounds to know. This resembles the requirement of fault, known to every national legal system. In greater detail, however, the notion of fault differs among Member States. With Article 13 of the Directive the European lawmaker stepped in and proposed a specific notion of fault. I am not sure if it was done knowingly but certainly with reasonable grounds to know. We can note from the wording of the Article 13 that what constitutes fault here is the tortfeasor's state of mind with respect to the infringement of another's right – that is to the action itself and to its legal classification[14] but not with respect to its consequences such as damage. This is also expressed in clear terms by recital 26:

---

[14] See *Thomas Dreier,* Ausgleich, Abschreckung und andere Rechtsfolgen von Urheberrechtsverletzungen – Erste Gedanken zur EU-Richtlinie über die Maßnamen und Verfahren zum Schutz der Rechte an geistigem Eigentum, GRUR Int 2004, 707; *Bodewig/Wandtke,* (n. 9), 223 ff.

Recital (26)
With a view to compensating for the prejudice suffered as a result of an infringement committed by an infringer who engaged in an activity in the knowledge, or with reasonable grounds for knowing, that it would give rise to such an infringement (...).

So an engagement in an infringing activity which is carried out knowingly, namely with knowledge that the act in question infringes another's right, is an intentional fault. Such an engagement carried out by the person who had reasonable grounds to know that his or her act may infringe another's right is negligence. As there is no limitation in the Directive, every form of negligence (not only gross negligence) amounts to fault and results in duty to pay damages under Article 13.[15]

3. Damages

a) Calculated damages

The most interesting part of the rule discussed here is the calculation of damages or rather the very notion of damages established by the Directive.[16] Two alternative methods of calculation are allowed and they both – according to the Directive – lead to the awarding of 'damages appropriate to the actual prejudice suffered (...) as a result of the infringement' so that they serve as a measure of compensation.

Under Article 13(1)(a), when the judicial authorities set the damages, they shall take into account all appropriate aspects, such as:

- the negative economic consequences, including lost profits, which the injured party has suffered,
- any unfair profits made by the infringer,
- in appropriate cases, elements other than economic factors, such as the moral prejudice caused to the rightholder by the infringement.

From the tort law point of view, the first element of calculation (negative economic consequences) is economic loss – burdens incurred, reduction

---

[15] See: *Walter/Goebel*, (n. 12), p. 1308.
[16] Cf. *Winfried Tilmann*, Schadensersatz bei der Verletzung von Rechten des Geistigen Eigentums, Zeitschrift für Europäisches Privatrecht (ZEuP) 2007, 290; *v. Ungern-Sternberg*, (n. 9), 461.

in the value of property and – expressly mentioned in the Directive – lost profit.[17] The last part of the rule (elements other than economic factors such as the moral prejudice caused by the infringement) bears close similarity to the tort law notion of non-economic loss. The element that diverges the most from the general tort law is the second one – unfair profits made by the infringer.

Firstly, it has to be noted that the 'unfairness' of the profit is not an additional condition of liability but only sort of indication that the rule concerns those profits that are linked to the infringement of the IP right.[18]

Secondly, the account of profits made by the infringer is a part of the mechanism of liability in damages. It is not a reference to the unjustified enrichment law.

Thirdly, disgorgement of profit is dependent on the infringer's fault. This was criticized by some authors who think that in any case of infringement the person in question should be deprived of any economic gains.[19] Even if this general observation were true, which I doubt, this would not mean that the profit gained by the bona fide infringer should be transferred to the right holder. It might lead to an economically unjustified enrichment of the right holder, especially in those cases where the nature and the range of his activity would never allow him to make comparable profits. Regardless of that, the account of profits as a mandatory rule applied to non-fault infringement could adversely affect the inventiveness by overdeterrence of marginally lawful conduct, especially in those areas where the attribution and scope of rights are not entirely clear. So in my opinion the Directive rightly counts the disgorgement of profits in the case of bona fide infringement among the non-mandatory measures in Article 13(2).[20]

By ordering the court to take into account all the above mentioned consequences of the infringement the Directive creates a kind of flexible system of liability. Flexibility appears here not with regard to the condi-

---

[17] See *Enrico Bonadio*, Remedies and sanctions for the infringement of intellectual property rights under EC law, (2008) 30(8) European Intellectual Property Review (E.I.P.R.), 324 ff.

[18] Rightly *Walter/Goebel*, (n. 12), p. 1308.

[19] See *Walter/Goebel*, (n. 12), p. 1309.

[20] Argument referring to Article 17(1)(b) of the product piracy regulation (raised by *Walter/Goebel*, (n. 12), p. 1312) is not convincing. The regulation has its specific, limited scope of application and it does not require Member States to provide for transfer of profits to the right holder but only to deprive a person guilty of piracy of his or her gains.

tions of liability but with regard to the amount of damages.[21] The exact scale of this flexibility depends, however, on the interpretation of Article 13(1). The question is whether the court has to choose between the three elements listed above or may cumulate them. And this is exactly the question of balance between compensation and prevention. In my view, there should be no doubt that the damages should cover both economic and non-economic consequences suffered by the harmed party as a result of the infringement (economic and non-economic loss). These are two different kinds of damage, concerning different kinds of interests of the harmed person and the principle of compensation itself requires them both to be repaired.[22] As to the infringer's profits, it is argued that the Member States are free to allow for cumulative damages but they are not obliged to do so.[23] In my opinion, different conclusions may be drawn from Article 3 and the requirement of proportionality. I do not deny the importance of prevention. But the economic analysis discussed above shows that the rule allowing the court to award the right holder the greater of the two: his lost profits or the infringer's profits, adequately increased to reach the necessary level of deterrence, should be an effective enough measure of prevention. Anything above this appropriate level of deterrence may result in reduction in creative or inventive activities. So there is no need to overburden the infringing person with double liability and to grant the injured person double benefit. The right way of interpreting Article 13(1)(a) should be, I think, that the court may award either the recovery of loss or the account of profits, whichever is higher.[24]

Finally it is worth noting that the phrase 'all appropriate aspects' in Article 13(1)(a) suggests that also some features or consequences of the infringing activity other than economic and non-economic loss and infringer's profits may have an influence on the amount of damages awarded. It is not easy to tell what they could be; maybe it is about intentional or negligent conduct.

---

[21] See *Tilmann*, (n. 16), 291.
[22] See to the same effect *Walter/Goebel*, (n. 12), p. 1310.
[23] See *Walter/Goebel*, (n. 12), p. 1309. I must confess that the authors' opinion on this matter is not entirely clear to me.
[24] Also other authors exclude the possibility of cumulating these two remedies. See: *von Ungern-Sternberg*, (n. 9), 461; *Tilmann*, (n. 16), 292.

b) Lump sum or pre-established damages

Even the flexible method of calculation applied in Article 13(1)(a) cannot release the right holder from the duty of proving either the scope of loss suffered or the amount of profit gained by the infringer and, what is often more troublesome, the attribution of loss or profit to the infringing activity. The infringer may have earned some of his profit without infringing and it is hard to measure the part of the profit which is unfair. Difficulties in proving damage and cost of investigation hinder the compensation process. Also the prevention provided by damages rules may be ineffective because the damage suffered in result of or profits attributable to a single act of infringement may be too small to justify the cost of monitoring and detecting wrongful acts.[25] For these reasons there is a need for damages that are not closely related to the actual loss or profit attributable to the infringement. A rule on lump sum damages gives the right holder the possibility of recovering damages higher than the actual loss and infringer's profit or at least provides a minimum amount of damages awarded irrespective of circumstances.

The Directive provides for such an alternative in Article 13(1)(b), according to which the court may, in appropriate cases, set the damages as a lump sum on the basis of elements such as at least the amount of royalties or fees which would have been due if the infringer had requested authorization to use the intellectual property right in question. Member States are thus obliged to introduce into their legal system the possibility to award lump sum or pre-established damages. The method of calculation is in principle left to the Member States, with only one limitation. The minimum set by the Directive is the amount of royalties or fees which would have been due – the market price of the licence.[26] Indeed, reasonable royalties are the most convenient measure of lump sum damages. It is, however, quite clear that the payment equal to royalties that would have been due in the case of legitimate use of the right totally fails as a preventive tool.[27] No one would be interested in investing time and money in negotiating the licence contract if he or she could use the IP right without authorization and pay the licence fee anyway. Of course, the lump sum is only an alternative to calculated damages. However, given that, for the reasons discussed above, it is often hard to pursue a claim for calculated damages, the alternative should be equally serious and deterrent.

---

[25] See *Blair/Cotter*, (n. 7), 1651 ff.
[26] See *Bonadio*, (n. 17), 325.
[27] See *Ohly*, (n. 10), pp. 267 ff.; *Walter/Goebel*, (n. 12), p. 1311.

It may be argued that the second limitation of the Member States' discretion in implementing the lump sum damages stems from the final sentence of recital (26) of the Directive:

Recital (26)
(...) The aim is not to introduce an obligation to provide for punitive damages but to allow for compensation based on an objective criterion while taking account of the expenses incurred by the right holder, such as the costs of identification and research.

This would rather be a misconception. One argument raised in the literature against this view is that the Directive is a minimum harmonization tool and Member States are free to raise the standard of protection as high as they find appropriate.[28] This is, however, not fully convincing given the requirement of proportionality (Article 3(2)). In my opinion, there is some limit in raising the amount of pre-established damages, but it cannot be derived directly from recital (26). Generally speaking, this part of the recital complicates rather than clarifies the matter. We can notice that the criterion of reasonable royalties itself does not include the cost of identification or research. The cost in question is variable and simply cannot be translated into any pre-established damages. And the notion of 'punitive damages' is too vague to serve as a boundary of Member States' freedom in implementing the Directive. What makes damages punitive is not its amount but the function it performs and the characteristics of a wrongful act for which it may be awarded.[29] One cannot classify damages as punitive only by use of criterion whether they are equal to single, double or even triple royalty. Punitive damages are qualified by their purpose, to foremost punish the wrongdoer and secondarily to deter him and others from similar behaviour in the future. Damages in the form of multiple royalties are a clear example of pre-established damages for which the amount is not dependent on the nature of a specific wrongful act of a specific tortfeasor. It would also not be true to say that the European law generally rejects punitive damages. Lack of any rules on punitive damages in the Rome II Regulation and very restrained wording of its recital 32 do not support such a firm thesis.[30] To

---

[28] See *Walter/Goebel*, (n. 12), p. 1309.
[29] See *Bodewig/Wandtke*, (n. 9), 222.
[30] (...) *the application of a provision of the law designated by this Regulation which would have the effect of causing non-compensatory exemplary or punitive damages of an excessive nature to be awarded may, depending on the circumstances of the*

the contrary, some passages of the ECJ *Manfredi* decision may support the opposite view.[31]

So the only limit is the requirement of proportionality and, in deciding whether double or triple royalty is a proportionate remedy, account should be taken not only of the relationship between the amount of damages and the scope of damage but also of the dissuasive effect of damages. While assessing the proportionality of a protective measure we should take into consideration both compensation and prevention. From this point of view both double and sometimes even triple royalty may be acceptable. The final decision should be left to the court which should – according to Article 3(2) and recital (17) – take account of the specific characteristics of the case, including the specific features of the infringed right as well as the intentional or unintentional character of the infringement.[32]

As to the nature of pre-established damages equal to the licence fee, it is sometimes argued that from the dogmatic point of view this kind of payment may be treated as compensation for the loss in the form of lost profits.[33] The similarity is only illusive and should not overshadow substantial differences. To claim lost profit, the infringed person has to establish that the profit would have been gained with a certain degree of probability. Reasonable royalties are awarded with no regard to whether conclusion of any licence contract by the right holder was likely or not at all.[34]

4. Damages in case of a bona fide infringement

Article 13(2) authorises Member States to provide for monetary claims of the harmed person also in the case of infringement done not by fault *('not knowingly, or with reasonable grounds know')*. The sanction is described here as *'the recovery of profits or the payment of damages, which may be pre-established'*. This brief description of remedies seems to refer to paragraph (1).[35] Recovery of profits or the payment of damages, including pre-established

---

case and the legal order of the Member State of the court seised, be regarded as being contrary to the public policy (ordre public) of the forum. Cf. Kellner, (n. 13), 138.

[31] See *European Court of Justice* 13.7.2006, joined cases C-295/04 to C-298/04, *Vincenzo Manfredi and Others v Lloyd Adriatico Assicurazioni SpA and Others*, [2006] ECR I-6619, especially at No. 7.
[32] See *Ohly*, (n. 10), p. 273. Cf. *Tilmann*, (n. 16), 292.
[33] See *Walter/Goebel*, (n. 12), p. 1310.
[34] Cf. *Bodewig/Wandtke*, (n. 13), 225.
[35] See *Walter/Goebel*, (n. 12), p. 1311.

damages, probably means here the calculated damages, disgorgement of profit and lump sum damages applied in the case of culpable infringement (this further backs up the thesis that the recovery of loss and the account of profits are alternative remedies and cannot be applied cumulatively). When understood this way, the provision simply allows Member States to shape the liability for the infringement of intellectual property right as a strict liability, not based on fault. As mentioned earlier, a provision like this is important as a confirmation that such an enhancement of protection of the rightholder is not disproportionate per se.

VI. Conclusions

As we can see from the short discussion above, both the scope of application of the harmonized rules and their content are relatively broad. The Directive regulates the consequences of infringement of every kind of intellectual property right. This probably makes it more practically important than the other piece of harmonized tort law, the Directive on product liability. The Directive's rules on damages determine the grounds of liability and method of compensation. It has to be noted, however, that this area of liability is not fully harmonized because some important parts of the liability rules still have to be decided on by national law. In the first place this concerns the notion of causal link between the infringement and the damage. Also the notion of damage may be treated differently in terms of specific details by different national legal orders.

The Significance of the Law of Tort with the Example of the Civil Liability for Erroneous ad hoc Disclosure

Matthias Casper

I. Background and matter of concern of this article

The significance of the law of tort within the law of capital markets has already been the subject matter of many papers.[1] In respect of the space here available, the subsequent discussion has to be limited to a summarising overview. At the same time, it will concentrate on a partial aspect of the discussion by means of which shows the significance of the law of tort for the capital market law especially well: the liability for erroneous ad hoc disclosure. In this context, the article draws a direct line to several previous works of the author and expands on them.[2] The primary reason why a limitation is necessary is that many rules in the capital market law do not intend a protection of the individual. The insider rules stand pars pro toto as they only want to protect the functionality of the capital market as such. In such cases, no requirement for a civil liability exists. In particular, a claim supported by s. 823 subs. 2 BGB [Bürgerliches Gesetzbuch, the German Civil Code] in conjunction with a protective law will fail.

This is closely related to the Janus-headed target dualism of the capital market law.[3] In each particular case an analysis is necessary to determine

---

[1] Two fundamental analyses by *Alexander Hellgardt*, Kapitalmarktdeliktsrecht, 2008, and *Klaus J. Hopt/Hans-Christoph Voigt,* Prospekt- und Kapitalmarktinformationshaftung – Recht und Reform in der Europäischen Union, der Schweiz und den USA, 2005, shall be highlighted here.

[2] *Matthias Casper,* Persönliche Außenhaftung der Organe bei fehlerhafter Information des Kapitalmarkts?, Zeitschrift für Bank- und Kapitalmarktrecht (BKR) 2005, 83; *id.*, Haftung für fehlerhafte Informationen des Kapitalmarktes, Der Konzern 2006, 32; *id.*, in: Kölner Kommentar zum Kapitalanleger-Musterverfahrensgesetz, 2008, §§ 37b, c WpHG Rn. 63 ff.

[3] *Eberhard Schwark,* in: Eberhard Schwark/Daniel Zimmer (ed.), Kapitalmarktrechts-Kommentar, 4th edition, 2010, § 1 WpHG Rn. 4 ff.; *Arne Wittig,* in: Sieg-

whether a rule serves to protect the particular individual investor or whether it rather has only the protection of the institutions as its goal. Only insofar as the protection of the individual is intended, the protection of third parties necessary for s. 823 subs. 2 BGB exists.

For three reasons the duty, established in s. 15 WpHG [Wertpapierhandelsgesetz, German Securities Trading Act], to disclose insider information to the public forthwith, is especially suitable for an exemplary investigation of the role of the law of tort in the capital market law. Firstly, it was controversial for a long time whether in this respect individual protection was standard.[4] It is now widely recognised that the duty for an ad hoc disclosure is only serving the protection of the capital market as an institution.[5] Secondly, because the legislator in Germany nonetheless decided to introduce a liability for erroneous, omitted or belated ad hoc disclosure. To what extent this form of liability by special legal provision has to be located within the law of tort will have to be investigated (also see infra). Finally, this sphere which has to be taken as emblematic for the many duties to furnish in-

---

fried Kümpel/Arne Wittig (eds.), Bank- und Kapitalmarktrecht, 4th edition, 2011, Rn. 1.10 ff.; *Klaus Hopt,* Vom Aktien- und Börsenrecht zum Kapitalmarktrecht? Teil 2: Die deutsche Entwicklung im internationalen Vergleich, Zeitschrift für das gesamte Handels- und Wirtschaftsrecht (ZHR) 141 (1977), 389, 431.

[4] The assumption that s. 15 WpHG is aimed at protecting the individual investor is supported by: *Heinz-Dieter Assmann,* Das künftige deutsche Insiderrecht, Die Aktiengesellschaft (AG) 1994, 196, 203; *Stefan Tippach,* Marktdaten im künftigen Insiderrecht, Zeitschrift für Wirtschafts- und Bankrecht (WM) 1993, 1269, 1272 (regarding the Directive on insider dealing – 89/592/EEC (O.J. L 334 of 18.11.1989)); *Barbara Grunewald,* Neue Regeln zum Insiderhandel, Zeitschrift für Bankrecht und Bankwirtschaft (ZBB) 1990, 128, 130 (regarding the Directive on insider dealing – 89/592/EEC (O.J. L 334 of 18.11.1989)); it is rejected by: *Mark Oulds,* in: Kümpel/Wittig (n. 3) Rn. 14.265; *Siegfried Kümpel,* in: Heinz-Dieter Assmann/Uwe H. Schneider (eds.), Wertpapierhandelsgesetz (WpHG), 2nd edition, 1999, § 15 Rn. 188; *Jörg Rodewald/Mathias Siems,* Haftung für die "frohe Botschaft" – Rechtsfolgen falscher Ad-hoc-Mitteilungen, Betriebs-Berater (BB) 2001, 2437, 2439; *Karl-Burkhard Caspari,* Die geplante Insiderregelung in der Praxis, Zeitschrift für Unternehmens- und Gesellschaftsrecht (ZGR) 1994, 530, 533 (with regard to s. 14 WpHG).

[5] *Daniel Zimmer/Dominik Kruse,* in: Schwark/Zimmer (n. 3) § 15 WpHG Rn. 6; *Heinz-Dieter Assmann,* in: Heinz-Dieter Assmann/Uwe H. Schneider (ed.), Wertpapierhandelsgesetz (WpHG), 5th edition, 2009, § 15 Rn. 28; *Casper* (n. 2) §§ 37b, 37c WpHG Rn. 3; contrary opinion: *Peter Versteegen,* in: Kölner Kommentar zum Wertpapierhandelsgesetz, 2007, § 15 Rn. 12.

formation, is an eminently useful tool as there is a multitude of judicial decisions available which were almost all delivered on the legal position previous to the introduction of the liability in ss 37 b, c WpHG and which are discussing a liability specifically in terms of the damage by means of a violation of bonos mores according to s. 826 BGB.[6] Therefore, also case material exists which focuses on individual issues such as causation and the extent of the damage.

II. Requirements set by European law

There are no requirements set by European Law for a liability for tort on the capital market. For example, Art. 14 I Market Abuse Directive (2003/6/EC) only stipulates that the member states have to provide effective regulations for the enforcement of the rules. It is not indicated whether this needs to be done by means of a civil liability or by means of penal or administrative regulations. When passing the Market Abuse Directive, the EU Commission even desisted explicitly from setting forth civil law penalties as it reckoned that for this purpose it would lack the necessary authority.[7] This

---

[6] This view has first been held by *Landgericht Augsburg* 24. 9. 2001, NJW-RR 2001, 1705, 1706; *Bundesgerichtshof* (BGH) 19.7.2004, BGHZ 160, 134, 142 = NJW 2004, 2664, 2666 – Infomatec I; *Bundesgerichtshof* (BGH) 19.7.2004, BGHZ 160, 149, 151 = NJW 2004, 2971, 2972 – Infomatec II; *Bundesgerichtshof* (BGH) 19.7.2004, WM 2004, 1726 = ZIP 2004, 1593 – Infomatec III; *Bundesgerichtshof* (BGH) 9.5.2005, WM 2005, 1269, 1270 = ZIP 2005, 1270 – EM.TV; *Bundesgerichtshof* (BGH) 28.11.2005, WM 2007, 683 = ZIP 2007, 681 – ComROAD I; *Bundesgerichtshof* (BGH) 15.2.2006, WM 2007, 684 = ZIP 2007, 679 – ComROAD II; *Bundesgerichtshof* (BGH) 26.6.2006, WM 2007, 486 = ZIP 2007, 326 – ComROAD III; *Bundesgerichtshof* (BGH) 4.6.2007, WM 2007, 1557, 1558 ff. = ZIP 2007, 1560, 1563 f.– ComROAD IV; *Bundesgerichtshof* (BGH) 4.6.2007, WM 2007, 1560 = ZIP 2007, 1564 – ComROAD V; *Bundesgerichtshof* (BGH) 7.1.2008, WM 2008, 395, 396 ff. = ZIP 2008, 407, 408 ff. – ComROAD VI; *Bundesgerichtshof* (BGH) 7.1.2008, WM 2008, 398, 399 ff. = ZIP 2008, 410, 411 ff. – ComROAD VII; *Bundesgerichtshof* (BGH) 3.3.2008, WM 2008, 790, 791 f. = ZIP 2008, 829, 830 f. – ComROAD VIII.

[7] Explanation of Art. 14 of the Proposal for a Directive of the European Parliament and of the Council on insider dealing and market manipulation (market abuse) of 30.5.2001, COM/2001/0281 final; the fact that this reasoning has been given up in more recent Directives is analysed by *Thomas Möllers/Franz Leisch*, in: Kölner Kommentar zum Wertpapierhandelsgesetz, 2007, §§ 37 b, 37 c Rn. 18.

open ruling on the European level is also typical for other requirements on transparency on the capital market, such as the regulations on investment transparency stipulated in capital market law according to ss 21 et seq. WpHG by means of which the requirements from the Transparency Directive (2004/109/EC) are transposed. Art. 24 thereof also leaves it to the member states to decide on the sanctions. Within Europe, in a comparative overview the whole sphere of the enforcement of the rules ('Normdurchsetzung') is also characterised by a great inconsistency. Recently, several papers by *Rüdiger Veil* have demonstrated this in an impressive manner.[8] A liability pertaining to civil law and on top of that a liability under the law of tort is, in this context, not the centre-point. In view of these open European initial findings, the question arises whether a liability under the law of tort of the issuer, or its acting board members ('Organmitglied') for the violation of regulations stipulated in the capital market law is an adequate mechanism. In the following, this shall be examined with the help of the example of the liability for erroneous and omitted ad hoc information respectively. In this context, the chosen prerequisites and the legal consequences of the liability in accordance with the special legal provision in ss 37b, c WpHG shall be compared to the information liability based on s. 826 BGB. The legal nature of the liability in ss 37b, c WpHG has to be determined only at the end, whereupon, in particular, the question has to be pursued whether a classification under the law of tort may achieve any benefits.

III. Liability of the issuer: comparison of the basis for liability and causation in ss 37b, c WpHG and s. 826 BGB

1. Misconduct threatened with sanctions

For now, if one takes a look at the misconduct threatened with sanctions it has to be concluded that under ss 37b, c WpHG any omitted, belated or erroneous ad hoc information will be sufficient for a liability of the issuer. On the other hand s. 826 BGB requires an infringement by means of a violation

---

[8] *Rüdiger Veil*, Französisches Kapitalmarktrecht. Eine rechtsvergleichende Studie aus der Perspektive des europäischen Kapitalmarktrechts, 2010; *id.*, Schwedisches Kapitalmarktrecht. Eine rechtsvergleichende Studie aus der Perspektive des europäischen Kapitalmarktrechts, 2010; *id.*, Englisches Kapitalmarktrecht. Eine rechtsvergleichende Studie aus der Perspektive des europäischen Kapitalmarktrechts, 2010.

of bonos mores. In the previous landmark decisions regarding erroneous information, the acting board member always acted for a personal gain, for instance, to push the price higher as he held shares of his own.[9] However, in the literature a controversy arose whether also the erroneous information, deliberate but not for personal gain, causes a liability according to s. 826 BGB[10] or even whether the omission of disclosure of information has to be put under the verdict of the violation of bonos mores, insofar as it was a deliberate omission.[11] If both is recognised, the element of s. 826 BGB in

---

[9] BGHZ 160, 149, 157; *Oberlandesgericht Frankfurt a.M.* 21.2.2006, AG 2006, 584, 585.

[10] This is assumed by: *Daniel Zimmer/Marc Grotheer*, in: Schwark/Zimmer (n. 3) §§ 37b, c WpHG Rn. 118b; *Rolf Sethe*, in: Assmann/Schneider (n. 5) §§ 37 b, 37 c Rn. 118; *Ulrich Ehricke*, in: Hopt/Voigt (n. 1) p. 280; *Holger Fleischer*, Zur deliktsrechtlichen Haftung der Vorstandsmitglieder für falsche Ad-hoc-Mitteilungen, Der Betrieb (DB) 2004, 2031, 2033; *Olaf Gerber*, Die Haftung für unrichtige Kapitalmarktinformationen – Zugleich eine Besprechung der BGH-Entscheidungen vom 19.7.2004 "Infomatec", Deutsches Steuerrecht (DStR) 2004, 1793, 1798; *Rüdiger Krause*, Ad-hoc-Publizität und haftungsrechtlicher Anlegerschutz, Zeitschrift für Unternehmens- und Gesellschaftsrecht (ZGR) 2002, 799, 823; *Thomas Möllers*, Der Weg zu einer Haftung für Kapitalmarktinformationen, JuristenZeitung (JZ) 2005, 75, 76; *Thomas Möllers/Franz Leisch*, in: Thomas M. J. Möllers/Klaus Rotter (ed.), Ad-hoc-Publizität, 2003, § 15 Rn. 17 ff.; *Knut Sauer*, Haftung für Falschinformation des Sekundärmarktes, 2004, p. 54; *Matthias Dühn*, Schadensersatzhaftung börsennotierter Aktiengesellschaften für fehlerhafte Kapitalmarktinformation, 2003, p. 139; *Eberhard Schwark*, Kapitalmarktbezogene Informationshaftung, in: Franz Häuser/Horst Hammen/Joachim Hennrichs (ed.), Festschrift für Walther Hadding, 2004, p. 1117, 1131 f.; it is rejected by: *Gerald Spindler*, Persönliche Haftung der Organmitglieder für Falschinformationen des Kapitalmarkts – de lege lata und de lege ferenda –, WM 2004, 2089, 2092; *Rützel*, Der aktuelle Stand der Rechtsprechung zur Haftung bei Ad-hoc-Mitteilungen, Die Aktiengesellschaft (AG) 2003, 69, 73; *Matthias Casper*, Der Konzern 2006, 32, 33; *Timo Holzborn/Martin Foelsch*, Schadensersatzpflichten von Aktiengesellschaften und deren Management bei Anlegerverlusten – Ein Überblick, Neue Juristische Wochenschrift (NJW) 2003, 932, 939; *Jörn Kowaleski/Alexander Hellgardt*, Der Stand der Rechtsprechung zur deliktsrechtlichen Haftung für vorsätzlich falsche Ad-hoc-Mitteilungen, Der Betrieb (DB) 2005, 1839, 1842; *Hellgardt* (n. 1) 386 ff.

[11] The latter is assumed by *Möllers*, JZ 2005, 75, 76 if the duty to disclose is evident; whereas the majority of the academia demands particular additional circumstances such as self-interest, see for example *Holger Fleischer*, Konturen der kapitalmarktrechtlichen Informationsdeliktshaftung, Zeitschrift für Wirtschaftsrecht

the sphere of the deliberate breach of duty would be largely the same as that of ss 37b, c WpHG. Such harmony is unconvincing. The prevailing view in the literature establishes its opinion with an alleged parallelism to the recognised case group of the attentive wrong supply of information.[12] This comparison is unconvincing. The attentive wrong supply of information is tailor-made to a personal relationship between the persons involved which is not present on the capital market. Other than in the sphere of a contractual or pre-contractual relationship there is no existing special trust justifying the liability resulting from s. 826 BGB. However, above all on the capital market the trust focuses on market-pricing according to the regulations but not on the respective board member ('Organ') of the issuer as a person.

Therefore the mere deliberate breach of the duty to furnish information an additional factor is necessary for a liability according to s. 826 BGB. The verdict of the violation of bonos mores cannot be limited in itself to state breaches of statutory regulations.[13] On the top of that, the mere omission is unsuitable to state an injury by means of a violation of bonos mores, insofar as there are no additional special factors. In addition to the personal benefit such special factors for a violation of bonos mores are also the achievement of unfair advantages for the issuer.[14] Moreover, in addition to such cases of personal benefit one has to think of the "last-period-phenomenon" known from economics[15] in which attentive erroneous information is used

---

(ZIP) 2005, 1805, 1806 with further references in n. 17; *Casper,* Der Konzern 2006, 32, 34; *Fleischer,* DB 2004, 2031, 2033; *Krause,* ZGR 2002, 799, 824; *Sauer* (n. 10) p. 54; the applicableness of § 826 BGB is generally rejected, for example, by *Rützel,* AG 2003, 69, 73.

[12] For this case group see *Bundesgerichtshof* (BGH) 3.12.1973, WM 1974, 153; *Bundesgerichtshof* (BGH) 22.6.1992, NJW 1992, 3167, 3174.

[13] This is correctly emphasised by *Spindler,* WM 2004, 2089, 2091.

[14] In addition to the classic situation where incorrect information is published in order to drive up the market value and thereby being able to sell shares at a higher price, the situation where information is not disclosed in order to cover up mismanagement and avoid liability according to § 93 Aktiengesetz would also need to be included; similarly *Hellgardt* (n. 1) 390 ff.; against any kind of liability in case of omission of disclosure of information for example *Georg Maier-Reimer/Nikolaos Paschos,* in: Mathias Habersack/Peter O. Mülbert/Michael Schlitt (ed.), Handbuch der Kapitalmarkt-information, 2008, § 29 Rn. 174 f.

[15] The pioneers of this being *Reinier Kraakman,* Corporate Liability Strategies and the Costs of Legal Controls, (1984) 93 Yale Law Journal (YLJ) 857, 866 and *Donald Langevoort,* Capping Damages for Open-Market Securities Fraud, (1996) 38 Arizona Law Review 639, 654; empirically analysed by *Jennifer Arlen/William Carney,*

for the rescue of a business which got into a crisis as the executive board is expecting the loss of their position anyway. If it is further acknowledged in accordance with the decision on "Infomatec" that also a blatantly erroneous or purely fictional ad hoc information indicates the violation of bonos mores,[16] the fact remains that there is no major difference between both of the opinions in the practical application.

2. Causation between erroneous information and the investment decision

There is a special focus in the discussion on the causation substantiating the liability between the erroneous information and the investment decision. Prior to the introduction of the reversal of the burden of proof with the German Third Financial Markets Promotion Act [*Drittes Finanzmarktförderungsgesetz*] for the prospectus liability in the primary market in s. 45 subs. 2 No. 1 BörsG [Börsengesetz, German Stock Exchange Act] by the legislator the concept of the so-called "Anlagestimmung" (Investment Climate) had been developed by jurisprudence and academia. This involves a refutable assumption that the investor bought or sold as a result of the erroneous information.[17] With the recourse to the efficient capital market hypothesis ('Theorie effizienter Kapitalmärkte') significant voices in the literature spoke in favour of expanding this facilitation to the liability for erroneous ad hoc information.[18]

Vicarious Liability for Fraud on Securities Markets: Theory and Evidence, (1992) University of Illinois Law Review (U Ill L Rev) 691, 720 ff.; *Donald Langevoort*, Selling Hope, Selling Risk: Some Lessons for Law from Behavioral Economics About Stockbrokers and Sophisticated Customers, (1996) 84 California Law Review (CLR) 627, 643.

[16] BGHZ 160, 134, 146 = ZIP 2004, 1599, 1603 – Infomatec I.
[17] Instead of all see *Fleischer*, ZIP 2005, 1805, 1807 with further references.
[18] See for example *Baums*, Haftung wegen Falschinformation des Sekundärmarkts, ZHR 167 (2003), 139, 180 ff.; *Fleischer*, DB 2004, 2031, 2034; for a more detailed analysis see *Sauer* (n. 10) 121 ff.; *id.*, Kausalität und Schaden bei der Haftung für falsche Kapitalmarktinformationen, Zeitschrift für Bankrecht und Bankwirtschaft (ZBB) 2005, 24, 27 ff., though he regards referring to the "Anlagestimmung" (Investment Climate) as dispensable since according to the theory of price-efficient markets it is proven that investors only rely on the incorrect price; similarly *Rü-*

While it is widely recognised for the liability according to ss 37b, c WpHG that a causation between the misinformation and the investment decision is at least not essential in those cases, in which the reparation of the damage is limited to the damage of the difference of the prices[19], a widely spread different opinion, especially in the jurisprudence, can be found with regard to a liability according to s. 826 BGB. After the BGH [Bundesgerichtshof, German Federal Court of Justice] allowed in its decision on Infomatec the recourse to the investment climate at least in particular cases for a period of two months,[20] it requested, beginning with the EM.TV decision,[21] then still tacitly,[22] and later very vehemently in its seven decisions to the ComRoad complex, a causation between the breach of duty and the investment decision and rejected a recourse to the concept of the investment climate even for purely fictional ad hoc information. The BGH, repeating this almost like a mantra, established that the recognition of the investment climate, respectively the recourse to the fraud-on-the-market-theory, which would waive any requirement of causation and merely rest upon the "disappointed general investor trust in the integrity of the market-pricing", would be inadmissible. This would result in an "unlimited extension of the basis for liability of the already far-reaching deliberate infringement by violation of bonos mores".[23] The literature is increasingly consenting to this opinion.[24]

In the end, we will nonetheless have no other choice than making a recourse to the concept of the investment climate if we do not want to cause substantial difficulties of proving matters for the investor who suffered dam-

---

diger Veil, Die Ad-hoc-Publizitätshaftung im System kapitalmarktrechtlicher Informationshaftung, ZHR 167 (2003), 365, 380 ff.

[19] See for example *Daniel Zimmer/Marc Grotheer*, in: Schwark/Zimmer (n. 3) §§ 37b, 37c WpHG Rn. 90; *Rolf Sethe*, in: Assmann/Schneider (n. 5) §§ 37b, 37c WpHG Rn. 83 ff.; *Casper* (n. 2) §§ 37b, 37c WpHG Rn. 51; *id.*, Der Konzern 2006, 32, 34.

[20] BGHZ 160, 134, 146 = ZIP 2004, 1599, 1603 – Infomatec I.

[21] BGH ZIP 2005, 1270 ff.; this has also been rejected by *Christian Duve/Denis Basak*, Welche Zukunft hat die Organaußenhaftung für Kapitalmarktinformationen?, BB 2005, 2645, 2648 f.

[22] Convincing interpretation by *Fleischer*, ZIP 2005, 1805, 1806 f.

[23] BGH ZIP 2007, 681, 682 – ComROAD I; BGH ZIP 2007, 679, 680 – ComROAD II; BGH ZIP 2007, 326 – ComROAD III; BGH WM 2007, 1557, 1558 f. – ComROAD IV; BGH WM 2007, 1560, 1561 = ZIP 2007, 1564 – ComROAD V; BGH WM 2008, 395, 396 ff. = ZIP 2008, 407, 408 ff. – ComROAD VI; BGH WM 2008, 398, 399 ff. = ZIP 2008, 410, 411 ff. – ComROAD VII.

[24] See for example *Daniel Zimmer/Marc Grotheer*, in: Schwark/Zimmer (n. 3) §§ 37b, c WpHG Rn. 118 with further references.

age or loss and to turn the liability for misinformation into a hardly effective weapon.[25] The objection of a boundless length of the liability can be met on two levels. Firstly, the easing of the burden of proof by means of a recourse to the investment climate has to be limited to cases in which only the damage of the difference of the prices is required and not also the rescission of the contract as a form of restitution in kind ('Naturalrestitution'). *Carsten Schäfer* was the first to point out this distinguishing criterion.[26] Insofar as the investor may require a rescission of the concluded contract on the shares by way of restitution in kind, it is consistent to adhere to the requirement that the investor has to prove causation. This is due to the fact that in case of a real or commercial rescission of the whole transaction it is the trust in the investment decision underlying the contract which is only justifying these legal consequences if the omitted failure to provide information would have kept the investor from the whole transaction. The evidence of this specific trust has to be presented by the investor as the investor's freedom of decision as such is then protected.[27] In other words, insofar as only the compensation of the damage of the difference of the prices is being

---

[25] As a compensation for this strict approach the Bundesgerichtshof (BGH) offers investors the possibility to prove causality by way of interrogation of a party if the breach of duty is grave; see for example *BGH* WM 2007, 1557, 1559 – ComROAD IV.

[26] *Carsten Schäfer*, Effektivere Vorstandshaftung für Fehlinformation des Kapitalmarkts, Neue Zeitschrift für Gesellschaftsrecht (NZG) 2005, 985, 990 f. = Der Gesellschafter – Sonderheft (GesRZ-SH) 2005, 25, 33 f.; in principle also assumed by *Stephan Hutter/Florian Stürwald,* EM.TV und die Haftung für fehlerhafte Ad-hoc-Mitteilungen, NJW 2005, 2428, 2430; with a similar approach but differing in the conclusion: *Duve/Basak,* BB 2005, 2645, 2649 f. This assumption has been prominently supported by *Gerhard Wagner,* Schadensberechnung im Kapitalmarktrecht, ZGR 2008, 495, 527 ff.; similarly *Lars Leuschner,* Zum Kausalitätserfordernis des § 826 BGB bei unrichtigen Ad-hoc-Mitteilungen, ZIP 2008, 1050, 1054 ff.; *Maier-Reimer/Paschos* (n. 14) § 29 Rn. 171 ff.; it is in principle also supported by *Daniel Zimmer/Matthias Cloppenburg,* Haftung für falsche Information des Sekundärmarktes auch bei Kapitalanlagen des nicht geregelten Kapitalmarktes?, ZHR 171 (2007), 519, 539 f.

[27] *Schäfer,* NZG 2005, 985, 990 f. = GesRZ-SH 2005, 25, 34; partly dissenting *Hellgardt* (n. 1) 519 ff., 528 f., who wants to allow a rescission of the contract in case of market disturbance that prevents efficient pricing but still applies the figure of 'Anlagestimmung' (Investment Climate).

requested (or may be requested), the evidence of the concrete causation by the investor is not necessary.[28]

On the other hand, the danger of a boundless length can be reduced by means of a short determination of the period in which the figure of investment climate is applied. Even if it will be difficult to find a fixed length of time, it remains the fact that periods of time of two months[29] or even longer[30] can be ruled out even for cases of extremely dubious reporting. The typical period of time has to be estimated at one to two weeks. In addition, the recourse to the investment climate gives only reasons for a refutable assumption. Accordingly, the issuer retains the freedom to demonstrate that his breach of the legal obligation to the ad hoc disclosure did not have a lasting negative effect, and therefore did not give reasons for an investment disposition in particular cases.

3. Extent and calculation of the damage

Whereas according to the predominant understanding, only the damage of the difference of the prices is restituted under ss 37b, c WpHG,[31] the BGH also allows a restitution in kind in the case of s. 826 BGB.[32] As a result, the

---

[28] During the period of 'Anlagestimmung' (Investment Climate) the investor further does not have to prove that the market value has been influenced by the erroneous information, see *Hutter/Stürwald*, NJW 2005, 2428, 2430 with further references regarding dissenting opinions.

[29] See *Oberlandesgericht München* 28.04.2005, ZIP 2005, 1141- previous instance in ComROAD III.

[30] See as an example of the case-law of lower instances *Landgericht München* 25. 7. 2006, BKR 2006, 465, 466 f.

[31] See for example *Casper* (n. 2) §§ 37 b, c WpHG Rn. 54 ff. with further references also regarding dissenting opinions as well as *Maier-Reimer/Paschos* (n. 14) § 20 Rn. 98 ff., particularly 129 ff. with further references.

[32] BGHZ 160, 149, 153; *BGH* ZIP 2005, 1270, 1272; *Michael Beurskens*, in: Ulrich Noack/Matthias Casper/Carsten Schäfer (ed.), Gesellschaftsrecht case by case, 2006, p. 349; *Florian Engelhardt*, Vertragsabschlussschaden oder Differenzschaden bei der Haftung des Emittenten für fehlerhafte Kapitalmarktinformationen, Zeitschrift für Bank- und Kapitalmarktrecht (BKR) 2006, 443, 447; *Fleischer*, ZIP 2005, 1805, 1809; *Gerber*, DStR 2004, 1793, 1797; *Eckart Gottschalk*, Die deliktische Haftung für fehlerhafte Ad-hoc-Mitteilungen, DStR 2005, 1648, 1651; *Klaus Hopt/Hans-Christoph Voigt*, in: Hopt/Voigt (n. 1) p. 133; *Hutter/Stürwald*, NJW 2005, 2428, 2430; *Michael Kort*, Die Haftung von Vorstandsmitgliedern für falsche Ad-

investor is entitled to request the revocation of the contract of sale. This is in itself compatible with the general rule based on tort in s. 249 BGB. However, the objection could be made that the investor did, in fact, not buy the shares from the issuer or the acting board.[33] Even if the restoration of the property of the person who suffered damage or loss and not the interest of the tortfeasor[34] is the primary concern of the restitution in kind only the damage of the difference of the prices should be awarded under s 826 BGB as well.[35] In the end, in the case of the erroneous capital market information the reproach targets the possible manipulation of the market price and not the erroneous establishment of a membership right as it is the case with the entry into a company as a result of fraudulent misrepresentation. Once more, it has to be made clear that s. 15 WpHG does not convey an individually protective character,[36] but only serves for the formation of prices according to the regulations.[37] Therefore, the loss of the investor lies in the fact that he had bought the shares at a price too high (or sold the shares too

---

hoc-Mitteilungen, Die Aktiengesellschaft (AG) 2005, 21, 24; *Franz Leisch*, Vorstandshaftung für falsche Ad-hoc-Mitteilungen, ZIP 2004, 1573, 1575; *Möllers*, JZ 2005, 75, 77; *Möllers/Leisch* (n. 7) §§ 37 b, 37 c Rn. 430 ff, 436; *Josef Sethe* in: Assmann/Schneider (n. 5) §§ 37 b, 37 c Rn. 123; *Spindler*, WM 2004, 2089, 2093.

[33] *Dühn* (n. 10) 157 ff.; *Andreas Fuchs/Matthias Dühn*, Deliktische Schadensersatzhaftung für falsche Ad-hoc-Mitteilungen, BKR 2002, 1063, 1069; *Holger Fleischer*, Der Inhalt des Schadensersatzanspruchs wegen unwahrer oder unterlassener unverzüglicher Ad-hoc-Mitteilungen, BB 2002, 1869, 1873; *Michael Kort*, Die Haftung der AG nach §§ 826, 31 bei fehlerhaften Ad-hoc-Mitteilungen, Neue Zeitschrift für Gesellschaftsrecht (NZG) 2005, 708; *Jochem Reichert/Marc-Philippe Weller*, Haftung von Kontrollorganen: Die Reform der aktienrechtlichen und kapitalmarktrechtlichen Haftung, ZRP 2002, 49, 55.

[34] *Fleischer*, ZIP 2005, 1805, 1809; *Spindler*, WM 2004, 2089, 2093; *Möllers*, JZ 2005, 75, 77.

[35] *Fuchs/Dühn*, BKR 2002, 1063, 1069; *Casper*, Der Konzern 2006, 32, 35; *Duve/Basak*, BB 2005, 2645, 2648; *Rützel*, AG 2003, 69, 76; *Sauer*, ZBB 2005, 24, 33; in principle also *Hellgardt* (n. 1) 492 ff.; also regarding this as "desirable": *Hutter/Stürwald*, NJW 2005, 2428, 2430; *Fleischer*, DB 2004, 2031, 2036; differentiating in accordance with the relevance of the ad-hoc publication: *Christoph Teichmann*, Haftung für fehlerhafte Informationen am Kapitalmarkt, Juristische Schulung (JuS) 2006, 953, 958.

[36] See supra.
[37] See supra.

cheap) at the capital market.[38] It is also difficult to see why the liable board member should bear the risk of prices dropping due to exogenous factors as he would then be imposed with the role of an insurer against disadvantageous market development trends.[39] It would not make much sense if the investor could speculate on the expense of the issuer by delaying the enforcement of the rescission of the contract.

Moreover, in practice, the problem of the ascertainment of the loss still remains. The difference in prices is determined by the difference between the purchase price actually paid and the hypothetical purchase price based on information according to the rules.[40] Therefore, it has to be asked by how much the price at which the investor bought or sold the shares was too high or too low. In this context, the effect which the true information has on the price after it becomes known can be classified as an indicator and can be counted back to the date of the investment decision. Of course, in practice, the ascertainment of the hypothetical purchase price nevertheless frequently requires an expert opinion.[41] A lump-sum compensation, as it was intended in the bill for a law on the liability for information on the capital market [Kapitalmarktinformationshaftungsgesetz, abbreviated in German as KapInHaG] presented in 2004,[42] is therefore urgently needed from the point of view of legal policy. Of course, the solution presented therein was

---

[38] In contrast, the assumption made by *Oberlandesgericht München* ZGR 2002, 1110, 1111 – EM.TV that it would be impossible to determine damages this way has rightfully been harshly criticised. But contrary to what *BGH* ZIP 2005, 1270, 1272 – EM.TV assumes this would not lead to restitution in kind being the standard legal remedy.

[39] These concerns are widely recognised, see for example *Fleischer*, ZIP 2005, 1085, 1809; *Hutter/Stürwald*, NJW 2005, 2428, 2430; *Sauer*, ZBB 2005, 24, 32 f.

[40] Instead of all see *Fleischer*, ZIP 2005, 1805, 1809 with further references; in-depth analysis of the financial aspects of determining damages this way in *Christina Escher-Weingart/Alexander Lägeler/Christoph Eppinger*, Schadensersatzanspruch, Schadensart und Schadensberechnung gem. der §§ 37 b, 37 c WpHG, WM 2004, 1845, 1850 ff.; though this is partially criticised by *Carsten Schäfer/Martin Weber/Peter Wolf*, Berechnung und Pauschalierung des Kursdifferenzschadens bei fehlerhafter Kapitalmarktinformation, ZIP 2008, 197, 200 f.

[41] For a too optimistic interpretation of the theory of information-efficient capital markets see *Sauer*, ZBB 2005, 24, 34; like here *Maier-Reimer/Paschos* (n. 14) § 29 Rn. 138.

[42] See the draft version of s. 37a subs. 4 WpHG printed in: NZG 2004, 1042.

all too simplistic.[43] Accordingly, the creditor should have been reimbursed with the balance between the purchase price and the weighted average stock market price in the period of the first thirty days after the publication of the erroneous information. The collapse of prices by virtue of exogenous factors would have then been passed on to the issuer.[44] One possibility to determine the loss, as shown in previous comparative law works of *Holger Fleischer*, is to count back the price fluctuations on the day of the publication by means of a backward induction ('rückwärtige Induktion') to the true value of the security on the day of the publication of the erroneous information.[45] If, for example, the stock price was at 100 on the day of the erroneous information and fell to 50 by the time the faultiness of the information became public and, as a result of the public knowledge, drops once more to 45, i.e. by another 10%, then the true price at the time of the erroneous information can be estimated at 90. In other words, the determination primarily has to start at the date at which the erroneous or omitted information is deemed to be common knowledge in order to be able to measure the break of the price at that time. In this respect, the Capital Asset Pricing Model from the modern monetary-economic discussion may provide assistance.[46] Likewise worthy of being discussed is the model of the lump-sum determination of the damage ('Modell der Schadenspauschalierung') suggested by *Schäfer/*

---

[43] The first draft proposal is crafted after sec. 21D(e) Securities Exchange Act but misses that this provision is aimed at limitation of damages and not at lump-sum compensation, see convincing criticism in *Möllers*, JZ 2005, 75, 80.

[44] For criticism of this see *Rüdiger Veil*, Die Haftung des Emittenten für fehlerhafte Information des Kapitalmarkts nach dem geplanten KapInHaG, BKR 2005, 91, 96f.; *Sauer*, ZBB 2005, 24, 32f.; *DAV-Handelsrechtsausschuss*, NZG 2004, 2348, 2350 as well as those named in n. 35.

[45] *Fleischer*, BB 2002, 1869, 1872; see further *Sauer* (n. 10) 357 ff.; also in favour of this: *Casper*, Der Konzern 2006, 32, 35; *Maier-Reimer/Paschos* (n. 14) § 29 Rn. 138; regarding the discussion in the US see *Lars Klöhn*, Problem Schadensberechnung: Neues vom US Supreme Court zur Haftung wegen fehlerhafter Kapitalmarktinformation, Recht der internationalen Wirtschaft (RIW) 2005, 728 ff. This is however rejected by *Schäfer/Weber/Wolf*, ZIP 2008, 197, 200 ff.

[46] Details in *Fleischer*, BB 2002, 1869, 1873; *Escher-Weingart/Lägeler/Eppinger*, WM 2004, 1845, 1852 ff. and especially *Jay Eisenhofer/Geoffrey Javis/James Banko*, Securities Fraud, Stock Price Valuation, and Loss Causation: Toward a Corporate Finance-Based Theory of Loss Causation, (2994) 59 The Business Lawyer 1419, 1441 ff.; *Martin Weber*, Börsenkursbestimmung aus ökonomischer Perspektive, ZGR 2004, 280 ff. For the entire issue see *Zimmer/Cloppenburg*, ZHR 171 (2007), 519, 537 ff.

Weber/Wolf, where the average price of the last 10 trading days up to the second day before the publication shall be compared with the weighted average price of the ten days from the second day after the publication.[47] In both models the slow publication of the inaccuracy of an ad hoc disclosure which is gradually reflected in the price structure is difficult.

IV. Do we need a cumulative external liability of the board ('Organaußenhaftung')?

1. Question

At the initial point, the liability of the acting board member to the issuer according to s. 93 subs. 2 AktG [Aktiengesetz, German Stock Corporation Act] or on grounds of a breach of the employment contract for an erroneous or omitted ad hoc disclosure has never been doubted. This liability can also be classified as an internal liability of the board. Furthermore, from the point of view of legal policy, the question is decided whether the issuer or the acting body shall be primarily liable externally towards the investors. In this respect, with the German Fourth Financial Markets Promotion Act [Viertes Finanzmarktförderungsgesetz] introducing the liability according to ss 37b, c WpHG, the legislator has opted for a liability of the issuer. Under the heading of cumulative external liability, in particular following the draft for discussion on the KapInHaG[48], it was controversially discussed whether the acting board members, in addition to the issuer, should not be liable towards the investors. De lege lata, this is only the case if, at the same time, a liability according to s. 826 BGB exists, as this primarily affects the member of the board and only by means of the imputation according to s. 31 BGB also the issuer. Even if this discussion from the point of view of legal policy had at first flattened out, it has restarted since then following the financial market crisis. As the author has already positioned himself

---

[47] *Schäfer/Weber/Wolf*, ZIP 2008, 197, 200 ff. Yet another model is proposed by *Wagner*, ZGR 2008, 495, 526 f. though the details of this cannot be discussed here.

[48] See *Casper*, Der Konzern 2006, 32, 38 f.; *Schäfer*, NZG 2005, 985, 987 ff.; *Fuchs/Dühn*, BKR 2002, 1063, 1068; *Duve/Basak*, BB 2005, 2645, 2647, 2650 f. speak in favour of a specific provision for cases of contingent intent, which so far have been solved under s. 826 BGB, in order to be able to integrate these cases into the WpHG.

in another context,[49] the following ideas are nonetheless limited to a short summery of the arguments exchanged.

2. Refutation of the central reasons for an external liability of the board

In the first place, it is often said by the advocates of a cumulative external liability that the current legal situation would not develop *enough preventive effect* to curb erroneous ad hoc disclosure. Despite the existing liability of the issuer in ss 37b, c WpHG and despite the jurisdiction on the liability according to s. 826 BGB, the current system of the liability of the issuer is not deemed as sufficient to discipline executive boards not abiding the law. Against this, the fact has to be raised that the current legal situation is already suitably appropriate to develop a sufficient preventive effect. De lege lata, members of the boards are already liable to be fined when breaching the duty of ad hoc publicity by means of s. 39 WpHG and s. 30 OWiG [Ordnungswidrigkeitengesetz, German Administrative Offences Act] and in exceptional cases may also be sued by the investors according to s. 826 BGB. Apart from that, the internal liability according to s. 93 subs. 2 AktG develops a sufficient deterrent effect. Indeed, Directors' & Officers'-insurances are capable of limiting the preventive effect of the internal liability of the board. However, this limitation is counteracted with the law regarding the adequacy of the remuneration of the members of the board, in force since 9 August 2009, with the duty to agree on an adequate deductible set in s. 93 subs. 2 c. 3 AktG. Since then, directors have to bear at least 10 % of the damage caused, though the deductible may be capped to 1.5 times of the annual fixed salary of the member of the board. Above all, in particular the danger of a loss of the position and reputation has a deterring effect. Besides, frequently, in the event of a deliberate action of the member of the board the insurance will not stand. Therefore, the supporters refer primarily to the so-called Last-Period-Constellation, which is claimed to be in need of an intensified deterrence.[50] This can be countered by the general law of tort in the form of s. 826 and s. 823 subs. 2 BGB in conjunction with

---

[49] Casper, BKR 2005, 83, 85 ff.

[50] Fleischer, Gutachten zum 64. DJT 2002, p. F 102 f.; *id.*, Die persönliche Haftung der Organmitglieder für kapitalmarktbezogene Falschinformationen – Bestandsaufnahme und Perspektiven, BKR 2003, 608, 612; Baums, ZHR 167 (2003), 139, 174.

s. 400 AktG and the liability for a delay in filing a petition for insolvency ('Insolvenzverschleppungshaftung'), both containing a sufficient deterrent potential.[51] It was already pointed out that the liability resulting from s. 826 BGB applies in the Last-Period-Constellations even without a special personal interest.[52]

Moreover, there is a call for an additional liability fund for the investors who suffered damage or loss. The background is the previous pathological cases which all took place at the 'New Market' of the Stock Exchange in Frankfurt ('Neuer Markt'), which has since then been laid to rest. Shortly after the publication of the erroneous information, some issuers such as Infomatec, ComROAD or Met@box were already insolvent. For the rare case of an insolvency without any assets ('masselose Insolvenz') the weaknesses of the model of the internal liability according to s. 93 AktG have been pointed out.[53] Meanwhile, upon a closer look, the private property of the executives directors is in general an insufficient additional liability fund for the investor who suffered a damage or loss. A claim against the directors only makes economical sense if, by means of this, the investor wants to take hold of the sum of the D&O-Insurance. However, this claim can only be made by the company as the policy holder and not e.g. by the member of the board personally. Apart from that, a D&O-insurance is not intended to secure the risk of insolvency of the issuer for the investors who suffered damage or loss. Furthermore, it would not be sensible, neither from the legal-dogmatic perspective nor from the economic point of view, to develop the external liability of the board as a contingent liability in the event of insolvency ('Insolvenzausfallhaftung').[54] Anyone who wants to relieve the investors from the risk of an insolvency has to stipulate an insurance comparable to s. 651k BGB for the issuer.

---

[51] It can further be pointed out that even the discoverers of the last-period-phenomenon are not entirely convinced by the effectiveness of a threat of liability for the management, see *Arlen/Carney*, (1992) U Ill L Rev, 691, 701 ff.; *Langevoort*, (1996) 38 Arizona Law Review 639, 654 ff.

[52] See supra.

[53] *C. Schäfer*, NZG 2005, 985, 989 = GesRZ-SH 2005, 25, 29 f.

[54] This is suggested as a "legislative makeshift" in the statement by the commercial law commission of the German Lawyer Association (Deutscher Anwaltverein, DAV) on the report of the Corporate Governance government commission, NZG 2003, Sonderbeil. zu Heft 9, p. 18; similarly *Kurt Kiethe*, Persönliche Organhaftung für Falschinformationen des Kapitalmarktes – Anlegerschutz durch Systembruch, DStR 2003, 1982, 1987.

There is also the call for a standardisation of the primary and secondary market as according to the undisputed interpretation of s. 44 subs. 1 BörsG. With the prospectus liability on the primary market a personal liability of the members of the issuer's board is possible. However, in terms of systematic consistency, the liability of the board under the law for prospectuses on the primary market does not make it compulsory to hold the directors personally liable for failures to provide information in the sphere of the secondary market as well. Under ss 44, 45 BörsG only those initiators who have a personal interest are liable.[55] As mentioned above, the case group of self-interest ('Eigeninteresse') is on the secondary market already encompassed by s. 826 BGB.

Finally, a generalised reference is made to the much stricter law of other well developed capital market legal systems, especially to that of the USA.[56] The opponents of an external liability of the board rightly counter this with the fact that an explicit external liability of the board exists almost nowhere in Europe.[57] Other than in the USA, there is the widely spread tendency to take action against the acting board members – in addition to the issuer – at best by virtue of the general civil law. Prevention is primarily seen as a duty of the law governing supervision and criminal sanctions.[58]

---

[55] *Eberhard Schwark*, in: Schwark/Zimmer (n. 3) §§ 44, 45 BörsG Rn. 8 f.

[56] SEC-Rule 10b-5; instead of all see *Louis Loss/Joel Seligman*, Securities Regulation, 3rd edition, 2001, p. 3481 ff.; *Thomas Lee Hazen*, The Law of Securities Regulation, 4th edition, 2002, § 13.10; for case-law, which is primarily directed against the issuer, see for example *Herman & MacLean v. Huddleston*, 459 US 375, 382 (1983); *Musick, Peeler & Garrett v. Employers Insurance*, 507 US 286 (1993); *Baker v. Latham Sparrowbush Assocs* 72 F.3d 346 (2d Cir. 1995) as well as the case-law cited in *Loss/Seligman*, p. 3510.

[57] Even though Austria has headed for an approach similar to the draft proposal of s. 37a WpHG, for further details see *Schäfer*, NZG 2005, 985, 989 = GesRZ-SH 2005, 25, 27.

[58] Overview in *Casper*, BKR 2005, 83, 84 f.; details can be found the comprehensive comparative law study in *Hopt/Voigt* (n. 1) 120 f. as well as the individual country reports.

3. Further arguments against a cumulative external liability of the board

Further arguments against a cumulative external liability of the board have already been presented in another context[59] in more detail and are only summarised here in brief statements:

As the ad hoc disclosure is a duty of the issuer he has to be the primary addressee of a liability. If the liability according to ss 37b, c WpHG is seen as a legal liability based on principles of reliance and not as a special form of a liability for tort,[60] it also lacks a suitable element of trust for a liability of the executives ('Managerhaftung').

The corporate law is characterised by the concept of internal recourse ('Binnenregress').[61] An external liability is limited to exceptional cases (ss 93 subs. 5, 117 AktG). There is no doubt that the legislator has the ability to break with this concept by providing a cumulative external liability of the board as the legal rule in capital market law. However, from the point of view of legal policy, such a legal provision would only be convincing if there were good reasons for it. In particular, this could be the case if only a cumulative external liability of the acting board members is able to prevent the board members to stray off the path of the integrity stipulated in capital market law. A judgement on this would be the task of the economic analysis of the law. As there is no empirical data existing with regard to this, the burden of proof for legal necessity is on the advocates of cumulative external liability. In the meantime, one is only able to argue on the basis of plausibility. The discussion under the aspect of prevention above has insofar been sufficient in order to cast doubt on this plausibility.

And lastly, in the event of insolvency, a cumulative external liability of the board sabotages a suitable distribution method. The recourse to the board members has to be reserved for the liquidator ('Insolvenzverwalter'). The assets which have to be recovered from executives not abiding the law must flow into the assets involved in the insolvency proceedings and must not be reserved for individual, especially quick acting, investors. Above all, a privilege of the investors in the form of an external liability of the board only for failures to provide information at the secondary market vis-à-vis

---

[59] See in particular *Casper*, BKR 2005, 83, 85 ff. and further *Spindler*, WM 2004, 2089, 2093 ff.; *Daniel Zimmer*, Verschärfung der Haftung für fehlerhafte Kapitalmarktinformation, WM 2004, 9, 10 ff.

[60] See the reference below in n. 65.

[61] This has gained assertiveness through the Gesetz zur Unternehmensintegrität und Modernisierung des Anfechtungsrechts (UMAG).

other creditor groups is hardly justifiable. Again, it has to be warned that this discussion cannot be geared towards the case of an insolvency without any assets as this is extremely rare.

V. Is the liability according to ss 37b, c WpHG a special kind of tort law ('Sonderdeliktsrecht')?

With regard to the legal nature of the liability according to ss 37b, c WpHG basically three opinions are being considered and discussed. Subsequent to the parallel discussion on the prospectus liability, ss 37b, c WpHG could be seen as a form of an assumed liability by virtue of a legal transaction.[62] As a consequence, this approach is not suitable for the liability for erroneous information of the secondary market as there is regularly no contractual relationship existing with the issuer. Based on this, a wide-spread opinion within the academia rejects the classification as a special case of liability based on principles of reliance[63] and argues in favour of a qualification as a 'special kind of tort law' ['Sonderdeliktsrecht'].[64] In particular, as a consequence, board members could be liable in addition to the issuer as accomplices according to s. 830 subs. 1 cl. 1 BGB which, as explained above, would serve little purpose. Originally, this controversy had in particular consequences for the dogmatic classification of the ss 37b, c WpHG and, besides this, prior to the introduction of s. 32b ZPO [Zivilprozessordnung, German Civil Procedure Code] with regard to the place of jurisdiction. Due to the lack of practical relevance this question can be disregarded nowadays. Today, from the legal nature, primarily evaluations for disputed questions can be deduced. Therefore, from the viewpoint of the classification under

---

[62] With regard to prospectus law see *Johannes Köndgen*, Zur Theorie der Prospekthaftung, AG 1983, 85, 90 ff.

[63] Though this classification is assumed for example by *Peter Mülbert/Steffen Steup*, Emittentenhaftung für fehlerhafte Kapitalmarktinformation am Beispiel der fehlerhaften Regelpublizität, WM 2005, 1633, 1638 ff.; *Veil*, BKR 2005, 91, 92; *Daniel Zimmer/Marc Grotheer*, in: Schwark/Zimmer (n. 3) §§ 37 b, 37 c WpHG Rn. 8 f.

[64] See for example *Rolf Sethe*, in: Assmann/Schneider (n. 5) §§ 37b, 37c Rn. 23; *Möllers/Leisch*, in: Möllers/Rotter (n. 10) § 13 Rn. 12; in principle also *Hellgardt* (n. 1) 20 ff.

the law of tort e.g. a priority of the ss 37b, c WpHG over the regulations for the maintenance of capital can be maintained.[65]

In the end, none of the hypotheses are completely convincing. As it came to light in the cases of ComROAD or EM.TV, there is an argument for a special form of a liability based on principles of reliance stipulated in the capital market law as the issuer is certainly able to create a situation of trust with an erroneous ad hoc disclosure.[66] On the other hand, in general, a special legal relationship ('Sonderrechtsbeziehung') is missing so that a comparison to s. 311 subs. 3 BGB has to be drawn for justification. By contrast, in the event of omitted or belated ad hoc disclosure an element of trust is hardly recognisable. On the other hand, a classification under the law of tort is more of a stopgap. It might be argued that ss 37b, c WpHG contains a preventive sanction for the infringement of a code of conduct stipulated in the capital market law. Yet, this obligation is just not a protective law within the meaning of the law of tort; the infringement of an object of absolute legal protection cannot be considered a priori. Therefore, there is only the reference to the systematic position of s. 32b ZPO and the rather evasive description as a special form of the liability under the law of tort stipulated in the capital market law. In the end, the better reasons unveil that the legislator created a hybrid with the avoidance of a liability for intentional damage contrary to public policy [contra bonos mores] and the creation of a special element of liability, legitimated only partially by trust, which could be best described as a basis for liability stipulated in capital market law sui generis. In any case, it has to be emphasised that the classification as a rule under the law of tort does not automatically require the application of s. 830 BGB or the assumption of a restitution in kind in the shape of the rescission of the contract which was completed as a result of the erroneous information. As a result, this opinion coincides with *Hellgardt's* point of view which promotes on the one hand an interpretation under the law of tort, however, on the other hand, regards the property of the investor as the only subject of protection of the liability under the law of tort within capital market law in connection with the duty to disclose information:[67] For *Hellgardt* – other than on the primary market – the freedom of decision of the investor is not protected, meaning that he is basically coming to the same conclusions for

---

[65] This question shall not be discussed in depth here, for more details see *Casper,* Der Konzern 2006, 32, 36 ff. with further references.
[66] See references above in n. 6 and 39.
[67] *Hellgardt* (n. 1) 33 ff.

the extent of damage[68] and the causation as those drawn herein. Moreover, despite the qualification under the law of tort, for him, the liability of the participant according to s. 830 subs. 2 BGB is not applicable.[69] Insofar as this cornerstone under the law of tort is abandoned, the hypothesis of the law of tort within capital market law is acceptable. However, the question remains what the benefit of a law of tort with a reduced density might then be. In its essence, it seems to be more consistent to call a spade a spade and acknowledge that ss 37b, c WpHG contain a specific liability within the capital market law which has to be suited to fit its particular necessities.

VI. Conclusion: Is the law of tort a suitable fundamental element for the enforcement of duties of disclosure?

As mentioned above, the European law does not enforce a civil liability in order to implement the duty of disclosure. In the sphere of capital market law, the European law does not recommend specific requirements for the so-called 'Enforcement'. Nonetheless, the civil liability could be an important element for the achievement of an adequate preventive effect. However, for the reasons pointed out above, the liability for intentional damage contrary to public policy [contra bonos mores] is hardly able to serve this purpose. Rather, it should be relied upon special elements of liability stipulated in capital market law which can be tailor-made for and adjusted to the requirements of the capital markets. Of course, from the legal point of view it would be desirable that a standard method for the determination of the damages caused by the difference of the prices is found and that it is clarified that causation between the breach of duty and the investment decision by the investor is not required.

Besides this, attention must be paid to an efficient enforcement of the liability in the form of a collective legal protection. Not only does the German Capital Investors Model Proceedings Act (Kapitalanleger-Musterverfahrensgesetz, KapMuG) have to be finally freed from its time limit,[70] it has, in particular, to be extended to a proper class action with

---

[68] Hellgardt (n. 1) 492 ff., though with the constraint that restitution in kind and therefore a rescission of the contract shall be applicable in case of market disturbances (so-called 'hot markets').

[69] Hellgardt (n. 1) 442 ff.

[70] After a test term of five years, which has expired in 2010, the regulation has been extended for another two years, see Art. 5 of the Gesetz zur Einführung einer Mus-

an Opt-In-Model, which cannot be substantiated here as this would be beyond the scope of this volume. Only as a footnote, it should be noted that one of the most spectacular cases of a belated ad hoc information had been a lawsuit according to the KapMuG. The supposedly belated announcement of the resignation of the former chairman of the executive board of Daimler, Jürgen Schrempp, had been contested by means of the KapMuG up to the BGH.[71]

VII. Twelve theses as a summary

1. The European capital market law is geared to increase the confidence in the capital markets. An important tool to reach this goal is information requirements. Beyond the ss 37b, c WpHG, however, the legislator has not provided any liability regulations in civil law.

2. In this respect, the European capital markets law specifies no further requirements. It only requires that the member states have to provide effective regulations for the so-called enforcement. It is not prescribed if this has to be done by civil law liability, penal provisions or administrative regulations. (cf. e.g. Art. 14 I Market Abuse Directive 2003/6/EC).

3. Considering these open European initial findings, the question is if a tort law liability of the issuer or of his acting board members ('Organe') for the breach of capital market law provisions is an adequate mechanism.

4. The existent liability of the issuer in ss 37b, c WpHG is no special implementation of tort law. The regulations about perpetration and participation in s. 830 BGB are not applicable.

5. S. 823 subs. 2 BGB in conjunction with a protective law as well as s. 826 BGB (liability for intentional damage contrary to public policy [contra bonos mores]) come into consideration as liability norms within the general

---

terwiderrufsinformation für Verbraucherdarlehensverträge v. 24. Juli 2010 (BGBl I, 977), Art. 9 II des Gesetzes zur Einführung von Kapitalanleger-Musterverfahren v. 16. August 2005 (BGBl I, 2437 [3095]).

[71] *Bundesgerichtshof* (BGH) 25.02.2008, WM 2008, 641 = ZIP 2008, 639; *Oberlandesgericht Stuttgart* 15.02.2007, WM 2007, 595 = ZIP 2007, 481; *Oberlandesgericht Stuttgart* 22.04.2009, WM 2009, 1233 = ZIP 2009, 962.

law of tort. For liability because of erroneous capital market information, s. 823 subs. 2 BGB requires the violation of a capital market law regulation that also aimed at protecting third parties. This has to be negated for transparency requirements. Only s. 826 BGB has become important, yet. The immoral behaviour that provokes the liability within the scope of s. 826 BGB is the denial of information as well as the publication of erroneous information for the capital market. According to the correct understanding, another element that constitutes the moral blemish is necessary. A conditional intent concerning the violation of the law – the disregard of the duty of information concerning the capital market – cannot itself be considered immoral. Other indications, e.g. an action because of self-serving motifs, are necessary.

6. There are also difficulties concerning the legal consequences. Due to the principle of restitution in kind, liability titles in tort law are barely suitable for an adequate liability regime. The receipt of the securities that have been purchased because of the erroneous information by the issuer is not only problematic under the aspect of capital maintenance and of the prohibited purchase of own stocks. The return of the securities to the issuer would cause the economic risks to be shifted to the issuer. This breach of duty, however, usually justifies only the compensation of the price spread damage ('Kursdifferenzschaden') and not of the damage for breach of contract ('Vertragsschaden').

7. Contrary to the judicature of the Federal Court of Justice (Bundesgerichtshof), compensation should be limited to price spread damage, not only in the context of ss 37b, c WpHG but also in case of liability for intentional damage contrary to public policy (contra bonos mores – s. 826 BGB).

8. The fact that the existent tort liability regime stipulated in capital market laws either lacks in effectiveness or is even void of it also becomes apparent with regard to causation and the rules of evidence. The jurisprudence in Germany requires that the investor substantiates concrete causation between false capital market information and the investment decision. Usually, the investor will not succeed in proving that causal link. If, however, the damage to be compensated is limited to the price spread damage, causation could be refutably presumed without any difficulty referring to the institution of 'investment climate' (fraud-on-the-market-theory).

9. Neither European nor German law currently stipulates personal liability of organ members in addition to the issuer. The only exception is – as

mentioned above – the mostly inefficient liability for damage contrary to public policy.

10. Moreover, cumulative external liability of acting board members is not necessary. The primary addressee of the duty of ad hoc disclosure is the issuer, not the board. The liability estate or assets of the board members generally do not suffice to cover liability claims of the investors. The deterrent potential of a threatening internal liability towards the issuer is sufficient. The so-called *Last-Period*-phenomenon is not suitable to legitimise general external liability of the board members.

11. Furthermore, it is, neither from a legal-dogmatic nor from a legal-economic perspective, reasonable to shape cumulative external liability in the form of accountability for omitting to file for insolvency ('Insolvenzausfallhaftung'). The risk of insolvency faced by investors can be mitigated by obliging the issuer to procure insurance similar to an insurance scheme as provided in s. 651k BGB.

12. Civil liability in the field of capital markets law is an expedient way to comply with the European imperative for an efficient sanction mechanism. However, the capability of general tort law in reaching this goal is restricted. Consequently, special liability norms modelled after ss 37b, c WpHG need to be put in place. They should only be directed at issuers. Besides this, attention should be focused on enforcement of liability in the form of collective legal protection. The KapMuG has not only to be freed from the time limit, i.e. extended for an indefinite period of time, but also has to be expanded to a class action (with an Opt-in-System).

Infringement of the Prohibition of Unfair Commercial Practices and Tort Law

Giovanni De Cristofaro

I. The private-law consequences of the infringement of the prohibition of unfair commercial practices under the Directive 2005/29/EC

The prohibition of unfair commercial practices, established by Art. 5, par. 1 of the Directive 2005/29/EC[1], is a general rule that shall apply to any action or conduct on the part of a business directly connected with the promotion, sale or supply of a product to consumers, before, during and after a commercial transaction[2].

The legal effects of the violation of such prohibition are not precisely fixed by the Directive: Art. 11 generically requires Member States to ensure the existence of "adequate and effective means" to combat unfair commercial practices in order to enforce compliance; Art. 13 merely orders Member States to lay down effective, proportionate and dissuasive penalties for the

---

[1] Directive 2005/29/EC of the European Parliament and of the Council of 11 May 2005 concerning unfair business-to-consumer commercial practices in the internal market (OJ 2005 L 149/22). For a general overview of the Directive, see: *G. De Cristofaro* (ed.), Le «pratiche commerciali sleali» tra imprese e consumatori. La direttiva 2005/29/CE e il diritto italiano, Turin, 2007; *E. Minervini/L. Rossi Carleo* (eds.), Le pratiche commerciali sleali. Direttiva comunitaria e ordinamento italiano, Milan, 2007; *M. Radeideh*, Fair Trading in EC law, Information and Consumer Choice in the Internal Market, Groningen, 2005; *C. Handig*, Harmonisierung des Lauterkeitsrechts in der EU, Wien, 2005; *G. Howells/H-W. Micklitz/T. Wilhelmsson*, European Fair Trading Law. The Unfair Commercial Practices Directive, Aldershot, 2006; *J. Massaguer*, Nuevo derecho contra la competencia desleal. La directiva 2005/29/CE sobre las praticas comerciales desleales, Madrid, 2006; *S. Weatherill/U. Bernitz* (eds.), The Regulation of Unfair Commercial Practices under EC Directive 2005/29. New Rules and New Techniques, Oxford, 2007; *H-W. Micklitz,* in: H.-W. Micklitz/N. Reich/P. Rott, Understanding EU Consumer Law, Antwerp – Oxford – Portland, 2009, p. 61 ff.

[2] See Art. 1, Art. 2 (d) and Art. 3 (1) of the Directive.

infringements of national provisions adopted in the application of the Directive, and to take all necessary measures to ensure that these are enforced. The Member States are also free to decide if the infringement of the prohibition of unfair commercial practices shall be sanctioned only with fines or penalties, or should also have special consequences for national private law, especially in the field of contract and tort law[3].

Indeed, EU institutions have ruled out that the introduction of the prohibition of unfair commercial practices towards consumers in national legal systems and the transposition of the EC-directive shall necessarily influence the general principles of the national contract law. The Directive should be without prejudice to contract law and, in particular, to the rules concerning the validity, formation or effects of a contract, as stated in Art. 3, par. 2, of the Directive[4].

Therefore it is unnecessary, for the correct implementation of the Directive, either to modify the general national rules concerning contracts (especially the rules concerning contract formation and grounds of invalidity), or to derogate such rules by introducing new, special rules applicable only to consumer contracts[5]. Particularly, the Directive does not oblige Member States to qualify a contract as void or voidable just because it has been concluded after and/or by virtue of an unfair commercial practice[6].

---

[3] *H.-W. Micklitz*, Legal Redress, in: G. Howells/H.-W. Micklitz/T. Wilhelmsson (cit. n. 1), p. 230.

[4] This provision has been criticised by *T. Wilhelmsson*, Scope of the Directive, in: G. Howells/H.-W. Micklitz/T. Wilhelmsson (cit. n. 1), p. 72, who has correctly stressed that despite art. 3 (2) there may be crossover effects from the content of the Directive to contract law. See also the critical remarks of *Augenhofer*, Ein "Flickenteppich" oder doch der "große Wurf"?, Zeitschrift für Rechtsvergleichung 2005, 206 and *Whittaker*, The Relationship of the Unfair Commercial Practices Directive to European and National Contract Laws, in: S. Weatherill/U. Bernitz (cit. n. 1), p. 144.

[5] *M. R. Maugeri*, Pratiche commerciali scorrette e disciplina generale dei contratti, in: A. Genovese (ed.), I decreti legislativi sulle pratiche commerciali scorrette, Padua, 2008, p. 268.

[6] *H. Köhler/T. Lettl*, Das geltende europäische Lauterkeitsrecht, der Vorschlag für eine Richtlinie über unlautere Geschäftspraktiken und die UWG-Reform, Wettbewerb in Recht und Praxis, 2003, p. 1049; *H. Collins*, The Unfair Commercial Practices Directive, (2005) European Review of Contract Law 425; *M. Schmidt*, Zur Annäherung von Lauterkeitsrecht und Verbraucherprivatrecht, Juristen Zeitung 2007, 83; *G. Abbamonte*, The Unfair Commercial Practices Directive and its General Prohibition, in: S. Weatherill/U. Bernitz (cit. n. 1), p. 16; *A. Mirone*, Pub-

Furthermore, recital 9 clarifies that the Directive 2005/29/EC is "without prejudice to individual actions brought by those who have been harmed by an unfair commercial practice". The aforementioned "individual actions" are, in my opinion, actions based on national rules, different from the general rules concerning the formation and the (in)validity of contracts (to which Art. 3, par. 2, already refers). This means, first and foremost, the actions to which consumers are entitled by virtue of national rules concerning precontractual liability, tort liability and liability for breach of contract duties and obligations.

This recital means to me that whenever the conduct of a trader towards a consumer is to be qualified as an unfair commercial practice under the Directive, yet at the same time gives the consumer concerned the right to a remedy against the trader based on a national rule, this "individual action" – for example an action in tort – is safeguarded. In this way, the consumer is and remains entitled to such a remedy even if the sanctions and penalties specifically forseen for the infringement of the prohibition of unfair commercial practices are applied.

Just because of its negative formulation ("the Directive is without prejudice ...") this recital cannot mean that the Directive obliges the Member States to introduce new and special rules to their legal systems which give consumers an individual right of action against the trader only because the latter has behaved in a way which can be qualified as an unfair commercial practice[7]. Most of the European authors therefore correctly rule out that, for the transposition of the Directive, it is necessary for the Member States to expressly qualify every commercial practice as a (civil) tort and consequently as a source of an obligation to damages for the liable trader and of a corresponding right to damages for every single consumer affected by the practice[8].

---

blicità e invalidità del contratto: la tutela individuale contro le pratiche commerciali sleali, in Annali italiani del diritto d'autore, della cultura e dello spettacolo, 2008, p. 309 f.; U. Salanitro, Gli obblighi precontrattuali di informazione: le regole e i rimedi nei principi acquis, in: G. De Cristofaro (ed.), I "Princìpi" del diritto comunitario dei contratti. Acquis communautaire e diritto privato europeo, Turin, 2009, p. 253.

[7] C. Alexander, Schadensersatz und Abschöpfung im Lauterkeits- und Kartellrecht, Tübingen, 2010, p. 185.

[8] H. Gamerith, Der Richtlinienvorschlag über unlautere Geschäftspraktiken – Möglichkeiten einer harmonischen Umsetzung, Wettbewerb in Recht und Praxis 2005, at 403; H. Collins (cit. n. 6), p. 425; H. Köhler/J. Bornkamm, Gesetz gegen den unlauteren Wettbewerb: UWG, Munich, 2010, sub § 9 UWG, p.1146; S. Augen-

I do not agree with the few authors who assert that consumers should in every case be considered entitled to an individual action for damages against the trader directly based on Art. 5-9 of the Directive[9]. At the same time I do not agree with the authors[10] who believe that the same arguments used by the European Court of Justice with regard to antitrust law in the "Courage"[11] and "Manfredi"[12] Judgments[13] could be used for the Directive on unfair commercial practices: that is, the attribution of an individual right of action (in damages) upon consumers should be considered as a measure necessarily requested by the need to ensure and maintain the effectiveness of the prohibition of unfair commercial practices in the national legal systems.

---

hofer, Individualrechtliche Ansprüche des Verbrauchers bei unlauterem Wettbewerbsverhalten des Unternehmers, Wettbewerb in Recht und Praxis 2006, 171; T. *Wunderle*, Verbraucherschutz im Europäischen Lauterkeitsrecht, Tübingen, 2010, p. 258.

[9] U. *Berlit*, Unlautere Geschäftspraktiken in der EG und das Gesetz gegen den unlauteren Wettbewerb, Recht der Internationalen Wirtschaft, 2005, Heft 5, Die erste Seite; K.-H. *Fezer*, Plädoyer für eine offensive Umsetzung der Richtlinie über unlautere Geschäftspraktiken in das deutsche UWG, Wettbewerb in Recht und Praxis 2006, 788.

[10] J. *Keßler/H.-W. Micklitz*, Das neue UWG – auf halbem Wege nach Europa?, Verbraucher und Recht 2009, 95; C. *Twigg-Flessner/D. Parry*, The Challenges Posed by the Implementation of the Directive into Domestic Law, in: S. Weatherill/ U. Bernitz (cit. n. 1), p. 231.

[11] Judgment of 20 September 2001, in the Case C-453/99 *(Courage Ltd and Bernard Crehan* [2001] ECR I-6297).

[12] Judgment of 13 July 2006, in joined Cases C-295/04 *(Manfredi v. Lloyd Adriatico Assicurazioni)*, C-296/04 *(Cannito v. Fondiaria Sai Spa)*, C-297/04 *(Tricarico v. Assitalia Spa)* and C-298/04 *(Mugolo v. Assitalia Spa)* [2006] ECR I-6619.

[13] See what the European Court of Justice has stated in the Judgement *"Courage"* (points 26 and 27): "The full effectiveness of Article 85 of the Treaty and, in particular, the practical effect of the prohibition laid down in Article 85(1) would be put at risk if it were not open to any individual to claim damages for loss caused to him by a contract or by conduct liable to restrict or distort competition. Indeed, the existence of such a right strengthens the working of the Community competition rules and discourages agreements or practices, which are frequently covert, which are liable to restrict or distort competition. From that point of view, actions for damages before the national courts can make a significant contribution to the maintenance of effective competition in the Community".

Unfair Commercial Practices and Tort Law

Indeed, as long as the means of "combatting unfair commercial practices" introduced in their legal systems are "adequate and effective", and as long as the penalties for the infringements of the prohibition of unfair commercial practices laid down by their national legislation are "effective" and "dissuasive" enough, it can be said with certainty that the Member States have correctly transposed the Directive, even if no individual right of action to damages is given to consumers. The introduction of a rule through which consumers harmed by an unfair commercial practice have an individual right of action to damages towards the trader is without any doubt a measure which *can* be taken to ensure that the national provisions adopted in application of the Directive are enforced, but it is not a measure that absolutely *must* be taken by the Member States in order to reach this goal[14].

Since the Directive is "without prejudice" to national contract and tort law, its transposition does not require their reform but, at the same time, does not prohibit their reform. National contract and tort law do not fall into the field covered by the full-harmonization pursued by the Directive, so Member States are and remain free to decide their content[15].

Member States are also allowed to introduce – by the implementation of the Directive – new provisions by virtue of which the infringement of the prohibition of unfair commercial practices shall have private-law effects which are exceptional in comparison with the general principles of contract and tort law.

It could, for example, be established that a contract whose conclusion has been preceded and influenced by an unfair commercial practice is void[16]

---

[14] G. *Howells*, Introduction, in: G. Howells/H.-W. Micklitz/T. Wilhelmsson (cit. n. 1), p. 23; H. *Köhler/J. Bornkamm* (cit. n. 8), sub § 9 UWG, p. 1146.

[15] T. *Wilhelmsson*, Scope of the Directive, in: G. Howells/H.-W. Micklitz/T. Wilhelmsson (cit. n. 1), p. 52; H. *Collins (cit. n. 6)*, at 431; S. *Whittaker*, The Relationship of the Unfair Commercial Practices Directive to European and National Contract Laws, in: S. Weatherill/U. Bernitz (cit. n. 1), p. 145 ff.; M. *Schmidt* (cit. n. 6), p. 83.

[16] That's what happened in France and in Luxembourg. Art. L. 122-15 of the French *code de la consommation* (as modified by Art. 39 of the Act n° 2008-3 of 3 January 2008 *"pour le développement de la concurrence au service des consommateurs"*, that has implemented the Directive in France) states in fact that when an aggressive commercial practice has led to the conclusion of a contract between a consumer and a trader, the contract is void and has no effect *("Lorsqu'une pratique commerciale agressive aboutit à la conclusion d'un contrat, celui-ci est nul et de nul effet")*. Furthermore, Art. L 122-8(2) of the *Code de la consommation* of Luxembourg (introduced by a law of 8 April 2001) states that every clause or combination of

or voidable[17] or at any time cancellable by the consumer[18]. Otherwise, it could be stated that if the conclusion of a contract has been preceded and influenced by an unfair commercial practice, the consumer is entitled to claim, receive and retain the goods or service but has no obligation to pay the agreed consideration and is entitled to claim the restitution of any price he may have paid[19].

Finally, a provision could be introduced which expressly states that any unfair commercial practice always creates an obligation for the liable trader to pay compensation for the damages suffered by every single consumer whose ecomonic interests have been harmed by the practice[20].

Such provisions could easily be considered as measures taken in order to ensure the enforcement of the Directive in the Member States: private-law

---

clauses of a contract concluded in violation of the prohibition of unfair commercial practices is void *(est réputée nulle et non écrite)*.

[17] That's what happened in Portugal. Art. 14 of the Act that has transposed the Directive in Portugal *(decreto-lei n.º 57/2008 of 26 March 2008)* states that if the conclusion of a contract has been influenced by an unfair commercial practice, the consumer may sue the trader in order to obtain either the annulment of such a contract according to Art. 287 of the civil code or an equitable modification of the contents of the contract.

[18] That's what happened in Poland. Art. 12 (4) of the Polish Act on combating unfair commercial practices of 23 August 2007 states that "In the case of unfair commercial practices, the consumer whose interest has been jeopardized or violated may request that the contract be cancelled and the benefits mutually returned and the costs associated with the purchase of the product be reimbursed by the trader".

[19] That's what happened in Belgium. Art. 41 of the *"Loi relative aux pratiques du marché et à la protection du consommateur"* of 6 April 2010 (an Act that contains, among others, the provisions concerning unfair commercial practices towards consumers that transpose in Belgium the Directive) states that: *"Lorsqu'un contrat avec un consommateur a été conclu à la suite d'une pratique commerciale déloyale visée à l'article 91, 12°, 16° et 17°, et à l'article 94, 1°, 2° et 8°, le consommateur peut, dans un délai raisonnable à partir du moment où il a eu connaissance ou aurait dû avoir connaissance de son existence, exiger le remboursement des sommes payées, sans restitution du produit livré»*. However, *"Lorsqu'un contrat avec un consommateur a été conclu à la suite d'une pratique commerciale déloyale visée aux articles 84 à 86, 91, 1° à 11°, 13° à 15, 18° à 23°, et à l'article 94, 3° à 7°, le juge peut, sans préjudice des sanctions de droit commun, ordonner le remboursement au consommateur des sommes qu'il a payées, sans restitution par celui-ci du produit livré"*.

[20] See below, *sub* II.

instruments to prevent and sanction the infringement of the prohibition of unfair commercial practices.

However, even in the Member States who do not introduce new provisions through which the infringement of the prohibition of unfair commercial practices shall have special consequences of contract or tort law, the implementation of the Directive 2005/29/EC will certainly not remain without any influence on the interpretation and application of the general rules concerning contract and tort law[21].

In the Member States where the rules adopted to transpose the Directive have been integrated with the Acts regulating unfair competition in general, and where the acts of unfair competition are intended as a particular kind of civil tort, unfair commercial practices towards consumers should be seen as an act of unfair competition and consequently as a source of an obligation to repair the damages suffered by the competitors and possibly also by the consumers.

Furthermore, it seems likely that in applying the general principles of national contract or tort law, the national courts will qualify at least some of the commercial practices that prove to be "unfair" according to the Directive, such as cases of pre contractual liability, contractual liability or tort liability and, on the basis of such general principles, will consequently condemn the liable trader against whom the consumer has brought a civil action for damages[22].

---

[21] *T. Wilhelmsson,* Scope of the Directive, in: G. Howells/H.-W. Micklitz/T. Wilhelmsson (cit. n. 1), p. 53. With specific regard to contract law, see *E. Minervini,* Codice del consumo e direttiva sulle pratiche commerciali sleali, in: E. Minervini/ L. Rossi Carleo (cit. n. 1), p. 82; *V. G. Raymond,* Incidences possibles de la transposition de la directive n° 2005/29/Ce du 11 May 2005 sur le droit français de la consommation, in: Contrats, concurrence, consommation 2006, 6; *J. Stuyck/E. Terryn/T. Van Dyck,* Confidence through fairness? The new Directive on unfair business-to-consumer commercial practices in the internal market, (2006) Common Market Law Review 142.

[22] *S. Whittaker,* The Relationship of the Unfair Commercial Practices Directive to European and National Contract Laws, in: S. Weatherill/U. Bernitz (cit. n. 1), p. 152; *H. Collins (cit. n. 6),* p. 426.

II. Tort law and prohibition of unfair commercial practices after the implementation of the Directive: the different solutions adopted by the Member States

With specific regard to the relationships between tort law and prohibition of unfair commercial practices, and the possibility for the consumers harmed by an unfair commercial practice to bring a civil action for damages against the liable trader, the solutions adopted by the Member States are very different

In some Member States the Directive has been transposed by Acts that contain a provision that expressly states that consumers harmed by unfair commercial practices are, in every case, entitled to such action.

In Ireland, for example, *subsection (2) of Section 74 (Consumer's right of action for damages)* of the *Consumer Protection Act 2007*, states that: "A consumer who is aggrieved by a prohibited act or practice shall have a right of action for relief by way of damages, including exemplary damages, against the trader who commits or engages in the prohibited act or practice".

In Greece, the new Art. 9θ of the Consumer Protection Act establishes that if a trader violates the provisions of Artt. 9γ a 9η of such Act[23] both consumers associations and single consumers are entitled to bring a civil action in order to obtain the injunction of the practice and compensation of the damages caused by an unfair commercial practice[24].

Similar provisions are also to be found in Portugal[25] and in Poland[26], while in Lithuania Art. 26 of the Law on Advertising states that every per-

---

[23] These provisions implement Artt. 5-9 of the Directive and contain the "black list" of practices that shall in all circumstances be regarded as unfair.

[24] According to L. Alexandridou, The Harmonization of the Greek law with the Directive on Unfair Commercial Practices, (2008) European Review of Contract Law 189, this provision gives single consumers harmed by an unfair commercial practices the right to claim the compensation of the damages suffered.

[25] Art. 15 *(Responsabilidade civil –* civil liability) of the Portuguese legislative Decree of 26 March 2008 concerning unfair commercial practices states that the *consumer* harmed by an unfair commercial practices prohibited by virtue of this decree shall be indemnified according to the general principles *("O consumidor lesado por efeito de alguma prática comercial desleal proibida nos termos do presente decreto –lei é ressarcido nos termos gerais").*

[26] According to Art. 12, section 1, of the Polish Act on combating unfair commercial practices of 2007, in the case of unfair commercial practices the consumer whose interest has been jeopardized or violated may request the damage suffered to be restored as per general terms and conditions.

son whose rights and law-protected interests are violated while using the advertising prohibited by such Law[27] shall have the right to appeal in court with a claim on cessation of use of the advertising and compensation of the damage inflicted.

In other Member States, the right of consumers harmed by unfair commercial practices to claim damages is not expressly foreseen by an appropriate provision, but can easily be inferred from general provisions of the laws in which the regulation of unfair commercial practices has been integrated.

So, for example, Art. 3 of the general Consumer Protection Act of the Slovak Republic[28] (whose § 7 contains the prohibition of unfair commercial practices) states that "the person successfully asserting a breach of right or obligation stipulated in this Act has the right to adequate financial compensation from the party, whose breach of a right or obligation stipulated in this Act is capable of inflicting damage to the consumer".

In Denmark and in Sweden the provisions which transpose the Directives 2005/29/EC and 2006/114/EC have been integrated into the respective "Marketing Practices Acts": the Danish Marketing Practices Act *(lov om markedsføring)* of 21th December 2005 has been modified by the law that in 2006 implemented the Directive 2005/29/EC in Denmark; the new Swedish Marketing Practices Act *(Marknadsföringslag)* was adopted in June of 2008 (SFS 2008:486)[29] and has repealed and replaced the previous Marketing Practices Act of 1995. Both of these Acts apply to any practice carried out by a trader in connection with his own business in order to offer, sell or supply goods or services to consumers and/or to other traders: for such practices the Danish and the Swedish Marketing Practices Act establish a set of rules which have the purpose of promoting and protecting the interests of consumers and traders in connection with the marketing of products, and preventing unfair marketing practices. According to section 20 of the Danish Marketing Practices Act, any trader who infringes this Act shall pay "reasonable damages"; according to section 37 of the Swedish Marketing Practices Act, any person who intentionally or negligently violates the pro-

---

[27] According to Art. 5 of the Law on Advertising, "The use of misleading advertising shall be banned" (section 1) and "Advertising shall in all circumstances be regarded as misleading if it contains the attributes of a misleading commercial practice established in subparagraph 1-21 of article 7 of the Lithuanian Law on Prohibition of Unfair Business-to-Consumer Commercial Practices" (section 6).

[28] See the introduction to such Act by P. *Bohata*, Slowakische Republik: Gesetz zum Schutz des Verbrauchers, Wirtshafts- und Recht der Osteuropa 2008, 142.

[29] See J. *Ebersohl*, Das neue schwedische Wettbewerbsrecht, Recht der Internationalen Wirtschaft 2009, 215.

Giovanni De Cristofaro

hibition of misleading or aggressive marketing practices shall compensate any consumer or trader for any damage arising from such a violation.

Thirdly, in some other Member States, the right of consumers harmed by unfair commercial practices to compensation for the damages suffered is not expressly foreseen by an appropriate provision, but can be inferred from the fact that the provisions concerning unfair commercial practices towards consumers have been integrated into the national, general law regarding unfair competition. This is the case in the Netherlands, in Austria and in Spain.

In the Netherlands, unfair competition is regulated in the sixth book of the civil code of 1992, inside the section dedicated to the extra contractual liability: unfair competition is therefore considered as a particular kind of tort, and consequently as a source of an obligation to damages for the liable trader. In the same section, both the regulation of misleading advertising (towards professional traders) and illegal comparative advertising and the regulation of unfair commercial practices towards consumers have been subsequently inserted. Illegal advertising and unfair commercial practices constitute therefore, just like unfair competition, special forms of a civil tort: according to Art. 193b and 193j of book 6 of the civil code, the trader who commits an unfair commercial practice is liable for a tort towards the consumers who have been recipients of his conduct and is therefore obliged to pay compensation for the damages caused, unless he demonstrates that such damages are not a consequence of his fault.

In Austria, even before the transposition of the Directive 2005/29/EC it was recognized by legal literature and by the Supreme Court[30] that not only competitors, but also consumers to whom acts of competition contrasting with the *bonos mores (guten Sitten)* are directed to claim damages from the liable trader, according to Art. 1 of the national Act on unfair competition of 1984. The provisions which transpose the Directive 2005/29/EC in Austria have been integrated into this Act, whose § 1 (as modified by the *UWG-Novelle 2007*[31]) today states that if a trader commits an unfair practice that is contrary to the requirements of professional diligence and is likely to materially distort the economic behaviour of the average consumer who receives it or to whom it is directed, this trader can be sued for damages, unless he has no fault: and the Austrian Literature and courts agree that

---

[30] See the judgement of *OGH* of 24 February 1998, in: *ÖBl* 1998, p. 193 and in: *ecolex*, 1998, p. 497.

[31] *Bundesgesetz, mit dem das Bundesgesetz gegen den unlauteren Wettbewerb 1984 UWG geändert wird.*

action for damages can be brought by any consumer affected by such an unfair practice[32].

The same can be said about Spain, whose general Act on unfair competition of 1992 *(Ley 3/1991* of 1992, *de Competencia Desleal),* modified in 2009 by the Act[33] that has transposed the Directive 2005/29/EC[34], prohibits acts of unfair competition in order to protect the interests of all the subjects who are involved in the market, and not only the interests of competitors (Art. 1). According to the general clause laid down in Art. 4 of the Act on unfair competition, any conduct objectively contrary to the requirements of good faith is considered unfair. Within business-to-consumer relations, any conduct that is contrary to the requirements of professional diligence and is likely to materially distort the economic behaviour of the average consumer who receives it or to whom it is directed must be considered particularly in contrast with the requirements of good faith. Unfair commercial practices towards consumers are also qualified as a typical act of unfair competition. The different remedies suitable against the trader who has committed an act of unfair competition are listed in Art. 32 of the Act on unfair competition: under such remedies we find the action on damages, to which "every natural or legal person involved in the market whose economic interests have been directly harmed by the act of unfair competition" (and therefore also individual consumers) is entitled (Art. 33), provided that the trader has acted intentionally or with negligence.

Finally, there are Member States where the question has been neither expressly nor implicitly solved by the legislation in force.

In some of these States the absence of a clear legislative solution should not create problems for consumers, because the Directive has been transposed by national provisions that qualify as void or voidable any contract whose conclusion has been influenced by an unfair commercial practice (France, Luxembourg) or which gives consumers in such cases the right

---

[32] B. *Lurger/S. Augenhofer,* Österreichisches und Europäisches Konsumentenschutzrecht², Vienna – New York, 2008, p. 298; *H. Gamerith,* Handelsrecht – Wettbewerbsrecht I – UWG, Unlauterer Wettbewerb⁶, Vienna, 2008, p. 111; *L. Wiltschek/ K. Majchrzak,* Die UWG-Novelle 2007, Österreichische Blätter für gewerblichen Rechtsschutz und Urheberrecht 2008, 12.

[33] Act n. 29 of 30 December 2009 *"por la que se modifica el régimen legal de la competencia desleal y de la publicidad para la mejora de la protección de los consumidores y usuarios".*

[34] On the reformed Spanish Act on unfair competition, see *R. Peris* (ed.), La reforma de la ley de competencia disleal, Valencia, 2010, and *T. Plaza,* La reforma de la ley de competencia disleal, Madrid, 2010.

Giovanni De Cristofaro

to cancel the contract (Poland) or the right to claim the restitution of the price paid for the product offered or promoted by the unfair commercial practice (Belgium). In practice, in light of the availability of such special and exceptional contractual remedies, it seems not to be important to clarify if consumers are entitled to claim damages in addition to (or as an alternative to) such contractual remedies: in every case a strong contractual remedy is available, which is capable of protecting consumers' economic interests and preventing the infringement of the prohibition of unfair commercial practices.

In other Member States the silence of the legislation in force seems to suggest a preclusion, as is the case in Great Britain. Here, the Government has refused to introduce into the *Consumer Protection from Unfair Trading Regulations 2008* a provision by virtue of which traders shall be obliged to compensate consumers who suffer detriment as a direct result of an unfair commercial practice. The reason for this choice lies in the belief that "adopting a general private right of action" for the Regulations as a whole might have had "unintended consequences"[35].

In other cases, it is not clear what the lack of a provision that expressly enables consumers harmed by unfair commercial practices to claim damages should mean. This is what happens, for example, in Germany and Italy.

In Germany the rules concerning unfair commercial practices towards consumers have been integrated into the general Act on unfair competition of 2004[36]. This law aims to protect not only competitors, but also consumers and any subject involved in the Market (s. § 1). Art. 9 of the German Act on unfair competition states that the trader who intentionally or negligently

---

[35] So the *"Response"* of the British Government in relation to the *Consultation on Draft Consumer Protection from Unfair Trading Regulations* (p. 16): "Consumer organisations argued that unless there is provision for traders to compensate consumers who suffer detriment as a direct result of an unfair commercial practice the CPRs will only ever have the potential to be partially effective. This is because traders may remain undeterred from breaching the Regulations taking the view that profits made far exceed enforcement costs. However, the Government remains concerned that adopting a general private right of action for the Regulations as a whole might have unintended consequences. It considers that further analysis is needed in order to determine the basis on which any private right of action was justified, and in what specific circumstances consumers might be able to bring proceedings for breaches of the Consumer Protection from Unfair Trading Regulations".

[36] *Gesetz gegen unlauteren Wettbewerb* of 3 July 2004, as modified by the Act of 22 December 2008 that has transposed the Directive 2005/29/EC in Germany.

commits an unfair commercial practice is obliged to compensate the competitors for the damages caused by such a practice. The fact that this provision expressly gives the right to damages only to competitors induces most of the scholars and the Courts to deny such a right to individual consumers potentially affected and harmed by an unfair commercial practice[37]. Some scholars, however, argue[38] that the Act on unfair competition should be qualified as a *Schutzgesetz* according to § 823, section 2, of the civil code, and in this way assert that this general provision of the civil code concerning extra contractual liability entitles individual consumers to claim damages from the traders who infringe the prohibition of unfair commercial practices stated by Art. 3 of the aforementioned Act[39].

In Italy, on the other hand, the provisions concerning unfair commercial practices towards consumers have been integrated into the consumer code, while the rules concerning misleading advertising directed at traders and comparative advertising have been inserted in a separate, appropriate legislative decree and the general rules on unfair competition (that are inserted in the civil code: Art. 2598–2600) have not been modified. Unfair competition constitutes a particular kind of tort for the Italian law, which only entitles the competitors of the trader who commits an act of unfair competition to damages[40]. However, neither the consumer code nor the

---

[37] M. *Goldmann*, in: H. Harte-Bavendamm/F. Henning-Bodewig, UWG. Gesetz gegen den unlauteren Wettbewerb. Kommentar, Munich, 2009, p. 1904-1905; T. *Lettl*, Wettbewerbsrecht, Munich, 2009, p. 427; K. V. *Boesche*, Wettbewerbsrecht, Heidelberg, 2009, p. 5-6; C. *Alexander* (cit. n. 7), p. 201-202.

[38] With regard to the Act of unfair competition of 2004, before the implementation of the Directive, see F. J. *Säcker*, Das UWG zwischen den Mühlsteinen europäischer Harmonisierung und grundrechtsgebotener Liberalisierung, Wettbewerb in Recht und Praxis 2004, 1219 f.; R. *Sack*, Folgeverträge unlauteren Wettbewerbs, Gewerblicher Rechtsschutz- und Urheberrecht 2004, 629; K.-H. *Fezer* (cit. n. 9) p. 789. With regard to the German Act of unfair competition, as modified in 2008, see R. *Sack*, Individualschutz gegen unlauteren Wettbewerb, Wettbewerb in Recht und Praxis 2009, 1333 and V. *Emmerich*, Unlauterer Wettbewerb, Munich, 2009, p. 354.

[39] This interpretation has been criticized by many German authors, who deny that the Act on unfair competition is to be qualified as a *Schutzgesetz* for the purposes of § 823, section 2, of the German civil code: M. *Schmidt* (cit. n. 6), p. 82; H. *Köhler*/J. *Bornkamm* (cit. n. 8), sub § 9 UWG, 1145; H. *Piper*/A. *Ohly*/O. *Sosnitza*, UWG, Gesetz gegen den unlauteren Wettbewerb. Kommentar, Munich, 2010 *sub* § 9 UWG, p. 898; A. *Ebert-Weidenfeller*, in: H.-P. Götting/A. Nordemann (eds.), UWG. Handkommentar, Baden Baden, 2010, sub § 9 UWG, p. 1030.

[40] A. *Genovese*, Il risarcimento del danno da illecito concorrenziale, Naples, 2005.

Act of 2007 on misleading and comparative advertising contain provisions which expressly oblige the trader who resorts to unfair commercial practices or to illegal advertising to compensate the damages suffered by consumers or traders in receipt of such conducts. Nevertheless, since one of the rights envisaged in the list of the "fundamental rights of any consumer" contained in Art. 2, section 2, of the Consumer Code is the "right to commercial practices which comply with the requirements of fairness and good faith", some Italian Scholars[41] believe that the trader who commits an unfair commercial practice violates such fundamental rights and, for this reason, causes the consumers affected by such a practice an "unjust damage" *(danno ingiusto)* according to the general clause of Art. 2043 of the civil code, which concerns extra contractual liability[42].

As a result of the wide interpretation and application of this general clause, made in the last twenty years by the Italian courts and through which the scope of application of the tort liability has been greatly extended, it appears much less difficult in Italy as in Germany, to qualify unfair commercial practices towards consumers as a tort on the basis of the general rules of the civil code concerning extra contractual liability. The consumer whose economic interests have been harmed by a commercial practice shall therefore be entitled to claim compensation if he proves the unfair nature of the commercial practice directed at him, the chain of causation between such a practice and the damages suffered, as well as the fault of the trader who has resorted to the practice. The right to compensation for damages for consumers resulting from an unfair commercial practice can be exercised not only in normal judicial proceedings, but also with the Italian "class action" now regulated in Art. 140-*bis* of the consumer code, a new and controversial instrument for the collective exercise of the right to compensatory damages to which a plurality of consumers are entitled, due to the same tort.

---

[41] G. De Cristofaro, in: G. De Cristofaro/A. Zaccaria (eds.), Commentario breve al diritto dei consumatori, Padua, 2010, p. 142 ff.; A. Ciatti, in: G. De Cristofaro (ed.), Pratiche commerciali scorrette e codice del consumo, Turin, 2008, p. 424; A. Mirone (cit. n. 6), p. 332-333.

[42] This interpretation has been however criticized by other scholars: for some critical remarks see for example S. *Pagliantini*, Forma e formalismo nel diritto europeo dei contratti, Pisa, 2009, p. 176-177.

III. Concluding (and critical) remarks and future prospects: towards the attribution to every European consumer of an individual right to claim compensation for the losses caused by an unfair commercial practice?

As we have seen, the Directive 2005/29/EC does not expressly oblige Member States to grant an individual right to compensatory damages to consumers whose economic interests are harmed by an unfair commercial practice. However, at the same time it allows Member States to introduce or maintain provisions that foresee and regulate such a right to damages and/or different remedies in private law (and especially in contract law).

The choice of EC-Institutions not to adopt a clear and definite solution to this question appears wrong and criticisable, above all because of the nature of the Directive, that aims to achieve a full harmonization (and not only a minimum harmonization) of the national legislations of the Member States concerning unfair commercial practices towards consumers. It appears obvious to me that a directive which prohibits unfair commercial practices and harmonises in detail the criteria for the evaluation of the unfair nature of a commercial practice, but at the same time avoids harmonising the private- and public-law consequences of the infringement of such prohibition has no chance of achieving a real and complete harmonization of the national laws.

The negative effects of this wrong choice can be clearly seen today, after the Directive has been transposed in all the Member States. In fact, through the transposition of the Directive, exactly what we could have predicted in 2005 has happened. Each Member State has "gone his own way", adopting rules and provisions that are very different under many aspects.

The greatest difference is the one between the private-law remedies available to consumers harmed by unfair commercial practices. In many Member States the existence of an individual right to damages is expressly stated by an appropriate provision or can easily be inferred from the contents of the legislative Act in which the rules concerning unfair commercial practices have been integrated; in other Member States the existence of such a right is uncertain, but in some cases consumers have been provided with special contract-law remedies against unfair commercial practices; in other Member States consumers are definitely not entitled either to damages or to special remedies in contract law.

This situation creates great differences between European consumers, whose level of individual protection from unfair commercial practices depends entirely on the national law applicable to any single case. From another point of view, this situation creates problems and difficulties for

European traders, who are forced to face different costs and risks depending on the national market in which they carry out their commercial practices. This can, of course, generate appreciable distortions of competition and obstacles to the smooth functioning of the internal market, and will slow down the development of cross-border activities. The aims expressly pursued by the Directive are therefore unlikely to be achieved, and the attempt to fully harmonize the national legislations appears doomed to sensational failure.

This is probably the reason why the European Parliament, in its Resolution of 13 January 2009 on the transposition, implementation and enforcement of Directive 2005/29/EC concerning unfair business-to-consumer commercial practices[43], has noted that some Member States "have not made provision for a direct right of redress for consumers, who thus are not entitled to bring claims for damages resulting from unfair commercial practices" and has therefore called on Member States who have not already done so "to consider the necessity of giving consumers a direct right of redress in order to ensure that they are sufficiently protected against unfair commercial practices"[44].

What would happen if a Court of a Member State in which neither individual rights to damages nor special contractual remedies are available to consumers harmed by an unfair commercial practice (for example Great Britain or Germany) referred the question of the compatibility of such a national system with the Directive 2005/29/EC and with EU-law in general to the European Court?

I think that the Court of Justice would probably recognize that such a national legal system is in contrast with the EU-law. Not because of the fact that giving an individual right to damages is to be seen as an unavoidable and necessary measure to grant the effectiveness of the Directive and to ensure the compliance with the prohibition of unfair commercial practices, but just because the existence of great differences between the national laws of the Member States in relation to such a fundamental aspect of the regulation of unfair commercial practices is in radical contrast with the aims pursued by the Directive. Since many Member States have spontaneously chosen to introduce or maintain provisions that expressly or implicitly entitle consumers to claim compensation for the damages resulting from an unfair commercial practice, it cannot be tolerated that in some other Member States consumers are entitled neither to such a right to damages nor to a different but appropriate private-law remedy.

---

[43] OJ 2010 C 46/E/26.
[44] Point 12 of the Resolution, OJ 2010 C 46/E/26, at p. E/29.

Since the purpose of the Directive is to eliminate the disparities between the national laws of the various Member States which could be liable to cause distortions of competition between operators established in different Member States, it is indisputable that the existence in some Member States but not in others of an obligation for the trader to provide compensation for damages caused to consumers by an unfair commercial practice would cause significant distortions of competition.

The Court of Justice has already argued in this way in the judgement "Simone Leitner versus TUI Deutschland" of 2002, concerning the Directive 90/314/EEC on package travel, package holidays and package tours[45]. Although this Directive does not contain a provision that expressly obliges Member States to give consumers a right to compensation for non-material damage resulting from the non-performance or improper performance of the services constituting a package holiday, the European Court has recognized that the Directive is nevertheless to be interpreted as conferring, in principle, such a right to consumers: not only because "compensation for non-material damage arising from the loss of enjoyment of the holiday is of particular importance to consumers" (point 22), but also and mainly because "the existence in some Member States but not in others of an obligation to provide compensation for non-material damage would cause significant distortions of competition, given that non-material damage is a frequent occurrence in that field" (point 21).

The same arguments, in my opinion, could and should also be used with reference to the Directive on unfair commercial practices.

---

[45] Judgement of 12 March 2002, in the Case C-168/00 *(Simone Leitner and TUI Deutschland GmbH & Co. KG)* [2002] ECR I-2631.

Personenbeförderungs- und Reiserecht

Ansgar Staudinger

I. Einleitung

In den vergangenen Jahren hat der Europäische Gesetzgeber auf dem Gebiet der Passagierrechte[1] eine Reihe von Rechtsakten erlassen.[2] Modellcharakter kam insofern der Verordnung über die Fluggastrechte (fortan VO) zu.[3] Dem folgte eine Regelung über die Fahrgastrechte[4] im Bahnver-

---

[1] Hierzu *Jens Karsten/Angela Seidenspinner*, „Zum Vorteile des Verkehrsnutzers" – 20 Jahre EU – Passagierrecht im Spannungsfeld zwischen international governance und europäischer Nutzerrechte, Zeitschrift für Europäisches Privatrecht (ZEuP) 2010, 830 ff.; *Helga Kober-Dehm/Peter Meier-Beck*, Die Rechtsprechung des Bundesgerichtshofs zum Personenbeförderungs- und Reiserecht, ReiseRecht aktuell (RRa) 2010, 250 ff.; *Schulz*, Rechtsprechungsübersicht zum Reiserecht 2009 bis 2010, Verbraucher und Recht (VuR) 2010, 203 ff.; *Klaus Tonner*, Aktuelle Entwicklungen im Flug- und Fahrgastrecht, Verbraucher und Recht (VuR) 2010, 209 ff.; *Ronald Schmidt/Holger Hopperdietzel*, Die Fluggastrechte – eine Momentaufnahme, Neue Juristische Wochenschrift (NJW) 2010, 1905 ff.; *Ansgar Staudinger/Dominik/Schürmann*, Die Entwicklung des Reiserechts in den Jahren 2009/2010, Pauschalreise-, Luftverkehrs-, Seebeförderungs-, Gastschulaufenthalts- und Reiseversicherungsrecht, NJW 2010, 2771 ff.; *Beatrix Lindner/Klaus Tonner*, Fluggastrechte als Verbraucherrecht auf mehreren Ebenen, Zeitschrift für Gemeinschaftsprivatrecht (GPR) 2011, 15.

[2] Siehe auch *Hans-Georg Bollweg*, Die Kundenrechte des Flug-, Bahn- und Busverkehrs im Vergleich, RRa 2010, 106 ff.

[3] Verordnung (EG) Nr. 261/2004 des Europäischen Parlaments und des Rates vom 11.2.2004 über eine gemeinsame Regelung für Ausgleichs- und Unterstützungsleistungen für Fluggäste im Fall der Nichtbeförderung und bei Annullierung oder großer Verspätung von Flügen und zur Aufhebung der Verordnung (EWG) Nr. 295/91, ABl. EU Nr. L 46 v. 17.2.2004, S. 1.

[4] Verordnung (EG) Nr. 1371/2007 des Europäischen Parlaments und des Rates v. 23.10.2007 über die Rechte und Pflichten der Fahrgäste im Eisenbahnverkehr (ABlEU Nr. L 315 v. 3.12.2007, S. 14).

kehr, welche seit dem 3.12.2009 in Kraft ist. Im Anschluss an die Verordnung (EG) Nr. 392/2009[5] hat das Europäische Parlament am 6.7.2010 einen weiteren Rechtsakt im See- und Binnenschiffsverkehr angenommen.[6] Laut Artikel 31 wird die Verordnung[7] über die darin verankerten Fahrgastrechte ab dem 18.12.2010 gelten. Am 17.12.2009[8] erzielte ferner der Rat Einvernehmen über einen Verordnungsvorschlag zu den Fahrgastrechten im Kraftomnibusverkehr. Schließlich ist die Legislative auf supranationaler Ebene derzeit mit einer Reform der Pauschalreiserichtlinie[9] befasst.[10]

Nicht zuletzt wegen ihrer Modellfunktion soll der Fokus nachfolgend auf der VO im Luftverkehr liegen. Dies gilt um so mehr, als im Tatsächlichen gerade die Vulkanaschewolke wie auch das Schneechaos im Winter 2010 massenhaft zu Störungen und in der Folge zu einer Reihe von Rechtsfragen geführt haben. Deren Beantwortung anhand der VO fällt vielfach aufgrund ihrer handwerklichen Mängel schwer. So hat der Gemeinschaftsgesetzgeber teils Tatbestände wie etwa Annullierung[11] und Verspätung[12] nicht legaldefiniert und damit abgegrenzt. Teils erweist sich der Rechtsakt beispielsweise in Bezug auf Fragen der gerichtlichen Geltendmachung von Ansprüchen[13] oder ihrer Verjährung[14] als lückenhaft. Daher überrascht es

[5] Verordnung (EG) Nr. 392/2009 des Europäischen Parlaments und des Rates vom 23. 4. über die Unfallhaftung von Beförderern von Reisenden auf See, ABlEU Nr. L 131 v. 28.5.2009, S. 24; dazu Czerwenka, Neue Haftungs- und Entschädigungsregelungen in der Schifffahrt-Harmonisierung durch Europarecht, Transportrecht (TranspR) 2010, 165 (167 ff.).

[6] Legislative Entschließung des Europäischen Parlaments vom 6.7.2010 zu dem Standpunkt des Rates in erster Lesung im Hinblick auf den Erlass einer Verordnung des Europäischen Parlaments und des Rates über die Fahrgastrechte im See- und Binnenschiffsverkehr und zur Änderung der Verordnung (EG) Nr. 2006/2004, abrufbar unter: http://www.europarl.europa.eu.

[7] Verordnung (EU) Nr. 1177/2010 des Europäischen Parlaments und des Rates v. 24.11.2010 über die Fahrgastrechte im See- und Binnenschiffsverkehr und zur Änderung der Verordnung (EG) Nr. 2006/2004.

[8] Ratsdokument 15861/09 vom 19.11.2009, in der überarbeiteten Fassung vom 11.12.2009 (Ratsdokument 17412/09).

[9] Richtlinie 90/314/EWG des Rates vom 13.6.1990 über Pauschalreisen.

[10] *Klaus Tonner*, Wieviel Vollharmonisierung verträgt das Reiserecht?, VuR 2010, 201.

[11] Art. 5 der VO.

[12] Art. 6 der VO.

[13] Hierzu unter V.

[14] Hierzu unter VI.

nicht, dass der EuGH in der Vergangenheit immer wieder im Wege der Vorabentscheidung von nationalen Gerichten[15] aufgefordert wurde, Auslegungszweifel zu beheben oder Lücken der VO zu schließen. Im Zentrum der nachfolgenden Untersuchung zur VO steht dabei das Urteil des Europäischen Gerichtshofs vom 19.11.2009[16] in der Rechtssache *Sturgeon u.a.*,[17] welches auf Vorlagen des *BGH*[18] sowie *HG Wien*[19] erging. Es ist Auslöser heftiger Kontroversen, und zwar zum einen über die Reichweite der Befugnisse dieses Spruchkörpers, zum anderen über den Aussagegehalt seiner Entscheidung. Dies gilt insbesondere deshalb, weil der Gerichtshof im Wege der Rechtsfortbildung den Sanktionsmechanismus für die Annullierung auf bestimmte Abflug- und Ankunftsverspätungen übertragen hat. Nun stößt gerade der Art. 7 VO in direkter wie analoger Form deshalb auf Bedenken, weil hier der Sekundärrechtsgeber abhängig davon, ob es sich um einen Kurz-, Mittel- oder Langstreckenflug[20] handelt, einen pauschalen Ausgleich vorsieht. Anspruchsverpflichtet ist das ausführende Luftfahrtunternehmen, welches vertraglich gebunden sein kann, aber nicht muss. Die Forderung steht dem jeweiligen Kunden zu. Die Form der Sanktion knüpft dabei an keinen konkret erlittenen Schaden des Fluggastes an und ist überdies ticketpreisunabhängig. Die nachfolgenden Ausführungen stellen einen Versuch dar, die ratio des vom EuGH gefällten Urteils – soweit möglich – widerspruchsfrei mit den Vorgaben des Gemeinschafts-, wie Völker-

---

[15] Siehe etwa aktuell diejenige des *Bundesgerichtshofs* (BGH) zu den Ausgleichsansprüchen nach der VO bei verspäteter Ankunft am Endziel vom 9.12.2010 (Xa ZR 80/10).

[16] *Europäischer Gerichtshof* (EuGH), *Sturgeon/Condor u. Lepuschitz/Air France*, RRa2009, 282 = NJW 2010, 43.

[17] Dazu *Ansgar Staudinger,* Das Urteil des EuGH in den Rechtssachen Sturgeon und Böck, RRa 2010, 10. Vgl. auch *Daniela Schulz,* Urteilsanmerkung zum EuGH, Urt. v. 19.11.2009 – Ausgleichsansprüche des Flugreisenden bei Verspätung, LMK 2010, 295994. Zur Verspätungshaftung in der internationalen Luftbeförderung siehe zudem *Paul Dempsey/Svante Johansson,* Montreal v. Brussels: The Conflict of Laws on the Issue of Delay in International Air Carriage, Air & Space Law 2010, 207. Siehe auch *Stephan Hoke/Wolf Müller-Rostin/Anna Recker,* Fragwürdiges aus Luxemburg zur Verordnung 261/2004, Zeitschrift für Luft- und Weltraumrecht (ZLW) 2010, 149.

[18] *Bundesgerichtshof* (BGH) 17.7.2007, NJW 2007, 3437.

[19] *HG Wien,* 26.6.2007 – 60 R 114/06d.

[20] Art. 7 Abs. 1 S. 1, Abs. 4 der VO (analog).

vertragsrechts, insbesondere des Montrealer Übereinkommens[21] (MÜ)[22] in Einklang zu bringen. Ein besonderes Augenmerk gilt schließlich auch der Frage, ob und inwieweit die VO tatsächlich Modellcharakter im Hinblick auf die nachfolgenden Rechtsakte hatte oder etwa gerade im Hinblick auf die Fahrgastrechte im Eisenbahnverkehr oder die Pauschalreiserichtlinie bzw. ihrer Transformation Divergenzen bestehen.

II. Wirkung der Entscheidung des EuGH gegenüber nationalen Spruchkörpern

Das Urteil des Gerichtshofs in der Rechtssache *Sturgeon u.a.* bindet rechtlich ohne Zweifel die staatlichen Gerichte im betreffenden Vorlageverfahren. Zudem kommt jenem eine faktische Bindungswirkung gegenüber sämtlichen Spruchkörpern im gesamten Binnenmarkt zu. Der BGH[23] hat sich daher im Ausgangspunkt überzeugend in mehreren Entscheidungen dem vom Europäischen Gerichtshof eingeschlagenen Weg der Rechtsfolgenanalogie angeschlossen. In methodischer Hinsicht ist dem EuGH aus deutschem Blickwinkel wohl keine verfassungsrechtlich zu beanstandende Kompetenzüberschreitung vorzuwerfen. Hierfür lässt sich der Beschluss des BVerfG vom 6.7.2010 in der Rechtssache *Mangold*[24] auf dem Gebiet des Arbeitsrechts ins Feld führen. Wie nachzuweisen sein wird, droht bei zutreffender Lektüre der Entscheidung des EuGH ebenso wenig ein Widerspruch zu Art. 29 in Verbindung mit Art. 19 MÜ.

Natürlich steht es jedem Spruchkörper frei, eine abweichende Rechtsauffassung als der EuGH und BGH zu vertreten,[25] auch wenn es im In-

---

[21] Übereinkommen zur Vereinheitlichung bestimmter Vorschriften über die Beförderung im internationalen Luftverkehr v. 28. 5.1 999, ABl. EG Nr. L 194 v. 18.7.2001, S. 39.

[22] Beachte die veränderten Haftungshöchstgrenzen, BGBl. 2009, II 1258.

[23] *Bundesgerichtshof* (BGH) 10.12.2009, RRa 2010, 90 (91); 26.11.2009, RRa 2010, 85 (89); 18.2.2010, RRa 2010, 93 (94); 151. Die Bindungswirkung missachtend *AG Rüsselsheim*, 21.1.2010 – 3 C 1482/09 (32).

[24] *Europäischer Gerichtshof* (EuGH) 22.11.2005, *Werner Mangold/Rüdiger Helm*, NJW 2005, 3695 ff.; *Bundesarbeitsgericht* (BAG) 26.4.2006, Neue Zeitschrift für Arbeitsrecht (NZA) 2006, 1162 ff.; *Bundesverfassungsgericht* (BVerfG) 6.7.2010, NJW 2010, 3422 ff.

[25] Siehe etwa *AG Nürtingen*, 27.9.2010 – 11 C 1219/10, welches die Berufung zugelassen hat.

stanzenzug wenig zielführend sein dürfte. Gleichermaßen kann jedes nationale Gericht ein weiteres Vorlageverfahren initiieren, sofern die primärrechtlichen Voraussetzungen in Art. 267 AEUV[26] vorliegen. Nun mag eine Rechtsfrage mit Bezug zur VO erneut entscheidungserheblich werden. Es müsste sich aber zudem um eine offene Frage handeln, über die der Gerichtshof noch nicht entschieden hat und deren Antwort im Sinne der acte-claire-Doktrin nicht auf der Hand liegt.[27] Andernfalls droht, dass das Vorabentscheidungsersuchen als unzulässig erachtet wird. Genau dies liegt aber jedenfalls dann nahe, sollte ein nationales Gericht ein „overruling" des am 19.11.2009 vom Europäischen Gerichtshof gefällten Urteils allein unter Hinweis darauf zu erreichen suchen, dass die Rechtsfortbildung einen Bruch mit dem MÜ bedeute. Dies gilt umso mehr, als der EuGH die Frage der Völkerrechtskonformität des Sekundärrechtsakts vom Grundsatz schon in seiner Entscheidung vom 10.1.2006[28] bejaht hat und hierauf in der Rechtssache *Sturgeon u.a.*[29] mehrfach Bezug nimmt, ungeachtet der Tatsache, dass er Art. 19, 29 MÜ nicht ausdrücklich erörtert. Gleichermaßen steht außer Frage, dass der Gerichtshof eine Rechtsfolgenanalogie befürwortet, welche sich intertemporal auf Sachverhalte vom 17.2.2005 an erstreckt, da die VO an diesem Stichtag zeitlich zur Anwendung gelangte.[30] Ansonsten hätte der Gerichtshof als Ausnahmefall ausdrücklich eine zeitliche Begrenzung in seinem Urteil festlegen müssen. Vor diesem Hintergrund erscheint unklar, ob und inwieweit die jüngst vom High Court[31] of England and Wales sowie AG Köln[32] betriebenen weiteren Vorlagen zulässig sind und in der Sache zu einer Präzisierung oder gar Aufgabe seines Ansatzes in der Rechtssache

---

[26] Beachte die Veränderung des Vorabentscheidungsverfahrens durch den Vertrag von Lissabon, ABlEU Nr. C 306 v. 17.12.2007.
[27] Ein erneutes Vorlageverfahren mag auf der Grundlage eines abweichenden Sachverhalts angezeigt sein, um etwa bei einem Kurzstreckenflug im Sinne von Art. 6 Abs. 1, lit. a) VO dem Europäischen Gerichtshof die Möglichkeit zu eröffnen, das Erfordernis der Mindestankunftsverspätung von drei Stunden zu korrigieren; hierzu unter IV.
[28] *Europäischer Gerichtshof* (EuGH) 10.1.2006, *International Air Transport Association u. European Low Fares Airline Association/Department for Transport*, RRa 2006, 127.
[29] *Europäischer Gerichtshof* (EuGH), *Sturgeon/Condor u. Lepuschitz/Air France*, RRa 2009, 282 = NJW 2010, Rn. 48, 49, 51, 65.
[30] Hierzu Art. 19 der VO.
[31] High Court Queen's Bench Division, CO/6569/2010 (TUI et al/CAA), RRa 2011, 37.
[32] Amtsgericht Köln, 4.10.2010 – 142 C 535/08, RRa 2011, 42.

Ansgar Staudinger

Sturgeon u.a. führt. Faktisch werden die beiden Vorabentscheidungsersuche allerdings wohl zu unterschiedlichen Prozesssituationen führen. Infolge der Vorlage des High Court droht ein „stand still im United Kingdom", da britische Gerichte einstweilen Verfahren über Ausgleichszahlungen bei Verspätungen auf der Grundlage der VO aussetzen müssen. Dies privilegiert im Ergebnis dort ansässige Fluggesellschaften. Demgegenüber bleibt abzuwarten, ob ein inländischer Spruchkörper analog § 148 ZPO im Lichte der Vorabentscheidungsersuchen vom High Court sowie AG Köln ein Gerichtsverfahren aussetzt.

III. Abflugverspätung als *conditio sine qua non*

Die Leitsätze sowie Gründe der Vorlageentscheidung vom 19.11.2009 könnten dahin fehlinterpretiert werden, der Gerichtshof habe als Ersatzgesetzgeber den Tatbestand einer isolierten dreistündigen Ankunftsverspätung praeter legem geschaffen und damit entgegen Art. 19, 29 MÜ in den Regelungsbereich der Konvention eingegriffen.

Die Aufgabe des EuGH bestand zunächst darin, die in Art. 5 und 6 VO geregelten Fälle der Annullierung und Abflugverspätung voneinander abzugrenzen. Der Gerichtshof sieht sich allerdings nicht in der Lage, diese Lücke des Sekundärrechtsaktes selbst zu schließen. Nach seinem Lösungsansatz bedarf es einer solchen Differenzierung auch nicht, da er beide Tatbestände hinsichtlich der Entlastung nach Art. 5 Abs. 3 VO und den Rechtsfolgen in Art. 7 VO im Ergebnis gleichstellt. Die Gewährung eines pauschalierten Ausgleichsanspruchs entsprechend der zuletzt genannten Vorschrift bedeutet demzufolge – wie es auch beim BGH[33] anklingt – lediglich eine Rechtsfolgenanalogie. Erst wenn mithin der Tatbestand von Art. 6 VO erfüllt ist, also eine Abflugverspätung vorliegt, kommt als Rechtsfolge kraft Richterrechts ein pauschalierter Ausgleich in Betracht, sofern sich der Beförderer nicht entsprechend Art. 5 Abs. 3 VO[34] entlasten kann.

---

[33] *Bundesgerichtshof* (BGH) 10.12.2009 – Xa ZR 61/09, Rn. 11, RRa 2010, 90.

[34] Bedeutsam wird dies etwa bei bestimmten Wetteberbedingungen. Sicherlich zählt etwa Vulkanasche zu derartigen außergewöhnlichen Umständen. Hingegen ist nach Ansicht des BGH bei Nebel zu differenzieren: *Bundesgerichtshof* (BGH) 25.3.2010 – Xa ZR 96/09, RRa 2010, 221 = NJW-RR 2010, 1641. Beachtung verdient überdies, dass die Entlastung nach der VO nur Platz greift, wenn das ausführende Luftfahrtunternehmen alle zumutbaren Maßnahmen ergriffen hat. Kann der Flugverkehr im Winter nicht aufrecht erhalten werden, weil der Flughafenbetrei-

Nach der hier vertretenen Lesart muss die Formulierung des Europäischen Gerichtshofs, Fluggästen „*verspäteter Flüge*"[35] stünde eine Forderung analog Art. 7 VO zu, folglich dahin interpretiert werden, es handele sich um Kunden, welche zunächst verspätet den Flug angetreten haben. Diesem Ansatz zufolge ginge zumindest der Vorwurf gegenüber dem Gerichtshof fehl, er habe dogmatisch unzulässig und überdies völkervertragsrechtswidrig einen neuen Tatbestand der alleinigen Ankunftsverspätung kreiert und diesen obendrein mit einem verschuldensunabhängigen sowie pauschalierten Ausgleichsanspruch sanktioniert.

Schließt man sich der vorliegend favorisierten Interpretation an – so etwa jüngst das LG Frankfurt a.M. in zwei Urteilen vom 23.9.2010[36] –, muss zunächst abhängig von der Entfernung anhand von Art. 6 Abs. 1, lit. a) bis c) VO eine Abflugverspätung[37] vorliegen. Erst dann kann ein Kunde überhaupt in den Genuss einer Forderung analog Art. 7 VO gelangen, nämlich in derjenigen Konstellation, in welcher sich am Zielort der verspätete Antritt der Reise noch in einem Zeitverlust niederschlägt und damit letztlich perpetuiert. Erfolgt der Abflug nach den Schwellenwerten von Art. 6 Abs. 1 VO indes „*pünktlich*" innerhalb der tolerierten Abweichung, vermag eine isolierte Ankunftsverspätung keine Sanktion nach der VO auszulösen. Tatbestandlich unterfällt diese Leistungsstörung allein dem MÜ. Dementsprechend droht im Ausgangspunkt auch kein unmittelbarer Konflikt zwischen beiden Regelwerken. Ebenso wenig kommt es auf die schwierige Qualifikation des Ausgleichsanspruchs in Art. 7 VO (analog)

---

ber mangels hinreichender Bevorratung kein Enteisungsmittel und entsprechendes Personal einsetzen kann, ist ein solches „Missmanagement" dem Luftfahrtunternehmen womöglich zurechenbar mit der Folge, dass eine Entlastung fehl schlägt. Siehe hierzu auch *Stephanie Sendmeyer*, Alle Jahre wieder: Europäische Fluggastrechte im Schneechaos, NJW 2011, 808; *AG Königs Wusterhausen* 3.5.2011 – 20 C 83/11.

[35] Siehe die Formulierung im Leitsatz sowie etwa Rn. 61.

[36] *Landgericht Frankfurt a.M.*, 23.9.2010 – 2 – 24 S 28/10, RRa 2010, 273 ff. und 2-24 S 44/10 (Rev. zugelassen), RRa 2011, 44

[37] Angesichts des klaren Wortlauts kann der EuGH nicht dahin verstanden werden, er setze stets eine dreistündige „*Abflugverspätung*" voraus. Bei einem Langstreckenflug i.S.v. Art. 6 Abs. 1, lit. c) VO muss vielmehr tatbestandlich eine Abflugverspätung von mindestens vier Stunden vorliegen. Beträgt diese etwa nur drei Stunden, hat der Kunde selbst dann keinen Ausgleichsanspruch analog Art. 7 VO, wenn er drei oder mehr Stunden später den Zielort erreicht. Hingegen genügt bei einem Kurzstreckenflug eine Abflugverspätung i.S.v. Art. 6 Abs. 1, lit. a) VO von zwei Stunden oder mehr.

Ansgar Staudinger

sowie darauf an, ob Art. 29, 19 MÜ einer derartigen Forderung entgegensteht. Denn selbst wenn man in Art. 7 VO eine pauschalierte Entschädigung sieht, welche mangels eines konkret nachzuweisenden Schadens weniger eine Kompensationsfunktion, sondern vielmehr verhaltenssteuernde oder sogar abschreckende Wirkung wie punitive damages haben soll, scheidet ein Völkerrechtsverstoß aus. Demzufolge kann auch offen bleiben, wie der Begriff des Schadens im MÜ[38] selbst auszulegen ist.

IV. Mindestankunftsverspätung von drei Stunden?

Wenn sich nun aber die Abflug- in einer Ankunftsverspätung fortsetzen muss, stellt sich die Anschlussfrage, welcher Zeitverlust am Zielort notwendig ist, um einen Ausgleich entsprechend Art. 7 VO auszulösen. Zugegebenermaßen überzeugt die Auffassung des Europäischen Gerichtshofs, stets eine Mindestdauer von drei Stunden zu veranschlagen, insofern nicht, als doch bei der Annullierung in bestimmten Fallkonstellationen ein verspätetes Eintreffen am Ankunftsort von mindestens zwei Stunden laut Art. 5 Abs. 1, lit. c), iii) VO genügt. Der Gerichtshof[39] scheint diese Vorschrift dahin misszuverstehen, dass die Vorverlegung des Abflugs von maximal einer Stunde sowie die Ankunftsverspätung von höchstens zwei Stunden zu addieren seien. Der Gemeinschaftsgesetzgeber sieht indes die Annullierung tatbestandlich bereits dann für gegeben, wenn der Kunde etwa anderweitig befördert wird, zwar planmäßig abfliegt (oder wenige Minuten danach), aber 121 Minuten später sein Ziel erreicht. Abhängig von der Entfernung mag in einer solchen Konstellation allenfalls eine Kürzung nach Art. 7 Abs. 2 VO Platz greifen. Wenn jedoch für die Annullierung auf der Rechtsfolgenseite ein Ausgleichsanspruch dem Grunde nach laut Art. 5 Abs. 1, lit. c), iii) VO schon bei einem geringeren Zeitverlust als drei Stunden gewährt wird, nämlich bereits bei einem verspäteten Eintreffen am Zielort nach mehr als zwei Stunden, gebietet der primär- wie letztlich

---

[38] Auf ein Vorabentscheidungsersuchen des *Juzgado de lo Mercantil n°4 de Barcelona* zur Haftungsbegrenzung nach dem MÜ entschied der *Europäische Gerichtshof* (EuGH), der Art. 22 II MÜ zugrundeliegende Begriff „Schaden" sei dahingehend auszulegen, dass der festgelegte Höchstbetrag sowohl materielle als auch immaterielle Schäden umfasse. Die Haftungsgrenze sei unabhängig von der Art der Schäden sowie der Entschädigung: *Europäischer Gerichtshof* (EuGH), Rs. C-63/09 (ABlEU Nr. C 102 v. 1.5.2009, S. 11), NJW 2010, 2113.

[39] Vgl. Rn. 57 f.

verfassungsrechtliche Gleichheitsgrundsatz, dies ebenso im Fall der Verspätung im Sinne von Art. 6 VO bei Kurz-, Mittel- wie Langstreckenflügen. Zur Illustration mag folgendes Beispiel dienen: Fliegt der Kunde nach Art. 6 Abs. 1, lit. a) VO 140 Minuten verspätet ab – diese Prüfung ist dem analogen Ausgleichsanspruch im Lichte der vorangehenden Ausführungen zwingend vorgeschaltet – und erreicht 120 Minuten nach der avisierten Landung sein Ziel, so steht ihm entsprechend Art. 7 Abs. 1, lit. a) VO bei mangelnder Entlastung des Beförderers ein Ausgleichsanspruch zu, welcher analog Art. 7 Abs. 2, lit. a) VO der hälftigen Kürzung unterliegt.[40]

Einwenden mag man nun, die Entscheidung des Europäischen Gerichtshofs verbiete eine solche Forderung, da er explizit einen dreistündigen Schwellenwert als Ausgangspunkt für die Rechtsfolgenanalogie festgesetzt habe. Zu bedenken bleibt zunächst, dass ein Vorabentscheidungsverfahren gegenständlich durch den jeweiligen Sachverhalt konturiert wird,[41] auch wenn die rechtlichen Ausführungen des Gerichtshofs über die zwei verbundenen Anlassstreitigkeiten hinauszielen. Beide Ausgangsverfahren betrafen jeweils Langstreckenflüge, woraus sich die Bezugnahme des Gerichtshofes auf Art. 7 Abs. 2, lit. c) VO[42] erklärt. Losgelöst hiervon sind aber ebenso inländische Spruchkörper infolge des Anwendungsvorrangs dem (gemeinschafts- wie verfassungsrechtlichen) Gleichheitsgrundsatz sowie der VO unterstellt. Sofern sich ein hiesiges Gericht demzufolge etwa mit einem Ausgleichsanspruch analog Art. 7 VO bei einer mindestens zweistündigen Ankunftsverspätung eines Kurzstreckenflugs befasst, sollte eine weitere Vorlage initiiert werden, um dem Europäischen Gerichtshof ganz allgemein die Gelegenheit zu verschaffen, den Schwellenwert zu korrigieren.

V. Gerichtszuständigkeit

In grenzüberschreitenden Sachverhalten greift im Lichte der vorangehenden Ausführungen selbst dann, wenn die Abflugverspätung in Anbetracht eines Zeitverlustes am Zielort durch Art. 7 VO analog sanktioniert wird, Art. 33 MÜ als an sich nach Art. 71 Abs. 1 Brüssel I-VO[43] vorrangige Gerichtsstands-

---

[40] Erreicht er den Zielort 100 Minuten verspätet, scheidet ein pauschalierter Ausgleichsanspruch folglich aus.
[41] Zum Sachverhalt der beiden Vorlagen siehe Rn. 11 ff. und Rn. 19 ff.
[42] Siehe Rn. 63.
[43] Verordnung (EG) Nr. 44/2001 des Rates über die gerichtliche Zuständigkeit und Anerkennung und Vollstreckung von Entscheidungen in Zivil- und Handels-

regel nicht ein. Vielmehr kann sich der Kunde neben Art. 2 Abs. 1 ebenso auf Art. 5 Nr. 1 lit. b), 2. Spiegelstrich Brüssel I-VO und damit das Urteil des Europäischen Gerichtshofs[44] in der Rechtssache *Rehder* stützen. Danach steht ihm ein Wahlrecht zu, gegen das Luftfahrtunternehmen am Abflug- oder Ankunftsort zu prozessieren. Art. 5 Nr. 1 lit. a) Brüssel I-VO erfordert allerdings, dass der geltend gemachte Anspruch als vertraglich einzustufen ist; lit. b) dieser Vorschrift, dass das Rechtsgeschäft die Erbringung einer Dienstleitung betrifft. Der EuGH qualifiziert die Forderung aus Art. 7 der VO jedenfalls insofern als freiwillig eingegangene Verpflichtung, als sie gegen das vertraglich gebundene, ausführende Luftfahrtunternehmen gerichtet ist. Dies überzeugt, selbst wenn man in dem pauschalierten Anspruch Elemente eines Strafschadensersatzes erkennen mag. Über den Anlassstreit hinaus erscheint es sachgerecht, sämtlichen auf der VO basierenden Forderungen einen vertraglichen Charakter zuzusprechen, jedenfalls mit Blick auf den Vertragspartner des Kunden als ausführendes Luftfahrtunternehmen. Indes verbleiben Zweifel, wenn abweichend vom Vorlageverfahren vertraglicher und ausführender Luftbeförderer nicht zusammenfallen. So mag die VO materiellrechtlich dem Kunden ebenso einen Anspruch gegen den „faktischen" Beförderer einräumen, der im Rahmen einer rechtsgeschäftlichen Beziehung des Kunden zu einem Dritten als ausführendes Luftfahrtunternehmen laut Art. 2 lit. b) der VO tätig wird. Es erscheint jedoch zweifelhaft, ob tatsächlich jeder (un)mittelbar aus diesem Sekundärrechtsakt abgeleiteten Forderung eine vertragliche Rechtsnatur zukommt und damit ein pauschalierter Ausgleichsanspruch nach Art. 7 VO (analog) allein gegen das ausführende Luftfahrtunternehmen Art. 5 Nr. 1, lit. b), 2. Spiegelstrich Brüssel I-VO unterfällt.[45] Ebenso ist unklar,

---

sachen vom 22. 12 .2000, ABlEG Nr. L 12 v. 16.1.2001, S. 1. Voraussetzung ist stets, dass der zeitliche, sachliche und räumliche Anwendungsbereich des Sekundärrechtsaktes eröffnet ist. Zum letzten Prüfungsaspekt und damit Art. 4 Brüssel I-VO siehe *Bundesgerichtshof* (BGH) 18.1.2011 – X ZR 71/10, RRa 1011, 79.

[44] *Europäischer Gerichtshof* (EuGH) 9.7.2009, Rs. C 204/08 *(Rehder/Air Baltic)*, RRa 2009, 234f.; hierzu *Ansgar Staudinger*, Praktikertipps zum Erfüllungsortsgerichtsstand im Luftverkehr, RRa 2009, 219; *ders.*, Streitfragen zum Erfüllungsortsgerichtsstand im Luftverkehr, Praxis des Internationalen Privat- und Verfahrensrechts (IPRax) 2010, 140 ff. Unterstellt wird, dass keine wirksame abweichende Erfüllungsort- bzw. Gerichtsstandsvereinbarung vorliegt. Zum Gerichtsstand bei Klagen wegen Annullierung siehe auch *Matthias Lehmann*, Gerichtsstand bei Klagen wegen Annullierung einer Flugreise, NJW 2010, 655 ff.

[45] Hierzu *Ansgar Staudinger*, IPRax 2010, 140 ff.; siehe in weiterem Zusammenhang *Stefan Leible*, in: Rauscher, Europäisches Zivilprozess- und Kollisionsrecht, Neubearbeitung 2011, Art. 5 Brüssel I-VO.

ob es sich tatsächlich um eine freiwillig eingegangene Verpflichtung im Sinne der zuletzt genannten Vorschrift handelt, wenn ein Kunde im Zuge der Vulkanaschewolke den faktischen Beförderer auf Ersatz seiner Hotel- und Verpflegungskosten verklagt. Jedenfalls greift die Argumentation, es gebe ja eine bestätigte Buchung und damit wohl in der Regel einen Vertrag, welchen der Dritter erfülle, zu kurz. Denn maßgeblich sind allein Vorgaben der Brüssel I-VO und verwandter Rechtsakte wie diejenigen der Rom I-[46] und II-VO[47].

Nun betont der EuGH aber in der Rechtssache *Rehder* mehrfach sowie im Leitsatz explizit, dass es sich bei der Beklagten um die „einzige" Luftfahrtgesellschaft und zugleich das „ausführende" Luftfahrtunternehmen handelt. Nimmt man parallele Fallgestaltungen in den Blick, so dürfte insbesondere die Vorlageentscheidung des EuGH in der Rechtssache *Réunion*,[48] welche einen tatsächlichen Verfrachter betraf, den Schluss nahe legen, Art. 5 Nr. 1 Brüssel I-VO sei versperrt. Der Gerichtshof hatte damals jedenfalls Ansprüche gegen den „faktischen" Transporteur als unerlaubte Handlung qualifiziert, so dass es neben dem allgemeinen Gerichtsstand in Art. 2 Abs. 1 bei Art. 5 Nr. 3 Brüssel I-VO verblieb. Dem hat sich die herrschende Lehre[49] angeschlossen. Handelt es sich bei dem Anspruchsgegner aus der VO somit allein um das ausführende und nicht vertraglich gebundene Luftfahrtunternehmen, erscheint es naheliegend, anstelle einer freiwillig eingegangenen, von einer gesetzlichen Verpflichtung zu sprechen bzw. den Ansprüchen als Sanktion auf unerlaubte Verhaltensweisen eine deliktische Rechtsnatur zuzuschreiben. Demzufolge kommt in einer solchen Fallkonstellation, welche von der Rechtssache *Rehder* abweicht, die Anwendbarkeit von Art. 5 Nr. 3 Brüssel I-VO in Betracht. Hierfür spricht ferner das Gebot der harmonischen Interpretation der Brüssel I- und Rom I-VO, wie sich bereits dem Erwägungsgrund Nr. 7 Rom I-VO entnehmen lässt.[50] Auch innerhalb von Art. 5 Abs. 2

---

[46] Verordnung (EG) Nr. 593/2008 des Europäischen Parlaments und des Rates vom 17. Juni 2008 über das auf vertragliche Schuldverhältnisse anzuwendende Recht (Rom I), ABlEU Nr. L 177/6 v. 4.7.2008 i. d. F. der Berichtigung v. 24.11.2009, ABlEU Nr. L 309 v. 24.11.2009, S. 87.

[47] Verordnung (EG) Nr. 864/2007 des Europäischen Parlaments und des Rates vom 11. Juli 2007 über das auf außervertragliche Schuldverhältnisse anzuwendende Recht („Rom II"), ABlEU Nr. L 199/40 v. 31.7.2002.

[48] *Europäischer Gerichtshof* (EuGH) 27.10.1998, Rs. C-51/97 („*Réunion européenne SA u.a./Spliethoff's Bevrachtingskantoor BV*"), IPRax 2000, 210.

[49] Vgl. statt aller *Leible*, in: Rauscher, a.a.O., Art. 5 Brüssel I-VO Rn. 26.

[50] Siehe auch *Europäischer Gerichtshof* (EuGH) 7.12.2010, Rs. C-585/08 und C-144/09 (*Pammer/Reederei Karl Schlüter GmbH & Co. KG* und *Hotel Alpenhof GesmbH/ Heller*). Siehe hierzu *Ansgar Staudinger/Björn Steinrötter*, Verfahrens- sowie kol-

Rom I-VO befürwortet nämlich das Schrifttum[51], ein faktisches Luftfahrtunternehmen eben nicht mit dem Vertragspartner des Kunden gleichzusetzen. In der Gesamtschau[52] sollte dem EuGH alsbald die Chance gegeben werden, seine Grundsätze aus der Rechtssache *Rehder* zu präzisieren. Die Frage, ob ein (un)mittelbarer Anspruch aus der VO allein gegen den faktischen Beförderer Art. 5 Nr. 1 oder Nr. 3 Brüssel I-VO unterliegt, ist – ihre Entscheidungserheblichkeit unterstellt – ohne Zweifel derzeit offen. Dies gilt ebenfalls für die Frage, wo Handlungs- und Erfolgsort[53] im Sinne des Art. 5 Nr. 3 Brüssel I-VO liegen. Dem steht ebenso wenig die Judikatur des BGH[54] zu Art. 32 EGBGB entgegen.[55] Nach Art. 267 AEUV kann demnach jede Eingangs- bzw. Berufungsinstanz diese Frage zur Vorabentscheidung vorlegen und hat die in concreto letzte Instanz eine dahingehende Pflicht. Die Antwort des EuGH wäre dann zu übertragen auf das Parallelabkommen zwischen Dänemark und der EU.[56] Ihr käme überdies eine Aussagekraft für das am 30.10.2007 in Lugano unterzeichnete Übereinkommen über die gerichtliche Zuständigkeit und die Anerkennung und Vollstreckung von Entscheidungen in Zivil- und Handelssachen[57] zu, welches zwischen der

---

lisionsrechtlicher Verbraucherschutz bei Online-Geschäften, Europäisches Wirtschafts- und Steuerrecht (EWS) 2011, 70.

[51] *Peter Mankowski,* in: Christoph Reithmann/Dieter Martiny, Internationales Vertragsrecht, 7. Auflage 2010 Rn. 2634; *Dieter Martiny,* in: Münchener Kommentar zum Bürgerlichen Gesetzbuch, Band 5, 5. Auflage 2009 Art. 5 Rom I-VO Rn. 35; *Ansgar Staudinger,* in: Franco Ferrari, Internationales Vertragsrecht, 2. Auflage 2011, Art. 5 Rom I-VO Rn. 37.

[52] Schließlich zeigt ein kurzer, an sich nicht maßgeblicher Blick ins nationale Recht, dass derjenige, der als Erfüllungsgehilfe im Rahmen eines Vertrages agiert, selbst gerade nicht vertraglich, sondern in der Regel ausschließlich deliktisch haftet.

[53] Sollte der Erfolgsort bei dem Kunden als natürliche Person nicht am Flughafen, sondern an seiner Vermögenszentrale lokalisiert werden, eröffnete ihm dies eine ortsnahe Prozessführung, da eine solche Zentrale in der Regel an seinem Wohnsitz festzumachen sein dürfte.

[54] *Bundesgerichtshof* (BGH) 10.12.2009, RRa 2010, 90 (92); 12.11.2010, RRa 2010, 34 (36).

[55] Hierzu unter VI.

[56] Abkommen vom 19.10.2005 zwischen der Europäischen Gemeinschaft und dem Königreich Dänemark über die gerichtliche Zuständigkeit und die Anerkennung und Vollstreckung von Entscheidungen in Zivil- und Handelssachen, AB1EG 2005 L 299/62 ff.

[57] AB1EU Nr. L 147 v. 10.6.2009, S. 5.

EU sowie Norwegen und Dänemark am 1.1.2010[58] und seit dem 1.1.2011 auch gegenüber der Schweiz[59] in Kraft getreten ist[60]. Im Zuge der Reform der VO sollte in Erwägung gezogen werden, einen Gerichtsstand im Rechtsakt selbst aufzunehmen. Mit Blick auf die Brüssel I-VO[61] ist jedenfalls derzeit nicht angedacht, Art. 15 Abs. 3 oder Art. 5 Brüssel I-VO diesbezüglich zu verändern.

VI. Lückenschließung im Hinblick auf die Verjährung

Die Entscheidung des Gerichtshofs in der Rechtssache *Sturgeon u.a.* wirkt nicht erst pro futuro, sondern auf den 17.2.2005 als Stichtag zurück, von dem an die VO zur Anwendung gelangte. Abgesehen von rechtskräftigen Entscheidungen hat somit jeder Kunde bis zur Schranke der Verjährung bzw. des Rechtsmissbrauchs die Möglichkeit, den pauschalierten Ausgleich auch noch für vergangene Sachverhalte geltend zu machen. Zur Frage, ob und welche Verjährungsfristen gelten, schweigt der Verordnungsgeber. Der BGH[62] scheint sich jedenfalls mit Blick auf das Kollisionsrecht ganz allgemein dafür auszusprechen, sämtliche Forderungen aus der Verordnung vertraglich einzustufen und unter die damals intertemporal einschlägigen Art. 27 ff. EGBGB zu subsumieren. Mit Blick auf die Frage der Verjährung ist der BGH demgemäß, ohne den Gerichtshof um Vorabentscheidung anzurufen, zunächst zu dem Ergebnis gelangt, bei einer reinen Luftbeförderung sei weder Art. 35 Abs. 1 MÜ unmittelbar noch entsprechend heranzuziehen. Sofern die Art. 27 ff. EGBGB deutsches Recht zur Anwendung berufen, verbiete sich ebenso der Rückgriff auf § 49a S. 1 LuftVG (analog). Vielmehr verbleibe es bei der Anwendbarkeit der §§ 195, 199 BGB. Dabei beginne die dreijährige Verjährungsfrist kraft § 199 Abs. 1 Nr. 1 und 2 BGB[63] erst mit

---

[58] ABlEU Nr. L 140 v. 8.6.2010, S. 1.
[59] Die VO gilt ebenso für die Schweiz, vgl. das Abkommen zwischen der Schweizerischen Eidgenossenschaft und der Europäischen Gemeinschaft über den Luftverkehr vom 21. Juni 1999.
[60] Vgl. *Heinz-Peter Mansel/Kartsen Thorn/Rolf Wagner*, Europäisches Kollisionsrecht 2010, IPRax 2010, 1 (13). Das Inkrafttreten in Island steht ebenfalls in 2011 an.
[61] Siehe den Vorschlag der Kommission vom 14.12.2010, Kom (2010) 748 endg.
[62] *Bundesgerichtshof (BGH)* 12.11.2009 – Xa ZR 76/07, RRa 2010, 34 (36), Rn. 18.
[63] Vgl. *Sebastian Herrler*, Rückforderung von Nutzungsersatz beim Verbrauchsgüterkauf: Verzögerter Beginn der Verjährungsfrist wegen unübersichtlicher Rechts-

Ansgar Staudinger

dem Schluss des Jahres 2009, in dem der Europäische Gerichtshof seine Entscheidung gefällt habe. Diese Grundsätze seien gleichermaßen für den Anspruch im Falle der Annullierung laut Art. 5 VO wie für jenen richterrechtlich geschaffenen bei einer Verspätung gemäß Art. 6 VO zu beachten. Hierauf weist der BGH,[64] welcher bislang unmittelbar allein mit der ersten Konstellation befasst war, in einem obiter dictum hin.

Festzuhalten bleibt, dass der Ansatz des BGH, auf Art. 35 Abs. 1 MÜ bzw. § 49a S. 1 LuftVG weder unmittelbar noch entsprechend abzustellen, sondern das in der Sache anwendbare Verjährungsstatut mithilfe des Kollisionsrechts zu ermitteln, uneingeschränkt überzeugt. Ebenso erscheint die diesbezügliche Abstandnahme des BGH[65] von einer Vorlage an den EuGH zumindest im Ausgangspunkt zutreffend. Denn in der Tat ist wohl davon auszugehen, dass auch für die Gerichte der übrigen Mitgliedstaaten kein Zweifel daran besteht, dass „sich die zeitlichen Grenzen der Ausgleichsansprüche nach Art. 7 VO aus dem nach dem Kollisionsrecht berufenen nationalen Sachrecht ergeben". Nur welches Anknüpfungsregime einschlägig ist, erscheint offen. Im konkreten Fall des BGH fielen ausführendes und vertraglich gebundenes Luftfahrtunternehmen zusammen. Dies galt auch im Hinblick auf die erste Entscheidung[66] zur vertraglichen Qualifikation eines Anspruchs auf Verzugszinsen. Demgemäß verdient der BGH jedenfalls in den beiden Ausgangsverfahren ebenso Zuspruch für seine vertragliche Qualifikation[67] der Ansprüche aus der VO. Anstelle der Art. 27 ff. EGBGB ist in gleichgelagerten Sachverhaltsgestaltungen nunmehr auf die Rom I-VO maßgeblich. Sofern sich die Forderung indes allein gegen den faktischen Beförderer richtet, stößt das Etikett vertraglich im Sinne der Rom I-VO sowie die Anwendung ihres Art. 5 Abs. 2[68] jedoch auf Beden-

---

lage, NJW 2009, 1845 ff.; *Mark-Oliver Otto*, Rechtsunkenntnis und Verjährungsbeginn, Versicherungsrecht (VersR) 2009, 760 ff.

[64] *Bundesgerichtshof* (BGH) 10.12.2009, RRa 2010, 90 (91), Rn. 11.

[65] *Bundesgerichtshof* (BGH) 10.12.2009, RRa 2010, 90 (93). Siehe hierzu aber auch *Audiencia Provincial de Barcelona* (Spanien), C-139/11.

[66] *Bundesgerichtshof* (BGH) 12.11.2010, RRa 2010, 34 (36).

[67] Der *Bundesgerichtshof* qualifizierte anfangs die Ansprüche aus der VO als gesetzlich (s. etwa *Bundesgerichtshof* (BGH) 30.04.2009, RRa 2009, 239 (241), Rn. 13 = NJW 2009, 2740 (2741)), gab dieses aber in der Folge auf.

[68] Der BGH hatte in dem Ursprungsverfahren auf Art. 28 EGBGB und in dessen Rahmen auf den Sitz des faktischen und zugleich vertraglich gebundenen Luftbeförderers abgestellt. Gegenüber dem allein ausführenden Luftfahrtunternehmen wird indes Art. 5 Abs. 2 Rom I-VO wohl ausscheiden; siehe hierzu Ferrari a.a.O., Art. 5 Rom I-VO Rn. 37. Zu Art. 5 Abs. 2 Rom I-VO beachte im weiteren Zusam-

ken und erscheint eine Zuordnung zur Rom II-VO[69] naheliegend. Dies gilt erst recht, wenn man im Lichte der vorangehenden Ausführungen für das Europäische Zivilverfahrensrecht in solchen Fallkonstellationen den Gerichtsstand der unerlaubten Handlung in Art. 5 Nr. 3 Brüssel I-VO befürworten sollte. Laut Erwägungsgrund Nr. 7 der Rom I- sowie Nr. 7 der Rom II-VO ist nämlich eine übergreifende harmonische Auslegung[70] der Begriffe vertrag- bzw. außervertragliches Schuldverhältnis geboten. Demzufolge sollten Forderungen allein gegen den faktischen Luftbeförderer, welche auf der VO basieren, jedenfalls im Europäischen Zivilverfahrens- wie Kollisionsrecht übereinstimmend qualifiziert werden. Auslegungszweifel vermag letztlich allein wiederum der EuGH im Wege der Vorabentscheidung auszuräumen.

VII. Widersprüche innerhalb der VO

Auf den ersten Blick scheint ungereimt, dass dem Kunden bei einem drei- (oder sogar zwei-)stündigen Zeitverlust am Zielort womöglich ein Ausgleichsanspruch analog Art. 7 VO zusteht, er indes nach Art. 6 Abs. 1, lit. c) in Verbindung mit Art. 9 VO erst ab einer Verzögerung von vier Stunden Betreuungsleistungen beanspruchen kann. Auflösen lässt sich der Widerspruch wohl unter Hinweis darauf, dass es sich um unterschiedlich geartete Sanktionen handelt, welche zudem einerseits an die abflugbedingte Zeiteinbuße am Ankunftsort, andererseits an den verspäteten Abflug als solchen anknüpfen.

---

menhang *Bundesgerichtshof* (BGH) 20.5.2010 – Xa ZR 68/09, RRa 2010, 225 (226), Rn. 15 ff.

[69] Ob im Wege des Art. 4 Abs. 3 Rom II-VO eine akzessorische Anknüpfung an das Vertragsstatut erfolgen kann, erscheint schon deshalb zweifelhaft, da der Beförderungsvertrag gerade nicht gegenüber dem aus der VO verpflichteten rein tatsächlichen Beförderer besteht.

[70] Siehe in diesem Zusammenhang als Beispiel für einen solchen angestrebten Gleichlauf in der Terminologie die Entscheidung des *Europäischen Gerichtshofs* (EuGH) 7.12.2010, Rs. C-585/08 und C-144/09 *(Pammer/Reederei Karl Schlüter GmbH & Co. KG* und *Hotel Alpenhof GesmbH/Heller)*. Siehe hierzu *Ansgar Staudinger/Björn Steinrötter,* Verfahrens- sowie kollisionsrechtlicher Verbraucherschutz bei Online-Geschäften, EWS 2011, 70.

VIII. Widersprüche mit Blick auf verwandte (zukünftige) Verordnungen

Die Verordnung (EG) Nr. 1371/2007[71] gewährt Kunden im Eisenbahnverkehr bei Verspätungen und Zugausfällen u.a. Fahrpreiserstattungen.[72] Allerdings kann der Kunde laut ihrem Art. 17 bei einer verspäteten Ankunft allein einen pauschalen Anteil der Ticketkosten verlangen. Dies entspricht damit dem im deutschen Werkvertragsrecht bekannten Ansatz der Minderung. Demgegenüber stehen dem Kunden im Luftverkehr nach Art. 7 VO (analog) ticketpreisunabhängige pauschale Ansprüche ohne Nachweis eines konkreten Schadens zu. Wie bereits dargelegt, basiert ein solches Rechtsfolgensystem nicht vornehmlich auf der Kompensation unfreiwilliger Vermögenseinbußen. Vielmehr scheint der Sekundärrechtsgeber die Luftfahrtunternehmer dazu anhalten zu wollen, Annullierungen wie Verspätungen zu meiden, indem er sie abschreckt bzw. fühlbare Sanktionen im Sinne eines Strafschadensersatzes androht. Die pauschalen Beträge von 250/400/600 Euro je nach Flugentfernung können dabei das Entgelt für den Flugschein um ein Vielfaches übersteigen. Ungereimt erscheint überdies, dass die pauschalen auf den bei der Abfassung der VO ermittelten durchschnittlichen Flugpreisen basieren, derart versteinerte Beträge indes mit den aktuellen Marktbedingungen nicht übereinstimmen müssen.[73]

Abweichungen der Modelle ergeben sich ferner etwa beim Vergleich der Hilfe- bzw. Betreuungsleistungen. So sind diese nur nach der VO im Flugverkehr keinem Entlastungstatbestand unterworfen. Dies wird virulent in den Fällen der Vulkanaschewolke.[74] Hiervon weicht die Rechtslage nach der Verordnung (EG) Nr. 1371/2007[75] ab. Ferner statuiert die VO lediglich Mindestrechte, so dass der Kunde etwa aus dem nationalen Recht einen weitergehenden Schadensersatz geltend machen kann. Eine

---

[71] Hierzu: *Ansgar Staudinger*, in: Stephan Keiler/Brigitte Stangl/Ilona Pezenka (Hrsg.), Reiserecht (2008), S. 141 ff.

[72] Dazu im Einzelnen *Tonner*, VuR 2010, 209 (212 ff.).

[73] Kritisch auch *Edgar Isermann*, Flugverspätungen werden „sanktioniert" – Bahnverspätungen werden „entschädigt", Editorial RRa 2010, 249.

[74] Hierzu AG Rüsselsheim 11.1.2011 – 3 C 1698/10 (32), RRa 2011, 93.

[75] Hierzu sowie zum Folgenden siehe *Ansgar Staudinger*, Zweifelsfragen der Verordnung (EG) Nr. 1371/2007 des Europäischen Parlaments und des Rates vom 23.10.2007 über die Rechte und Pflichten der Fahrgäste im Eisenbahnverkehr, Europäische Zeitschrift für Wirtschaftsrecht (EuZW) 2008, 751 (754 f.); siehe im Übrigen die Angaben bei *Ansgar Staudinger*, in: Ansgar Staudinger, § 651a–§ 651m BGB, Neubearbeitung 2011, Vorbemerkungen zu §§ 651 c-g Rn. 46.

Anrechnung erfolgt dabei laut Art. 12 Abs. 1 der VO. Hingegen wird der parallele Sekundärrechtsakt im Bahnverkehr teils als abschließend bewertet.[76] Weitere Ungereimtheiten drohen im Schiffsverkehr sowie hinsichtlich der geplanten Verordnung über Fahrgastrechte im Kraftomnibusverkehr. Im ersten Fall gewährt der Sekundärrechtsgeber laut Art. 19 der Verordnung (EU) Nr. 1177/2010 den Kunden bei verspäteter Ankunft allein Fahrpreisnachlässe. Im Busverkehr wird bei der Ankunftsverspätung auf supranationaler Ebene wohl ebenso wenig eine pauschalierte, ticketpreisunabhängige und insofern vergleichbare Entschädigung wie im Luftverkehr vorgeschrieben.

Sicherlich hat der Unionsgesetzgeber eine Einschätzungsprärogative. Doch welche Sachgründe sollen etwa die gravierenden Unterschiede zwischen Luft- und Bahnverkehr rechtfertigen? Allein unterschiedliche Faktoren der Preisbildung reichen zur Legitimation nicht aus. Gerade im Lichte der abweichenden Modelle muss der Sekundärrechtsgeber vielmehr eingehend begründen, weshalb etwa ein ticketpreisunabhängiges pauschales Ausgleichssystem bei „Verspätungen" allein im Luftverkehr verhältnismäßig erscheint, und zwar sogar zu Lasten eines rein faktischen Beförderers, der dem Kunden nicht einmal als Vertragspartner gegenübersteht. Dies gilt nicht minder in Bezug auf die Unterstützungs- und Betreuungsleistungen, welche selbst bei außergewöhnlichen Umständen von solchen „Dritten" zu tragen sind, ohne einen konkreten Höchstbetrag vorzusehen. In der Gesamtschau erscheinen die zuvor genannten Sanktionen gerade bei Verspätungen im Lichte der übrigen Sekundärrechtsakte insbesondere rein ausführenden Luftfahrtunternehmen gegenüber als eine Ungleichbehandlung und als ein überzogener Eingriff in die Dienstleistungsfreiheit. Hiermit einher gehen in zweifacher Weise Wettbewerbsverzerrungen. So unterliegen Luftfahrtunternehmen mit Sitz außerhalb des Binnenmarkts nicht uneingeschränkt der VO im Luftverkehr; anders hingegen ihre europäischen Konkurrenten. Innerhalb des Binnenmarktes ergibt sich dann beispielsweise gerade im Fernverkehr ein weiterer Wettbewerbsnachteil zwischen Bahn- und Luftfahrtunternehmen.

---

[76] Vgl. die Ausführungen bei *Staudinger*, in: Staudinger, § 651a–§ 651m BGB, Neubearbeitung 2011, Vorbemerkungen zu §§ 651 c-g Rn. 46.

IX. Widersprüche mit Blick auf die Einstandspflicht des Pauschalreiseveranstalters

Einem Kunden steht bei der Nur-Luftbeförderung schon für den Fall einer Abflug- und daraus resultierenden mindestens drei- (bzw. zwei-) stündigen Ankunftsverspätung ein pauschalierter Ausgleich nach der VO zu, und zwar sogar gegen den faktischen Luftbeförderer. Demgegenüber soll ein Pauschalreisetourist nach bislang vorherrschender Ansicht[77] in Deutschland verspätete Beförderungen zu seinem Urlaubsdomizil bzw. zurück in das Ausgangsland von mehr als vier bis acht Stunden als bloße Unannehmlichkeit hinnehmen, ohne in den Genuss einer Minderung des Reisepreises gegenüber seinem Veranstalter als Vertragspartner zu gelangen. Im Ergebnis droht damit der Widerspruch, dass unter Umständen bei vergleichbarer „Leistungsstörung" der Reiseveranstalter als Vertragspartner in geringerem Umfange einstehen muss als das ausführende und vertraglich nicht gebundene Luftfahrtunternehmen. Anders gewendet: Es erscheint ungereimt, dass der Reiseveranstalter angeblich eine mangelfreie Reise erbringen soll, indes derselbe Sachverhalt erhebliche Forderungen gegenüber einem Dritten auslöst. Aus der VO im Luftverkehr folgt vielmehr, von welcher Zeitschwelle etwa bei Abflug- und Ankunftsverspätung die Grenze der sanktionslosen Unannehmlichkeit überschritten ist. Diese Wertung sollte man sim Wege übergreifender systematischer Auslegung in den Begriff des Mangels der Pauschalreiserichtlinie als Mindeststandard hineinlesen. Hierfür spricht zum einen, dass die VO selbst in ihrem Art. 2 lit. d), Art. 8 Abs. 2 auf diesen Rechtsakt Bezug nimmt. Zum anderen vermeidet die Übertragung der Erheblichkeitsschwelle aus der VO auf die andere Richtlinie Wertungswidersprüche[78] und schafft ein vergleichbares nicht zu unterschreitendes Schutzniveau. Der BGH[79] hatte zwar in der Vergangenheit eine dahingehende Vorlagepflicht am 7.10.2008 abgelehnt. In dem Anlassstreit ging es allerdings auf der Sachrechtsebene um § 651e Abs. 1 BGB und mithin um die Kündigung wegen eines erheblichen Mangels. Nach Ansicht der Revisionsinstanz könne nicht automatisch von einer fünfstündigen Verspätung im Sinne der VO auf eine erhebliche Beeinträchtigung geschlossen werden. Hiervon zu unterscheiden ist aber die Abgrenzung der

---

[77] Siehe dazu *Staudinger/Schürmann*, NJW 2010, 2571 (2775). *Ansgar Staudinger/Dominik Schürmann*, Pauschalreise-, Luftverkehrs- sowie Eisenbahnrecht – Rechtsprechung aus dem Jahr 2008/2009 sowie aktuelle Entwicklungen, NJW 2009, 2788 (2789 f.).

[78] Hierzu *Staudinger*, RRa 2010, 10 (13 f.).

[79] *Bundesgerichtshof* (BGH) 7.10.2008 – X ZR 37/08, RRa 2009, 40 (42 f.), Rn. 22.

hinzunehmenden Unannehmlichkeit vom Mangel. Der EuGH ist demnach dahin um Vorabentscheidung anzurufen, ob die Schwellenwerte der VO in die Pauschalreiserichtlinie insofern ausstrahlen, als sie das Vorliegen eines Mangels begründen. Diese Frage ist offen und ihre Antwort im Nachgang zur Rechtssache *Sturgeon* nicht im Sinne der acte-claire-Doktrin auf der Hand liegend. Sollte der Gerichtshof einen Gleichlauf bejahen, wäre wiederum das jeweilige inländische Umsetzungsrecht wie etwa die §§ 651a ff. BGB richtlinienkonform auszulegen. Mit der Vorlageentscheidung ginge demzufolge der Gewinn an Rechtssicherheit und -einheit im Binnenmarkt einher. Müsste nun wie in der VO auch im deutschen Pauschalreiserecht von einem Mangel ausgegangen werden, bedeutete dies im Ergebnis keinen fundamentalen Bruch. Denn in der Vergangenheit hatten bereits einige Spruchkörper[80] ihre Entscheidungen zu den §§ 651a ff. BGB mit Wertungen der VO unterfüttert oder vergleichbare Zeitspannen zugrunde gelegt.

Ungeachtet der harmonischen Auslegung von Pauschalreiserichtlinie und VO bzw. der richtlinienkonformen Interpretation der §§ 651a ff. BGB obliegt den nationalen Gerichten weiterhin eine Feinsteuerung, um dem Charakter der Pauschalreise als Bündel Rechnung zu tragen. So bleibt es allein den inländischen Gerichten vorbehalten, anhand der Einzelfallumstände etwa die Minderungsquote festzulegen oder zu bestimmen, ob in der Gesamtschau die verspätete Beförderung als ein Baustein des Pakets zu einem erheblichen Reisemangel im Sinne des § 651e Abs. 1 BGB führt. Eine solche Einzelfallkasuistik ist nicht Aufgabe des EuGH. Erst recht führt die harmonische Auslegung der VO und der Pauschalreiserichtlinie nur insofern zu einem Gleichlauf, dass dieselbe Leistungsstörung zumindest dem Grunde nach als Mangel auf der Rechtsfolgenseite eine Sanktion auslöst. Selbst wenn aber etwa der Begriff des Mangels im Sinne des Harmonisierungsinstruments bzw. kraft richtlinienkonformer Auslegung in den §§ 651a ff. BGB bejaht wird, ist hiervon etwa die Schadensersatzpflicht des Reiseveranstalters zu unterscheiden. So muss der Kunde für § 651f Abs. 1 über den Mangel in concreto einen Schaden[81] nachweisen und kann sich der Reiseveranstalter unter Umständen exculpieren.

Eine weitere Ungereimtheit besteht derzeit mit Blick auf die Betreuung und Unterstützung, welche ein nur faktisches Luftfahrtunternehmen nach der VO einem Kunden gegenüber selbst beim Vorliegen außergewöhnlicher

---

[80] Siehe etwa *LG Köln*, 18.11.2008 – 11 S 497/07; *AG Duisburg*, 11.1.2006 – 73 C 4598/05, RRa 2006, 132.
[81] *Europäischer Gerichtshof* (EuGH), Rs. C-32/10, ABlEG Nr. C 100 v. 17.4.2010, S. 18.

Umstände wie etwa der Vulkanaschewolke[82] schuldet. Denn ein Reiseveranstalter ist nach § 651j Abs. 1 und 2 BGB, obschon er Vertragspartner des Kunden ist, ihm gegenüber gerade nicht dazu verpflichtet, im Nachgang zur Kündigung wegen höherer Gewalt Hotel- und Verpflegungskosten zu tragen.[83]

X. Ergebnis

Die sicherlich teils kritik- und korrekturbedürftige Judikatur des Europäischen Gerichtshofs in der Rechtssache *Sturgeon u.a.* verschafft einer Vielzahl von Kunden – selbst bei Sachverhalten vor dem Stichtag der Entscheidung – pauschalierte Ansprüche analog Art. 7 VO gegen vertragliche wie faktische Luftbeförderer. Voraussetzung ist das Vorliegen einer streckenabhängigen Abflugverspätung i. S. v. Art. 6 Abs. 1, lit. a) bis c) VO, das mindestens zweistündige verspätete Eintreffen am Zielort sowie die fehlende Entlastung analog Art. 5 Abs. 3 VO. Die Höhe des Ausgleichsanspruchs und eine etwaige Kürzung richten sich entfernungsabhängig nach Art. 7 Abs. 1 und 2 VO analog.

Die Vorlageentscheidung des Europäischen Gerichtshofs zeigt darüber hinaus, dass der Unionsgesetzgeber in der Pflicht ist, die Lücken der Verordnung sinnstiftend zu schließen, andernfalls bleibt es bei der Flickschusterei der Judikative. Eine Reform muss allerdings verwandte Sekundärrechtsakte mit in den Blick nehmen. Denn der europäischen Legislative obliegt die Aufgabe, ein in sich widerspruchsfreies System des Reiserechts zu schaffen. Es gilt, Regulierungsstandards bei Leistungsstörungen zu entwickeln, welche den Unterschieden und Gemeinsamkeiten bei den einzelnen Transportmitteln ebenso Rechnung tragen wie den Grundzügen eines Europäischen Zivilrechts bis hin zum Verhältnismäßigkeitsprinzip. Dass derartige Modelle verkehrsträgerübergreifend gestaltet werden müssen, dient nicht nur dem Wohl des Kunden, der häufig in einer Reisekette wie bei Rail & Fly, verschiedene Transportmittel nutzt, sondern auch dem Ziel eines fairen Wettbewerbs zwischen allen konkurrierenden Akteuren. Es bleibt abzuwarten, welche Ergebnisse das vom EU-Verkehrskommissar *Tajani* eröffnete Konsultationsverfahren zur Novellierung der VO im

---

[82] Beachte dazu *AG Rüsselsheim* 11.1.2011 – 3 C 1698/10 (32), RRa 2011, 93; *Dublin Metropolitan District Court* (Irland), C-12/11, RRa 2011, 148; anders bei Ansprüchen gegen den Reiseveranstalter, *AG Rostock* 4.2.2011 – 47 C 410/10, RRa 2011, 74.

[83] *Staudinger*, in: Staudinger, a.a.O., Vorbemerkungen zu §§ 651 j Rn. 38.

Luftverkehr bringt. Eine Anstoßfunktion für Legislativakte auf nationaler wie supranationaler Ebene mag sicherlich auch den Empfehlungen des 48. Verkehrsgerichtstages vom 27. bis 29.1.2010 in Goslar zukommen. Darin wird der europäische Gesetzgeber aufgefordert, bei der Fortschreibung der Ansprüche von Reisenden sachlich nicht gerechtfertigte Unterschiede zu beseitigen, und zwar insbesondere bei der pauschalen Entschädigung für Verspätungen. Reformbedürftig erscheinen aber in der VO nicht nur der Gleichlauf von Annullierung und Verspätung bei den Sanktionen sowie ticketpreisunabhängige Pauschalen ohne konkreten Nachweises eines Schadens, sondern auch der Umfang der geschuldeten Unterstützungs- und Betreuungsleistungen, vor allem rein ausführenden Beförderern gegenüber etwa in Fällen außergewöhnlicher Wetterlagen.

Gerade im Reiserecht stellen Leistungsstörungen ein Massenphänomen mit erheblicher Standardisierung der Sachverhalte dar. Vielfach handelt es sich um Bagatellstreitigkeiten. Angesichts dessen bleibt schließlich die effektive außergerichtliche Streitbeilegung ein Desiderat. Bei Problemen mit Verkehrsbetrieben kann seit dem 1.12.2009 die „Schlichtungsstelle für den öffentlichen Personenverkehr" (söp) unter der Leitung von PräsOLG a. D. *Edgar Isermann* zu Rate gezogen werden. Zudem sieht die Koalitionsvereinbarung der amtierenden Bundesregierung neben der Überprüfung und eventuellen Verbesserung der Rechte von Fluggästen und Bahnkunden die gesetzliche Verankerung einer unabhängigen, übergreifenden Schlichtungsstelle für die Verkehrsträger Bus, Bahn, Flug und Schiff vor.[84] Formal spricht hierfür, dass bei allen Unterschieden die Rechtsakte, aus denen Kunden Ansprüche ableiten können, eben auch zum Teil übereinstimmen und in der Zukunft in noch größerem Maße parallele Strukturen aufweisen sollten. Aus dem Blickwinkel der Unternehmer hat ein übergreifendes Modell der Schlichtung den Vorteil der Kostenersparnis und beugt einer Wettbewerbsverzerrung vor, da ansonsten vergleichbare Entlastungstatbestände unterschiedlich ausgelegt und angewendet werden könnten. Hinzu kommt, dass ein Passagier gerade bei einer Reisekette mit mehreren Beförderungsmitteln womöglich gezwungen wäre, sich an verschiedene Stellen zu wenden. Unabhängig von einer solchen zuvor skizzierten Ideallösung erscheint jedenfalls die Etablierung einer Schlichtung im Luftverkehr als dringend notwendiger erster Schritt, möglichst unter Einbeziehung auch von in anderen Mitgliedstaaten ansässigen Luftfahrtunternehmen. Sollte es an besserer Einsicht auf Seiten der Beförderer fehlen, ist letzten Endes die nationale Legislative gefordert.

---

[84] Rn. 1936 ff. bzw. 1893 ff. des Koalitionsvertrags, abrufbar unter: http://Politikbeobachter.eu/wp-content/uploads/2009/10/koalitionsvertrag.pdf.

Part III
Private versus Public Enforcement

Private Losses in European Competition Law: Public or Private Enforcement?

Petra Pohlmann

I. Introduction

One of the most controversial subjects in competition law in Europe is the right balance of public and private enforcement. After the recent elections in the United States discussions about a changed climate in antitrust enforcement were calmed by the American Antitrust Institute. The elections, so the Institute predicted, would have relatively little impact on the enforcement of the antitrust laws. One of the reasons for this view was that enforcement by private plaintiffs would continue to account for more than 95 percent of antitrust cases.

In Europe we approach the field of enforcement from the other side. The law of the Member States does not have a private enforcement tradition that can be compared to the US tradition. It was only a decade ago that European law itself rediscovered[1] the importance of private enforcement, driven particularly by the Court of Justice.

The question we want to discuss today is how public and private enforcement instruments should be assessed with regard to private losses. I will pick out three aspects.

---

[1] In the 1960s the Commission published a study on private damage claims (Commission, La réparation des conséquences dommageables d'une violation des articles 85 et 86 du traité instituant la CEE, collection études, Serie concurrence no. 1, 1966, 7 ff.), but did not draw conclusions from its results *(Wolfgang Wurmnest,* Schadensersatz wegen Verletzung des EU-Kartellrechts – Grundfragen und Entwicklungslinien, 2010, www.jura.unihannover.de/fileadmin/fakultaet/Institute/INTIF/Wurmnest/Schadensersatz_wegen_Verletzung_des_EU_KartR.pdf, to appear in print in: *Oliver Remien* (ed.), Schadensersatz im europäischen Privat- und Wirtschaftsrecht, 2011).

II. Public versus private enforcement with regard to damages

I will start with the advantages and disadvantages of both tracks of enforcement, with particular reference to private losses.

Means of public enforcement are finding and terminating infringements, fines, criminal penalties, director disqualification, skimming off of the benefits and damage claims in favour of private parties. Means of private enforcement are voidness as a means of defence, and – as offensive means – actions for certain behaviours, including cease-and-desist proceedings, skimming off of the benefits and damage claims.

Accordingly both tool boxes, the public and the private, have two compartments that overlap: first, private damage claims on the one hand and public damage claims in favour of private parties on the other, and second, the skimming off of the benefits either in favour of private parties or in favour of the exchequer. These four instruments will be examined more closely.

Both enforcement regimes have their pros and cons. Private enforcement is not politically influenced and thus not exposed to rent-seeking. It enhances private market players' awareness of competition law, makes use of the specific market knowledge of private claimants[2] and is a necessary element of a market economy governed by competition.[3] At the same time it deters undertakings from infringing competition law. But it does not constitute a systematic, methodic approach. As private parties will choose the stony path to court only if they stand to gain more than they have to pay,[4] its success depends on the circumstances, e.g. the rules on civil procedure or the relationship between the parties, particularly their economic dependence.

Public enforcement offers better methods of investigation and detection of infringements. The costs of information and transaction are lower than in private enforcement, amongst other things because more specialized units decide. Further, a consistent competition policy is possible, which entails

---

[2] *Gerhard Wagner*, German Working Papers in Law and Economics, 2007, Paper 18, p. 2.
[3] The latter aspect is stressed by *Roman Guski*, Zeitschrift für Wettbewerbsrecht (ZWeR) 2010, 278, 302.
[4] *Hans-Wilhelm Krüger*, Öffentliche und private Durchsetzung des Kartellverbots von Art. 81 EG, 2007, p. 203.

better deterrence.[5] Public enforcement can also respond flexibly to changing circumstances.[6]

The other side of the coin is that the political dimension leads to legal uncertainty. Political changes may trigger changes in competition law enforcement. However, in the EU competition law is less influenced by politics than in the US, so this aspect might be disregarded. But public enforcement might be influenced by public opinion,[7] and the risk of rent-seeking exists. Another disadvantage is that market participants are not involved. As a consequence, awareness of competition law might be low.

Ultimately, both enforcement tracks should be combined to realize their positive effects and at the same time to compensate, at least partly, for their respective shortcomings.

Damage claims and skimming off of the benefits as means of enforcement bring – besides the pros and cons mentioned – specific risks and disadvantages. Private damage claims from individuals or representatives may create the dreaded "litigation culture" or "American conditions", the beneficiaries being above all the lawyers. Private claims may entail strategic or even abusive actions and have the potential for over-deterrence – hindering undertakings from taking entrepreneurial chances. Further, they have the potential for over-compensation[8] and endanger public enforcement strategies, particularly leniency programs. In addition, private enforcement brings about higher social costs[9] and investment in the civil court system might be necessary.[10]

These risks can be largely avoided by a clever design of the rules for private damage claims. Who can raise claims? What damages can be claimed for? Should the defendant be able to invoke the passing on defence?[11] The

---

[5] Hans-Wilhelm Krüger, Öffentliche und private Durchsetzung des Kartellverbots von Art. 81 EG, 2007, p. 260.
[6] Hans-Wilhelm Krüger, Öffentliche und private Durchsetzung des Kartellverbots von Art. 81 EG, 2007, p. 193 et seqq.
[7] Alexander Kruß, Kartellschaden und Verbraucherschutz, 2010, p. 270.
[8] Jeroen Kortmann/Christof Swaak, (2009) 7 European Competition Law Review (ECLR) 340, 344-347.
[9] Hans-Wilhelm Krüger, Öffentliche und private Durchsetzung des Kartellverbots von Art. 81 EG, 2007, p. 307 et seq.
[10] Kortmann/Swaak, (2009) 7 ECLR 340, 347.
[11] Justus Haucap/Torben Stühmeyer, Wirtschaft und Wettbewerb (WuW) 2008, 413, 421 et seqq.; Hans-Georg Kamann/Stefan Ohlhoff, ZWeR 2010, 303 et seqq.; Erik Kießling, Gewerblicher Rechtsschutz und Urheberrecht (GRUR) 2009, 733 et seqq.; Michael Reich, WuW 2008, 1046 et seqq.

answers to these questions decide how far the abovementioned risks will occur.[12] I will come back to this aspect in a moment. But one point should already be made clear: private claims should include claims of representatives as trade or consumer associations. This is, as the famous replica football shirts case in the UK showed, the only way to pay compensation for small damages spread among a large number of people.

Damage claims by state bodies on behalf of consumers are possible for instance in the UK and in Sweden, and were proposed in the draft regulation that was discussed within the competition community after the white paper, but never published. These claims have all the disadvantages of public enforcement that I have already mentioned. In addition, they do not fall within the scope of state functions because the state only has to provide means to enforce private rights, but does not have to enforce private rights itself. It must be added that public claims on behalf of consumers do not have the advantages of private claims. Nor do they open another chance for enforcement, as they will usually be follow-on claims as well. But one point might speak in their favour: the danger of over-compensation and over-deterrence as well as the risk for leniency programs might be lower, because it is easier to coordinate the different enforcement tools within the state.

Public skimming off of the benefits does not lead to compensation for the private claimant, but stops halfway. The benefits the infringer earns are in many cases, particularly cartel cases, the reverse of the damage the other party suffers. When the competition authority skims them off, the infringer is penalized, but the injured party gains nothing. In Germany we have public and private skimming off. The private form entitles trade associations to skim off, paradoxically in favour of the federal budget. Neither instrument has ever been used. Skimming off of the benefits in favour of the injured party would detach the legal consequences from the idea of compensation if the benefits were distributed without regard to the damage caused. What remains, and may be helpful, is damage quantification with the help of the infringer's benefits, as sec. 33 p. 3, 3 of the German Cartel Code stipulates.

Ultimately, a combination of private and public enforcement with regard to losses occurred is not convincing. Public skimming off of the benefits and public claims for private damages cannot replace and should not amend private remedies. For private losses private enforcement is the right option, but not in the form of skimming off.

---

[12] Cf. *Jürgen Beninca*, WuW 2004, 604-608; *Joachim Bornkamm*, GRUR 2010, 501-506; *Friedrich Wenzel Bulst*, Zeitschrift für europäisches Privatrecht (ZEuP) 2008, 178-195; *Johannes Dittrich*, GRUR 2009, 123-127.

Theses (1):
- Private claims for damages are an indispensable element of competition law enforcement.
- They should be accompanied by the possibility of non-profit consumer and trade organizations bringing a representative action for damages on behalf of the injured parties.
- State bodies should not be entitled to bring such action.
- Public and private skimming off of the benefits should not be used as an enforcement measure.

III. Which way should Europe go: pleading for competition of competition law systems

Our analysis refers to a typical one-dimensional competition law regime so far. In the EU the situation is more complex, however. Private enforcement lies in the hands of the Member States while public enforcement takes place on both levels. It is important to realize that any European statutory provision for private claims, be it a directive or a regulation, is to be applied by the Member States only. In the field of private enforcement any adoption of legal concepts from the US is adoption at the expense of third parties, the Member States. Thus within the EU, having realized that private enforcement is a necessary tool, we have to ask whether the EU should create new rules for these claims or whether this should be left to the Member States.

From my point of view the time has not yet come to harmonize this field of law. Assuming that the EU had a mandate to harmonize here – which is questionable[13] – it is too early to act in any case. There are other things on the to-do list that need prior attention.

The Commission must ascertain that its proposals do not disregard substantial differences between the tort law systems. The Ashurst study on private claims does not go deep enough to serve as a basis. The Commission must make sure that the system it proposes is consistent in itself and that its implementation does not endanger its own consistency and that of the national systems. Substantial matters such as the aim of tort law but also details such as limitation periods[14] have to be considered.

---

[13] Committee on Economic and Monetary Affairs, Report on the White Paper on damages actions for breach of the EC antitrust rules (2008/2154(INI)), A6-0123/2009, p. 9.

[14] *Kortmann/Swaak,* (2009) 7 ECLR 340, 347-349.

The Commission must also take the institutional circumstances into account. Procedural rules, the structure of the whole enforcement system, and its actors, differ in the individual Member States.

The reluctant response of the Member States to the EC white paper shows that it is too early to harmonize private enforcement. And the fact that the draft regulation the Commission developed from the white paper died an inglorious death after being leaked within the competition law community affirms this. A certain period of competition between the competition law systems of the Member States will help to find solutions. Five years is the minimum, because civil cases will take some time to pass all the levels of jurisdiction.

Theses (2):
- The EU should not take measures to harmonize private enforcement in the near future.
- There should be at least five years during which the competition law systems of the Member States should be developed according to the requirements of the Courage and Manfredi judgments.

IV. Quantification of antitrust damages: the Oxera study and lessons to learn

Shortly after the failure of Neelie Kroes' directive on private enforcement, a study on antitrust damages was published. It raised hopes that the Commission has now chosen the right path. As one of the obstacles of private enforcement is the uncertainty over the quantification of the harm suffered, the EU Commission thought it necessary to shed some light on this dark chapter of enforcement. The Commission wants to learn more about private enforcement in the Member States. On behalf of the Commission, Oxera, an independent economic consultant, published a report on quantifying antitrust damages a year ago.

But why did the Commission start with the quantification of damages? At first sight it might be surprising that the Commission stopped the approach it took in the draft directive, humbly retreating now to non-binding guidance for the calculation of damages. But the reason becomes clear if we read the Oxera report: the report has a mainly economic approach. It does not – or only marginally – take into account the different national laws, but focuses on economic methods to quantify damages. Some of these methods are simple, some are more sophisticated and some are really complicated, based on Industrial Organisation models, and it is hard to imagine a civil court applying them. Nevertheless, this economic approach is, compared to an assessment of 27 legal systems and their rules on the quantification of damages, an easy way for the Commission to do something for private enforcement, because economic science is the same everywhere in the EU.

The report is a step in the right direction. It starts from the situation in the Member States, gives some important economic insights and help,[15] and assembles more than 20 cases from different Member States. But for some reasons I am not very happy with it.

The first is that it is too economic, and leads to a reliance on mathematics and economics that is not appropriate when it comes to applying law.[16] It creates the illusion that a certain sum of damage can be calculated. But this will seldom be the case. The recent experiences with German case law show that the courts can deal with the calculation of damages only by using sec. 287 of the Civil Procedure Code which allows the damage to be estimated,[17] and by relying on so-called prima facie evidence that allows the gap of knowledge to be bridged when events typically entail certain damages.

The second shortcoming in the report is that it does not offer an in-depth-analysis of procedural instruments that help to quantify damages like the procedural rules on the distribution of burden of proof and the required level of proof mentioned earlier. As a consequence it misleads the reader, conveying the impression that all these complicated economic methods have to be applied.

The third failing is that the report is too schematic. Hardcore cartels, so it says, cause mainly overcharge damages. Hence there is not a word about lost profit in cartel cases, although this may play an important role.

Theses (3):
- The Oxera report is a step in the right direction, because it does not aim at imposing rules on the Member States but tries to develop rules bottom up from the Member States.
- The report nevertheless falls short of an in-depth-analysis of the legal background, particularly of the law of civil procedure, by focusing on economic methods of quantification of damages.

---

[15] Therefore some authors appreciate it, *Carlos Lapuerta/Richard Caldwell/Dan Harris,* (2010) Journal of European Competition Law & Practice 438-443.
[16] See also *Bruno Augustin,* (2010) Competiton Law Insight 14-16.
[17] Cf. *Gerhard Wagner,* German Working Papers in Law and Economics, 2007, Paper 18, p. 14, who advocates simple rules for the estimation of damages.

Petra Pohlmann

The Law of Damages and Competition Law: Bien étonnés de se trouver ensemble?

Willem H. van Boom

I. Introduction

One of the many French influences on Dutch society is the continued use in Dutch parlance of the expression "Bien étonnés de se trouver ensemble". This expression is used to denote a situation in which unlikely companions much to their own surprise find themselves having the same intentions, goals or interests. Are competition law and the law of damages such unlikely companions? In this contribution, I sketch the framework of the law of damages and then try to identify the touch points – if any – between the law of damages and (European) competition law.

First, a brief introduction of the actors and issues involved in breach of competition law may help clarify some points of definition. In the following, I will concentrate on simple horizontal anti-competitive practices such as price fixing and exclusionary practices. In a simple horizontal price cartel, competitors agree to keep prices at a certain level. Direct and indirect purchasers may suffer overcharge harm, i.e., a higher price than they would have had to pay if no cartel had existed. Possibly, end-users (consumers) suffer economic loss as well if the high prices are passed on through the chain. As far as exclusionary practices are concerned, existing competitors may be forced out of the market or seriously hindered in developing or sustaining their market share as a consequence of collusion to exclude. The excluded competitors may suffer pure economic loss (loss of market share, or even insolvency) as a result. This may in turn lead to a reduction in competition and therefore to higher prices and/or reduction of choice or quality for direct and indirect purchasers down the chain.

National tort law systems may first want to address the issue whether any of the injured parties involved in these cases will find a court willing to hear their case. In some legal systems, this is dealt with according to procedural rules of *standing*, while in others the key question (in tort law rather than in procedure) is whether the statutory duty breached by the infringers was owed vis-à-vis the current claimant. In either case, the ECJ

Manfredi decision (see infra III.) prescribes that a generous rule of standing has to be applied.

A particular issue in the law of damages is the *passing-on* defence. We will deal with this defence at a later stage; for now it suffices to give a brief description of the problem. If a direct purchaser would claim compensation for the overcharge caused by the cartel, the economic conditions may be such that the overcharge was in fact passed on to indirect purchasers. If that is true, then the direct purchaser will not have suffered any damage. The passing-on defence complicates the individual position of both direct and indirect purchasers and end-users.

So far, the actors were introduced and some of the definitions were explained. Now it is time to address some of the complications that arise as soon as the aforementioned 'unlikely companions' meet. The analysis that follows will be mostly abstract and isolated from real-life law. The reason for this is simply that the laws of damages in European legal systems differ extensively. By slightly ignoring this crucial point – which obviously is by no means a detail to be overlooked – I can largely ignore the question what we consider to be 'the' law of damages in European private law. As Rodger rightly notes, 'the most obvious practical dilemma is the appropriate ascertainment of damages'.[1] A comprehensive pan-European definition of what constitutes damage in competition cases and how it should be quantified, is absent.[2] Admittedly, in some legal systems the law of damages is considered to be part of the general (codified) principles of private law, in others there is no unified concept of damages and there are in fact several 'laws' of damages. These differences may be relevant when policymakers try to dovetail European competition law with national laws of damages. For instance, in those legal systems that operate a unitary concept of the law of damages, the functions and goals of damages may be more easily adjusted to the goals of compensation as set out by European law while in others breach of competition law may lead to the application of a specific set of rules on damages.

---

[1] B. Rodger, Private Enforcement and the Enterprise Act: An Exemplary System of Awarding Damages?, (2003) European Competition Law Review (E.C.L.R.) 112.

[2] Generally on the differences between the legal systems, see *D. Waelbroeck et al.*, Study on the conditions of claims for damages in case of infringement of EC competition rules – Comparative report, Brussels 2004.

II. Taxonomy of remedies in private law

Before turning to damage caused by competition law infringements and the legal aspects of compensating such damage, it may be useful to distinguish between several remedies in private law and the functions these perform. In my opinion, remedies in the law of obligations can be subdivided into prospective remedies, retrospective remedies and vindicatory remedies.[3] Any of these three remedies may well be operated in a given legal system by individuals or at an aggregate level by groups, a voluntary or compulsory representative or even by some state-appointed representatives (e.g., a public officer 'Ombudsman') for the benefit of multiple affected individuals and businesses.

Prospective are those remedies that aim at preventing (further) harm and may include mandatory and prohibitory injunctions in civil procedure.[4] As such, similar goals are served with public authority powers to order cessation and compliance ('command and control' orders) in the public interest. Naturally, prospective civil and public law remedies may differ principally as far as the interest underlying the respective remedies is concerned (private vs. public) but from the viewpoint of compliance with substantive law the differences may well be less accentuated. Fines and imprisonment of directors under criminal law or administrative law may have a prospective function as well. By fining or incarcerating the perpetrators after the event, the State aims at incentivizing potential infringers into abstaining from competition law infringements *(ex ante)*. This is not to say that criminal or administrative sanctions with a punitive element cannot be ascribed other functions as well; the functions of punitive sanctions are in fact manifold. Nevertheless, one of the functions of punishment through fining may be the prevention of the infringement in the first place. Thus, a prospective element can be discerned. The same is true of punitive damages (exemplary damages) in private law but since the role of this type of damages is far from compensatory, it seems to be far removed from the European legal culture (at this moment in time, that is).

---

[3] Note that the word 'remedy' is understood here to have a neutral meaning of and not to denote the 'actionable at law vs. equitable remedy' dichotomy in the common law jurisdictions.

[4] For the sake of simplicity I will not include the debate on whether injunctions are in fact part of the law of obligations or 'merely' a procedural tool belonging to the realm of civil procedure. On that debate, see, eg, W. *Van Boom*, Comparative notes on injunction and wrongful risk-taking, (2010) 17 Maastricht Journal of European and Comparative Law 10 ff.

Retrospective are those remedies that aim at putting things right. In the law of damages, the compensation of losses suffered subject to the principle of 'full compensation' is prototypical of the retrospective remedies. In principle, compensatory damages are harm-based damages. However, next to these harm-based damages, there are also gain-based damages which are subject to the paradigm of 'restitutio in integrum'. This latter category of damages do not concentrate on the losses suffered by the injured party but on the gains (profits) accrued by the infringer(s). By allowing a private action for skimming-off (disgorgement of profits) instead of or even in addition to claims for harm-based damages, a legal system would operate a two-faced system of retrospective remedies. Restorative injunction is also a remedy with a retrospective focus: the defendant is ordered to undo what he did and to bring the claimant into the position he would have been but for the infringement. In public law, retrospective remedies are less frequently found than in private law.

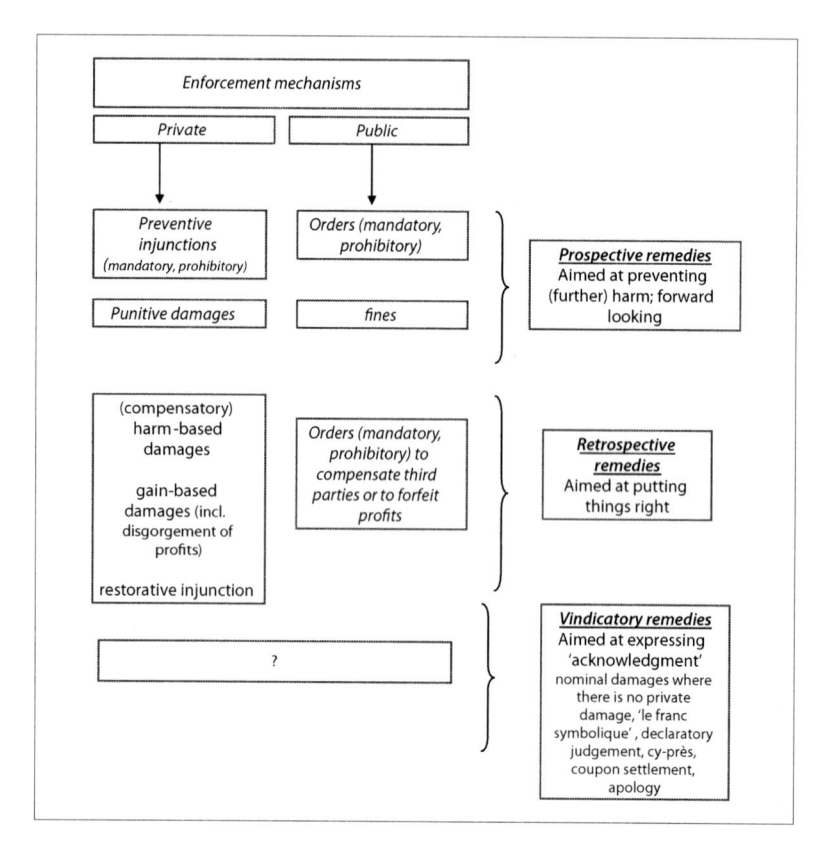

```
                    Enforcement mechanisms
                    ┌──────────┬──────────┐
                    Private              Public
                       │                    │
                       ▼                    ▼
              ┌─────────────────┐  ┌─────────────────┐
              │   Preventive    │  │Orders (mandatory,│ ⎫   ┌─────────────────────┐
              │   injunctions   │  │   prohibitory)  │ ⎬   │Prospective remedies │
              │(mandatory,      │  │                 │ ⎭   │Aimed at preventing  │
              │ prohibitory)    │  ├─────────────────┤     │(further) harm; forward│
              ├─────────────────┤  │     fines       │     │      looking        │
              │Punitive damages │  │                 │     └─────────────────────┘
              └─────────────────┘  └─────────────────┘

              ┌─────────────────┐
              │ (compensatory)  │
              │   harm-based    │  ┌─────────────────┐ ⎫
              │    damages      │  │Orders (mandatory,│ ⎪   ┌─────────────────────┐
              │                 │  │ prohibitory) to │ ⎬   │   Retrospective     │
              │   gain-based    │  │ compensate third│ ⎪   │      remedies       │
              │damages (incl.   │  │parties or to forfeit│ ⎭   │  Aimed at putting   │
              │disgorgement of  │  │     profits     │     │    things right     │
              │    profits)     │  └─────────────────┘     └─────────────────────┘
              ├─────────────────┤
              │restorative injunction│

                                                          ⎫   ┌─────────────────────┐
              ┌─────────────────┐                         ⎪   │ Vindicatory remedies│
              │        ?        │                         ⎬   │Aimed at expressing  │
              │                 │                         ⎪   │  'acknowledgment'   │
              └─────────────────┘                         ⎭   │nominal damages where│
                                                              │there is no private  │
                                                              │   damage, 'le franc │
                                                              │symbolique', declaratory│
                                                              │judgement, cy-près,  │
                                                              │ coupon settlement,  │
                                                              │       apology       │
                                                              └─────────────────────┘
```

Vindicatory remedies constitute a category of claims that seem to have little in common at first glance. Yet, what they share is the ambition to express acknowledgement by the legal system that harm has been done, that the legal order has been violated and amends must be made. Vindicatory remedies can be invoked concurrently or alternatively; they can help overcome evidentiary difficulties such as proof of damage or difficult to calculate losses. Nominal damages and symbolical amounts ('le franc symbolique') can have the function of vindicatory remedy, as can a declaratory judgement. Other than that, the category of vindicatory remedies is underdeveloped and undertheoretized.

If we put this into a graph, this is how the remedies in private and public law would add up (figure)

III. A short history of everything

The threefold division of remedies provides a useful tool when looking at the interplay between competition law and damages. In European competition law, the 2006 ECJ *Manfredi* decision has made clear that domestic laws of damages should at least fulfil their classical function of retrospective remedy.[5] In *Manfredi*, the ECJ was called to decide on the private law aspects of European competition law. Manfredi was one of several Italian consumers who took their insurance company to court, claiming reimbursement of the overcharge on their insurance policy when the Italian competition authorities declared the underlying insurance cartel agreement unlawful. To what extent would the national court be obliged by articles 81 and 82 EC (= articles 101-102 TFEU) to acknowledge a claim in private law? The ECJ took a principled approach to the matter. Briefly described, the *Manfredi* ruling sets forth the following principles:
- EU competition law necessitates Member States to respect the right of individuals to seek compensation;
- Any individual suffering harm as a consequence of breach of art. 81 EC, can claim compensation for that harm;
- It is for the domestic legal system to prescribe the detailed rules on damages, procedure and limitation periods, and to designate the appropriate courts, provided that the principles of equivalence and effectiveness are observed;

---

[5] ECJ Judgment, 13 July 2006 in the case *Vincenzo Manfredi and Others v Lloyd Adriatico Assicurazioni SpA and Others*, joint cases C-295/04 to C-298/04 [2006] ECR I-6619. Cf. Case C-453/99, *Courage Ltd. v Bernard Crehan* [2001] ECR I-6297.

- Individuals seeking compensation should be allowed to claim both actual loss and loss for profit, plus interest;
- National courts are allowed to ensure that individuals are not unjustly enriched by their actions.

Note that frictions between the EU principle of effectiveness and compensatory damages are foreseeable: effectiveness does not necessarily sit well with the traditional compensatory retrospective goals of the law of damages. The principle of effectiveness alludes to prospective goals underlying a substantive rule of EU law. EU law calls upon the court to judge the national remedy at stake according to this principle (as one of the yardsticks). If the prospective effect that EU law is pursuing is the eradication of anti-competitive behaviour while the national retrospective remedy merely aims to compensate, it fails in terms of prospective ambitions.[6]

A development that ran parallel to the judicially created 'access to justice' for individuals and businesses injured by competition law infringement was the Commission's 2005 inventory of the potential of private damages actions as a tool within the overall system of enforcement. First, there was the impetuous 2005 Green Paper by Commissioner Kroes highlighting the private enforcement paradigm, stressing deterrence as a private law value and suggesting trebling damages as an incentive against anti-competitive behaviour. Undeniably, the Commission was contemplating to convert the traditionally retrospectively oriented remedy of compensatory damages into a prospective tool.[7] The predominantly prospective approach of the Green Paper evoked a lot of criticism. The 2008 White Paper responded well to this criticism. In essence, the White Paper centred on truly accomplishing the retrospective ambitions of the law of damages in the competition law context. The paper postulated that indirect purchasers are to have standing in court, the fault requirement in tort law needs to be relaxed, national courts need to be given guidance to facilitate assessing quantum (through simplified and rough modelling of economic damage), claimants need to have access to documentary evidence, and that decisions by national competition authorities (e.g., the decision on the facts and the breach

---

[6] Perhaps this conundrum can be solved by interpreting the effectiveness principle in such a way that it alludes to something less than a prospective remedy and something more than a retrospective remedy.

[7] For further examples of how this conversion attempt would work out, *Centre for European Policy Studies/Erasmus University Rotterdam*/LUISS *Guido Carli*, Making Antitrust Damages Actions More Effective in the EU: Welfare Impact and Potential Scenarios, Brussels 2007.

of competition law) need to have binding authority in case of follow-on actions in civil courts. Furthermore, the Paper focused on access to justice for end-users by stressing that there is a clear need for aggregation of low-value claims by means of representative action and opt-in collective action. All in all, the 2008 White Paper emphasized the necessary interplay between public law enforcement as a source of prospective remedying and private law damages actions as a source of retrospective remedying.

A 2009 Draft Directive addressing most of these issues was shelved for political reasons. However, the basic idea of improving access to compensatory damages, was not. In a 2010 speech, the new Vice President of the European Commission responsible for competition policy, Joaquín Almunia, expressed the Commission's intentions as follows:

> "It is basic justice that customers harmed by cartel behaviour should obtain redress for the harm caused to them. I believe the current situation does not allow companies, often SMEs, and consumers to enforce this right. Certainly this is not possible throughout the EU. This is why the Commission is committed to proposing legislation on the matter". [8]

The new 2010 Commission seems to have decided to give priority to supporting the aggregation of claims, both in competition law cases and consumer law cases generally. In a recent 'joint information note' by the European Commission representatives Reding, Dalli and Almunia, five principles were put forward.[9] Future action by the EC needs to:

- Promote effective compensation for every individual who suffered damage;
- Avoid abusive litigation;
- Stimulate settlement and ADR;
- Ensure cross-border enforcement;
- Address the issue of adequate financing possibilities.

A new consultation round is now due.

---

[8] Speech Nov. 2010 at the occasion of the air cargo Cartel press conference.
[9] Renforcer la cohérence de l'approche Européenne an matière de recours collectif: prochaines étapes – Note d'information de Mme Reding, M. Almunia et M. Dalli, SEC(2010) 1192.

Willem H. van Boom

IV. Relaying with the law of damages

In the European civil law systems, the traditional role of the law of damages is mainly compensatory. Hence, if European law assigns the task of deterrence, punishment or generally prevention to the law of damages in private law, the goals and function of that part of private law need recalibration. For instance, as already mentioned the principle of effectiveness does not sit well with the classical concept of compensatory damages and would therefore need adjustment of some sort.

The more recent European policy documents seem to communicate the message that in the domain of competition law, the law of damages 'merely' needs to fulfil a function of a retrospective remedy. This does not answer, however, what it exactly is that damages has to 'put right'. In other words, what is the damage that needs redress? This question is pertinent because in this respect, competition law and policy and private law may not share the same concept of damage. Competition law aims at guaranteeing an adequate operation of the market economy in the abstract. Hence, it aims at preventing and redressing *losses to society* caused by anti-competitive behaviour. By contrast, however, there is little agreement on what the aims of private law, more in particular tort law and the law of damages, are. If one considers private law to be interested in offering remedies to protect or vindicate *private interests,* there can be several dogmatic gaps between competition law and the private law of damages. Here, I briefly address two of these 'gaps', namely the 'law/rights' and the 'social/private loss' divide.

1. Enforcement of what? Law or rights?

In tort law, there is a continuous debate on whether tort law merely protects legally acknowledged interests such as life, health, and property against infringements or whether tort law purports to offer compensation for wrongs of a broader kind, including wrongful acts leading to pure economic loss. The various legal systems have different positions in this debate – some are more forthcoming than others in offering retrospective remedies against infliction of pure economic loss.[10] Breach of competition law by definition causes pure economic loss. If a given tort system automatically imputes such acts as tortious breach of statutory duties vis-à-vis competitors, direct and indirect purchasers and end-users, then the relay from competition law to tort law is straightforward. Not all legal systems are so simple, however.

---

[10] Generally, C. *Van Dam,* European Tort Law, Oxford 2006, 141 ff.

Naturally, this does not imply that the European legislature is not allowed to nudge Member States into adapting their tort law systems. It does mean, however, that European policymakers may not always appreciate the subtle difference between 'law' and 'rights' in private law. I mention just one example. The Commission announced the forthcoming 2011 consultation on collective action as setting out "to ensure that rights are a reality for all" because "the effective rights of European citizens cannot vary depending of where they live in the EU". Moreover, the 2010 Joint Information Note states: "Rights which cannot be enforced in practice are worthless. Where substantive EU rights are infringed, citizens and businesses must be able to enforce the rights granted to them by EU legislation" and "EU citizens and businesses should be able to take action when harmed by a breach of any EU legislation creating substantive rights".[11]

These quotes raise a serious point of transposition from competition law to private law. The question for the law of tort and the law of damages would be whether competition law indeed creates substantive rights, and if so: what do these entail? Enforcement of competition law in a public law setting is merely seen as the enforcement of law. In a private law setting, suddenly the shift is made towards private *rights* and their enforcement. This begs the question whether and to what extent the European Commission envisages that competition law rules which protect general interest (the proper functioning of markets) can automatically convert into tort law rules protecting individual rights? Are these truly actionable substantive rights under private law rather than pure economic interests 'protected' by the retrospective remedy of compensation?

2. Social loss and private loss

Apart from the 'law/rights' divide, there is the 'social/private loss' divide. Not all losses to society also constitute private losses (and vice versa). Overcharge is a private loss suffered by businesses and/or individuals. Calculating the overcharge harm may be difficult, as may be the identification of who actually suffered it. The anti-competitive behaviour may also cause an additional loss, a so-called deadweight loss to society. In the figure "private and social loss", this latter loss is the area denoted as "B".

---

[11] Renforcer la cohérence de l'approche Européenne an matière de recours collectif: prochaines étapes – Note d'information de Mme Reding, M. Almunia et M. Dalli, SEC(2010) 1192, p. 3-4.

Willem H. van Boom

Part III: Private versus Public Enforcement

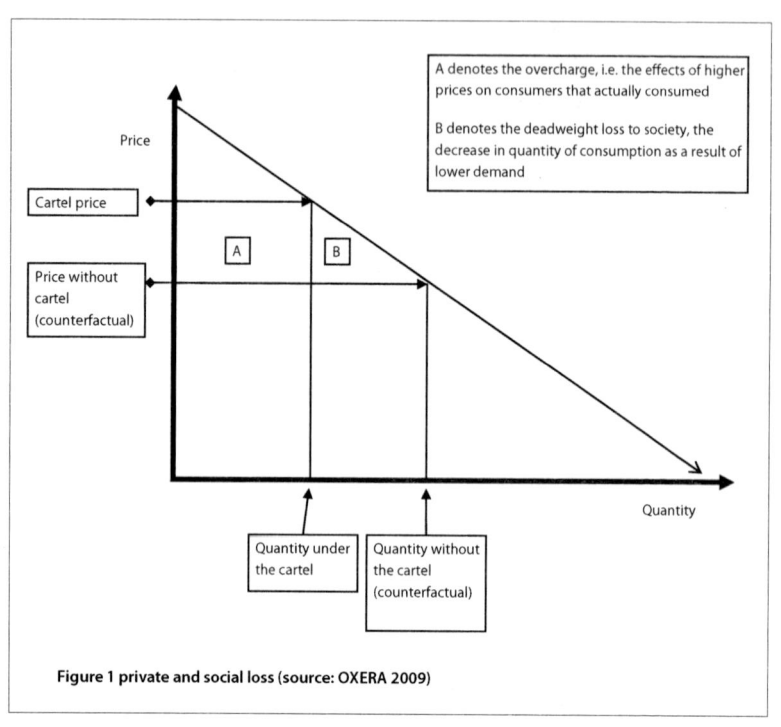

[Figure: Price/Quantity diagram with labels:
- A denotes the overcharge, i.e. the effects of higher prices on consumers that actually consumed
- B denotes the deadweight loss to society, the decrease in quantity of consumption as a result of lower demand
- Cartel price
- Price without cartel (counterfactual)
- Quantity under the cartel
- Quantity without the cartel (counterfactual)]

Figure 1 private and social loss (source: OXERA 2009)

Though in theory it may be possible to design economic models for the calculation of social losses, it seems unlikely that law can effectively bring the amount home to the injured individuals. These individuals do not exist since the economic model merely approximates the deadweight loss to society, not economic losses inflicted on individuals. Having lost out on welfare in the sense of 'experiencing' reductions in welfare does not cause harm to identifiable persons. Therefore, deadweight loss to society does probably not constitute actionable economic loss in private law.

Calculating damage "A" may be difficult enough. Especially challenging is the passing-on issue: who has in fact suffered damage A? Is it the direct purchaser or someone else in the chain to whom the overcharge was passed on? In the context of competition law enforcement, the passing-on defence may result in either of two problematic conditions: either every injury suffered by the remote end-user is too small and/or remote to constitute a sufficiently large claim worth pursuing (wide dispersion of loss towards the bottom of the chain causes dispersion of injury) or the pursuit of individual claims causes an uncoordinated stream of a multitude of claims which the legal system will have difficulty to process efficiently. So, there is a danger of either having too little claims going to court or too many! Barring the passing-on defence fits a system that ascribes deterrence functions rather than compensation functions to damages actions. One could argue that if private damages actions are merely to punish and deter (the prospective function), then the claims should be in the hands of those who are best equipped to initiate them. By restricting anti-trust actions to direct purchasers and by disallowing the passing-on defence, the claim is then effectively concentrated. This, however, does not fit the European Commission's approach to damages action as a retrospective remedy. The Commission has stated that, in line with the compensation principle, the passing-on defence should be permitted (but the onus lies on the defendant).

3. Guidance in assessing damages

The only guidance given by the ECJ in *Manfredi* as concerns quantum, is that injured persons must be able to seek compensation not only for actual loss (damnum emergens) but also for loss of profit (lucrum cessans) plus interest. Calculating actual losses and lost profits in case of anti-competitive behaviour, is, however, excruciatingly difficult and notoriously error-prone. The use of economic models may facilitate the calculations. In the context of anti-competition infringements, economic modelling seeks to identify statistically significant relationships while controlling for other plausible explanations, thus roughly isolating the causative element of a particular economic loss. The admission of such a quantitative approach to the calculation of damage may help to overcome a major obstacle in damage calculation, namely picturing the 'counterfactual': how would the relevant market have developed, what prices, quality, choice, and conditions for competitors would have existed if the infringement had not occurred?

However, the use of economic models comes at a cost: the myth of exactness. At best, these models are as good as the data that are used as input. The weaker the assumptions, the higher the error risk; the less parameters the model uses, the easier the model is to use. However, the final outcome may not at all approximate the real damage. Usually, there is no way of predicting the future that never was. As a rule of thumb concerning the calculation of damages, one can say that the more accurate one wants to emulate the holy grail of 'full compensation', the more costly the process is and the more likely it may be that the distribution (through rules of evidence) of the risk of uncertainty of the actual damage ends up with the wrong party. So, there is no ideal solution in the law of damages for calculating pure economic loss. Therefore, legal systems may want to take a pragmatic approach by granting courts a high degree of discretion in awarding damages and stimulating the use of economic models as guidelines.[12]

V. Mass damages issues

The Commission's attention seems currently focused on facilitating mass damages claims, not merely concerning competition law enforcement but in a broader perspective. There is much to be said for prioritising this area. In competition law infringement, chances are that end-consumers suffer small overcharge losses individually. The smaller the individual claim, the higher the likelihood that the individual claimant would rather wait for someone else to initiate the anti-trust procedure and the damages action. For this reason (and many others) a public authority is indispensable to initiate infringement proceedings, collect the evidence and have the perpetrators condemned by a court. But perhaps some form of public funding, facilitation or support of the follow-on damages procedure is needed anyway to overcome the 'freeriders dilemma' and collective goods problem.[13]

The Commission's 2011 consultation will have to be clearer on the exact goals the Commission would like to achieve in this area. If private overcharge losses are individually small, what good will a form of collective action (whether by means of opt-in or opt-out procedure) do? Redeem rates of 'coupon settlements' in the USA are deplorably low.

So, even the most sophisticated opt-out collective damages action would not succeed in bringing competition law 'to the people'. The question is: do we need coupon settlements in Europe, given that these will not serve prospective but merely retrospective purposes and that they are prone to fail this purpose? Collecting a large amount of money without any real prospect of actually handing out the money to the persons injured by the competition law violation, needs a different underpinning from a merely retrospective compensatory function. Perhaps collective damages actions in competition law should be defined in terms of a vindicatory remedy rather than a retrospective remedy. If a sophisticated system of cy-près were in place, collective damages action could serve a number of vindicatory functions. These would need to be accentuated. The key question then is whether Europe is

---

[12] Oxera et al., Quantifying antitrust damages – Towards non-binding guidance for courts (Study prepared for the European Commission), Luxembourg 2009, p. 21.

[13] J. Rüggeberg/M. P. Schinkel, Consolidating Antitrust Damages in Europe: A Proposal for Standing in Line with Efficient Private Enforcement, (2006) 29 World Competition 413.

able design a collective procedure that serves to redress social losses rather than (merely) private losses.

Moreover, if collective damages actions serve a compensatory goal, some form of aggregation of small claims is needed, but not necessarily through private law and not necessarily for all cases. As mentioned, aggregation will not guarantee full compensation of individuals in case of small-value claims and the interests of the business community will only be served if aggregation leads to effective and swift 'closure' at acceptable costs. Therefore, perhaps a more creative solution to this issue should be considered by departing here from the ideal of retrospective remedy and turning instead to the concept of 'vindicatory remedy'. Perhaps civil courts are traditionally less well equipped to do so but competition authorities may feel more at ease with ordering some sort of 'cy-près' compensation for social loss. Again, this area is in need of further theoretical development.

VI. Closing remarks

Antitrust damages claims are coming to Europe – that much is clear. The European Commission has moved from the initial idea of private enforcement of competition law to a more attenuated role for damages. By stressing the need to preserve strong public enforcement, the recent European Commission's communications seem better in tune with the European culture of the division of labour between private and public law. Hence, it seems probable that in the forthcoming policy proposal there will be no role for punitive or multiplied damages, but only for compensatory damages. That means that the full compensation principle will probably govern the assessment of damages in the years to come. What that actually means is unclear.

Take for instance interest on damages claims. There is no uniform approach in Europe as concerns the question whether the claimant has a right to interest ancillary to the claim for damages. Given the time-lag between violation and judgement, the claimant would prefer to have pre-judgement interest. There is, however, no consistency across Europe in rules regarding pre-judgement interest (both with regard to timing, percentage and compound/singular composition).[14] Would this be a good point for the EU to harmonize?

Another point of uncertainty concerns the role – if any – of the retrospective remedy of disgorgement of profits. European legal systems are

---

[14] D. Waelbroeck et al., Study on the conditions of claims for damages in case of infringement of EC competition rules – Comparative report, Brussels 2004, 84 ff.

dissimilar on this point; they struggle with two colliding principles of the retrospective remedy: the tortfeasor is not to profit from his wrongdoing while the claimant is not to be made better off than he was prior to the wrong. Disgorgement may also prompt the need for definition of what in fact constitutes a loss. Though deadweight losses will probably not be compensated through these retrospective remedies, there may still be some symbolic redress for these losses. As mentioned, by stimulating collective damages actions and some form of cy-près, the European legislature may actually promote the development of 'vindicatory remedies' in private law. Whether this also means that the concept of what exactly constitute private losses will be clarified, is doubtful.

If at the end of the day, it has proved unattainable for the EU to formally align the law of damages of Member States in the context of competition law, perhaps the EU could resort to soft law. Introducing non-binding guidelines as a tool, then consistently propagating the use and spread of this tool and fine-tuning it through informal procedures might be good way to overcome the impossibility to reach consensus at a political level. This seems to be exactly the way chosen by the Commission with the publication in 2009 of an informal tool 'non-binding guidance' drawn up by economic experts.[15] Perhaps a similar approach can be helpful in slowly aligning the law of damages concerning group actions and cy-près.

---

[15] *Oxera et al.*, Quantifying antitrust damages – Towards non-binding guidance for courts (Study prepared for the European Commission), Luxembourg 2009.

Private versus Public Enforcement of Laws – a Law & Economics Perspective[*]

Lars Klöhn

I. Introduction

When should laws be enforced by private actors and when should society rely on law enforcement by public authorities? This question has been analyzed in great detail in law & economics scholarship.[1] This article surveys the literature and outlines a framework of criteria for deciding whether private or public enforcement of laws is preferable.[2] To exemplify the criteria, the framework is then applied to some "real-life" enforcement issues.[3] As there are several contributions on specific areas of law such as antitrust, securities regulation, consumer protection and so forth in this book,[4] this exemplification is limited to two rather obvious cases – the enforcement of contract law and criminal law.

Several preliminary remarks are in order regarding the scope of this article: *First*, this article assumes that the adjudication of legal disputes will be carried out by public courts. While the issue of private adjudication, e.g. in the field of commercial arbitration,[5] is extremely interesting from an economic standpoint, it exceeds the scope of this article. *Second*, this article will not cover the economics of legal harmonization. An argument which might be invoked by supporters of private enforcement of laws in the Eu-

---

[*] I would like to thank Christian von Bar, Geraint Howells, Tim Kautz, Jeroen Kortmann, Petra Pohlmann and the other participants of the conference "Compensation of Private Losses – The Evolution of Torts in the European Business Law" for valuable comments. The usual disclaimers apply.

[1] For a short overview from the perspective of political theory *see Kent Roach/Michael Trebilcock*, Private Enforcement of Competition Laws, (1996) 34 Osgoode Law Journal (Osgoode L. J.) 461, 473 et seq.

[2] *Infra* IV-VI.

[3] *Infra* VII.

[4] *See* the contributions in this volume.

[5] From a Law & Economics perspective *see William Landes/Richard Posner*, Adjudication as a Private Good, (1979) 8 Journal of Legal Studies (J. Legal Stud.) 235.

ropean context could be that it better lends itself to harmonization because it does not require states to adjust their public enforcement apparatus. This argument would require an assessment of the advantages and disadvantages of legal harmonization within the EU, which have been discussed in great detail elsewhere[6] and shall be excluded in this article. *Third*, this article will focus on the general issue of whether private or public enforcement of laws is preferable. It will not discuss the optimal design of private rights of action (e.g. mechanisms to overcome collective action problems, the optimal regulation of adjudication costs and so forth) and hybrid institutions which combine aspects of private and public enforcement.

II. Optimal law enforcement as part of the economic theory of regulation

The debate over private versus public enforcement of laws is part of the economic theory of regulation. Within this theory it only concerns one aspect of the optimal structure of law, namely, who should be the actor initiating and prosecuting the enforcement of laws. Other aspects of an optimal legal system, which are not treated here, include

---

[6] See, e.g., *Thomas Apolte,* Die ökonomische Konstitution eines föderalen Systems, 1999; *Richard Buxbaum/Klaus Hopt,* Legal Harmonization and the Business Enterprise, 1988, pp. 1-23; *Emanuela Carbonara/Francesco Parisi,* The Paradox of Legal Harmonization, (2007) 132 Public Choice 367; *Wolfgang Kerber* in: Stefan Grundmann (ed.), Systembildung und Systemlücken in Kerngebieten des Europäischen Privatrechts, Gesellschafts-, Arbeits- und Schuldvertragsrecht, 2000, p. 67; *Christian Kirchner,* in: Stefan Grundmann (ed.), *supra,* pp. 99-113; *Hein Kötz,* Rechtsvereinheitlichung – Nutzen, Kosten, Methoden, Ziele, (1986) 50 Journal of Comparative and International Private Law (RabelsZ) 1; *Hans-Joachim Mertens,* Nichtlegislatorische Rechtsvereinheitlichung durch transnationales Wirtschaftsrecht und Rechtsbegriff, (1992) 56 RabelsZ 219; *Paul Stephan,* Regulatory Cooperation and Competition – The Search for Virtue (June 1999), University of Virginia Law School, Legal Studies Working Paper No. 99-12, http://ssrn.com/abstract=169213; *Henri Tjiong,* Breaking the Spell of Regulatory Competition: Reframing the Problem of Regulatory Exit, (2002) 66 RabelsZ 66; *Gerhard Wagner,* The Economics of Harmonisation, The Case of Contract Law, (2003) 39 Common Market Law Review (Common Market L. Rev.) 995; *Konrad Zweigert/Hein Kötz,* Einführung in die Rechtsvergleichung, 3rd edition. 2006, § 2 VI = pp. 27 ff.

- whether an issue should be governed by the law at all or left to (purely) social norms,
- the optimal timing of legal intervention (before an act, after an act or after harm has occurred),
- the optimal form of legal intervention (prevention, imposition of fines, liability for harm, imprisonment and so on).[7]

III. Different forms of private enforcement of laws

The following categories provide a useful overview of various different forms of private law enforcement, which will be referred to later in this article.

1. Rights of action versus rights of initiation

As to the nature of the *right granted to private parties*, it can be a *right of action*, i.e. the right to sue alleged violators of the law, or a mere *right of initiation*,[8] i.e. the right to sue the responsible agency to take action against an alleged violator. In the latter case, law enforcement against the supposed violator is administered by a public authority. Accordingly, the latter alternative shall not be understood as a private enforcement of laws in this article.[9] Even less power to privately enforce the law is granted by the *right of defense*, i.e. "the right of those regulated to obtain judicial review of allegedly unauthorized government controls"[10] and *hearing rights*. These rights are excluded from consideration here as well.

---

[7] For a concise overview *see Steven Shavell*, Foundations of Economic Analysis of Law, 2004, pp. 571 et seq.

[8] *See* also *Matthew Stephenson*, Public Regulation of Private Enforcement: The Case for Expanding the Role of Administrative Agencies, (2005) 91 Virginia Law Review (Va. L. Rev.) 93, 97: "agency forcing suits".

[9] For an extensive analysis *see Richard Stewart/Cass Sunstein*, Public Programs and Private Rights, (1982) 95 Harvard Law Review (Harv. L. Rev.) 1195.

[10] *Stewart/Sunstein*, (1982) 95 Harv. L. Rev. 1193, 1198.

2. Statutory versus implied rights of action

As to the *source of law*, we can distinguish rights of action granted by statute *(statutory rights of action, express private remedies)* from *implied rights of action* created by the judiciary.[11] European Union law sometimes grants express private remedies such as Art. 1 Product Liability Directive[12] or Art. 7 Transparency Directive[13]. The most important implied rights of action, perhaps, have been recognized under United States federal securities and investor protection laws.[14]

3. Victim rights versus common good rights of action

With regard to *how the (property) right to take action is allocated*, we can distinguish rights of action available only to the victims of the violation of law (victim rights[15], personal private rights of action[16]) from "common good" rights of action[17] which are granted to everyone and are usually assigned on a first-come-first-served basis. Of course, there are hybrid forms,

---

[11] Pamela Bucy, Private Justice, (2002) 76 Southern California Law Review (S. Cal. L. Rev.) 1, 14 (distinguishing between statutorily created private causes of action and court-implied private causes of action); *Stephenson*, (2005) 91 Va. L. Rev. 93, 98-106.

[12] Council Directive 85/374/EEC of 25 July 1985 on the approximation of the laws, regulations and administrative provisions of the Member States concerning liability for defective products, OJ L 210/29.

[13] Directive 2004/109/EC of the European Parliament and of the Council of 15 December 2004 on the harmonisation of transparency requirements in relation to information about issuers whose securities are admitted to trading on a regulated market and amending Directive 2001/34/EC.

[14] *Kardon v. National Gypsum Co.*, 73 F.Supp. 798 (E.D. Pa. 1947 [implying a private cause of action for violations of Securities Exchange Act Rule 10b-5]; *J.I. Case Co. v. Borak*, 377 U.S. 426 (1964) [implying a private cause of action under § 14(a) Securities Exchange Act].

[15] William Landes/Richard Posner, The Private Enforcement of Law, (1975) 4 Journal of Legal Studies (J. Legal Stud.) 1, 21 et seq.; *Bucy*, (2002) 76 S. Cal. L. Rev. 1, 13: „victim action".

[16] Philip Moremen, International Private Rights of Action: A Cost-Benefit Framework, (2006) 8 San Diego International Law Journal (San Diego Int'l L.J.) 5, 11.

[17] *Bucy*, (2002) 76 S. Cal. L. Rev. 1, 13: "common good private justice actions"; *Moremen*, (2006) 8 San Diego Int'l L.J. 5, 11: "public PRAs".

i.e. when the right to take action is formally reserved to victims but due to a very broad definition of the term "victim" can be invoked by many people.[18]

4. Rights of action as deterrents versus compensation mechanisms

As to the *goal* of private enforcement of laws, some private rights of action serve the primary goal of *deterrence,* as is clearly the case in securities regulation. Others are designed primarily to compensate the victims for losses resulting from violations of the law.[19]

5. Monopolistic versus competitive law enforcement

With regard to the number of parties who can enforce the law, we may speak of *monopolistic law enforcement* when there is only one party to enforce the law and of *competitive law enforcement* when parties compete to enforce the law.[20]

6. Profit-driven versus non-profit law enforcement

With respect to the incentives of private parties, we can speak of *profit-driven law enforcement* if the incentive to enforce the law is some monetary gain and *non-profit-driven law enforcement* if private parties enforce the law because of some non-monetary motive, such as fairness considerations, political or ethical convictions and so on.[21] While the first type of law en-

---

[18] Bucy, (2002) 76 S. Cal. L. Rev. 1, 17: „hybrid private justice actions".

[19] On this disctinction, *see.* e.g. *Bucy,* (2002) 76 S. Cal. L. Rev. 1, 15-17; *Stephenson,* (2005) 91 Va. L. Rev. 93, 96.

[20] *See,* e.g., *Landes/Posner,* (1975) 4 J. Legal Stud. 1, 16; *Mitchell Polinsky,* Private Versus Public Enforcement of Fines, (1980) 9 Journal of Legal Studies (J. Legal Stud.) 105, 106 et seq.

[21] Cf. *William Rubinstein,* On what a "Private Attorney General" is – And Why it Matters, (2004) 57 Vanderbilt Law Review (Vand. L. Rev.) 2129, 2136 et seq.(2004); *Moremen,* (2006) 8 San Diego Int'l L.J. 5, 12; *Amanda Rose,* Reforming Securities Litigation Reform: Restructuring the Relationship Between Public and Private Enforcement, (2008) 108 Columbia Law Review (Colum. L. Rev.) 1301, 1338.

forcement is prominent but not exclusive in securities and corporate litigation non-profit-driven private enforcers often bring citizen or qui tam suits.

IV. The case for government failure in public enforcement of laws *(Becker/Stigler)*

The discussion of the enforcement issue in law & economics commenced with a splendid argument by *Gary Becker* and *George Stigler* in favour of private enforcement of laws in areas typically reserved to public enforcement, such as criminal law and tax law.[22] They detect a "major error of the theory of rules" in the assumption that "rules provide any guidance or incentive to their enforcement". They ask: "society does not pretend to be able to designate who the bakers should be – this is left to personal aptitudes and tastes. Why should enforcers of laws be chosen differently?"[23]

Under the system they propose, "anyone could enforce statutes and receive as compensation a fine levied against convicted violators".[24] If violators cannot pay the fine, the state would impose on them some non-monetary punishment and compensate those enforcing the law.[25] If persons are acquitted of charges, they would be compensated by those who took them to court.[26] Impoverished enforcers would be required to post a bond or some other kind of "malpractice" insurance.[27] The right to use violence when enforcing the law would be granted "at least" to some licensed firms.[28]

According to *Becker* and *Stigler,* such system would offer some significant advantages over public enforcement: With compensation set at the right level, the incentives to enforce the law would be as high as the incen-

---

[22] Gary Becker/George Stigler, Law Enforcement, Malfeasance, and Compensation of Enforcers, (1974) 3 The Journal of Legal Studies (J. Legal Stud.) 1, building on some insights published previously; *see* Gary Becker, Crime and Punishment: An Economic Approach, (1968) 76 Journal of Political Economy (J. Pol. Econ.) 169; George Stigler, The Optimum Enforcement of Laws, (1979) 78 Journal of Political Economy (J. Pol. Econ.) 526.
[23] Becker/Stigler, (1974) 3 J. Legal Stud. 1, 14.
[24] Becker/Stigler, (1974) 3 J. Legal Stud. 1, 14.
[25] Becker/Stigler, (1974) 3 J. Legal Stud. 1, 15.
[26] Becker/Stigler, (1974) 3 J. Legal Stud. 1, 15.
[27] Becker/Stigler, (1974) 3 J. Legal Stud. 1, 15: "perhaps".
[28] Becker/Stigler, (1974) 3 J. Legal Stud. 1, 16.

tives of prospective violators to break the law,[29] thus solving one of the major problems of the traditional system of public enforcement.[30] Also, at this level of compensation there would be no danger of collusion between the violator and the enforcer of the law against the public; law enforcers could not be corrupted.[31] A competitive market for law enforcement would evolve; specialized firms would lower the overall enforcement costs of society,[32] taking advantage of technological innovation if this promises to enhance the efficiency of law enforcement.[33]

V. The case for market failure in private enforcement of laws *(Landes/Posner)*

One year later, *William Landes* and *Richard Posner* responded to the *Becker/Stigler*-argument for private enforcement of laws.[34] Focusing on the area of criminal law, they showed that a system of private enforcement will not be as efficient as a system of optimal public enforcement save by chance.[35] On the contrary, it will tend to too much enforcement relative to optimal enforcement (over-enforcement).[36]

To understand the counterargument, we must keep in mind that, from an economic standpoint, *optimal* law enforcement is not equal to *maximum* law enforcement. Rather, optimal law enforcement minimizes the sum harm to society caused by perpetrators and total enforcement costs.[37] Assuming that perpetrators will choose to violate the law when the expected benefits from breaking the law are higher than the expected costs, all society must

---

[29] Becker/Stigler, (1974) 3 J. Legal Stud. 1, 13.
[30] Becker/Stigler, (1974) 3 J. Legal Stud. 1, 2: "These so-called victimless crimes are highly remunerative, if undetected, when entry into their performance is restricted by the law. It is worth perhaps $500 a week to practice [drugs] trades in a neighbourhood, and we must ask: to whom is it worth $500 a week to suppress the traffic?".
[31] Becker/Stigler, (1974) 3 J. Legal Stud. 1, 14.
[32] Becker/Stigler, (1974) 3 J. Legal Stud. 1, 14.
[33] Becker/Stigler, (1974) 3 J. Legal Stud. 1, 15.
[34] Landes/Posner, (1975) 4 J. Legal Stud. 1.
[35] Landes/Posner, (1975) 4 J. Legal Stud. 1, 3-15.
[36] Landes/Posner, (1975) 4 J. Legal Stud. 1, 15.
[37] For a instructive introduction into the basic model see *Mitchell Polinsky/Steven Shavell*, The Theory of Public Enforcement of Law, in: Mitchell Polinsky/Steven Shavell (eds.), Handbook of Law and Economics, Vol. 1, 2007, pp. 403, 407 et seq.

do to reduce violations is to raise the "price" of breaking the law beyond the expected benefits of breaking the law.[38] This "price" $P_{(f,p)}$ is a function of the sanction f imposed on the violator (monetary or non-monetary) and the probability p of apprehension and conviction. Seen from the perspective of the perpetrator, the price can be raised either by increasing the likelihood of apprehension or by increasing the severity of the sanction, or both.

From the viewpoint of society, the calculation is slightly different. Assuming some fixed optimal price P* is sufficient to deter violations, the rational legislator will choose the combination of f and p which minimizes enforcement costs. Since the actual process of law enforcement is costly, this combination is likely to include a relatively high monetary sanction f and a *relatively low probability of apprehension and conviction p*.[39]

However, a system of private enforcement of laws will not permit regulators to undertake such "high sanction/low probability strategy". The reason is that in a system of private enforcement regulators can only adjust one variable, f, to achieve optimal enforcement but cannot control p. If regulators raise f, private enforcers cannot distinguish whether this is due to an increase in the value of law enforcement relative to other activities or an effort to lower p and save enforcement costs. Thus, private individuals are likely to *increase* the resources devoted to law enforcement when in a system of optimal public enforcement those resources would be *reduced*.

Landes and *Posner* stressed that their analysis should not be taken as a case for preferring public over private enforcement because this would require a comparison between private and *actual*, not *optimal* public enforcement.[40] Although their analysis has been contested and refined by other scholars in subsequent papers,[41] there seems to be little dispute that

---

[38] This insight had already been developed by *Jeremy Bentham,* Theory of Legislation, 1931. It was „reintroduced" in the seminal article on criminal behaviour and economic theory by *Becker,* (1968) 76 J. Pol. Econ. 169.

[39] *Becker,* (1968) 76 J. Pol. Econ. 169, 183 et seq. Regulators may not simply choose an (infinitely) high monetary sanction as f. The higher this sanction the more people will only suboptimally be deterred by it as they will not be able to pay the fee. Therefore, the higher the monetary sanction the higher the need for some supplementary non-monetary sanction such as imprisonment, which is more costly for society than the monetary sanction; *David Friedman,* Efficient Institutions for the Private Enforcement of Law, (1984) 13 Journal of Legal Studies (J. Legal Stud.) 379, 381.

[40] *Landes/Posner,* (1975) 4 J. Legal Stud. 1, 15.

[41] *Polinsky,* (1980) 9 J. Legal Stud. 105; *Friedman,* (1984) 13 J. Legal Stud. 379; *see also Milton Harris/Artur Raviv,* Some Results on Incentive Contracts with Applications

the choice between public and private enforcement means searching for a "second-best solution," requiring complex considerations of various criteria as well as being dependent on the factual context of regulation.[42] The following section gives an overview of those considerations.

VI. Framework of criteria for a second-best solution

1. Enforcement costs

a) Enforcement costs and the *Landes/Posner* over-enforcement-theorem

A major factor to be considered when choosing between public and private enforcement is enforcement costs. The *Landes/Posner* over-enforcement-theorem holds only if the probability of enforcement is sufficiently low. If the probability of enforcement is unity, there can hardly be any over-enforcement.[43] Therefore, in the *Landes/Posner*-model, private enforcement becomes more attractive as enforcement costs decrease, holding everything else constant.[44]

b) Enforcement costs in the real world

In reality, both private and public enforcement have several specific costs attached to them. Enforcement costs mainly consist of information costs necessary to detect whether, to what extent and by whom a law has been broken, and the costs of prosecuting and sanctioning the perpetrator. Public enforcement requires some centralized system of information gathering, whereas private enforcement relies on a "de-centralized" system, in which

---

to Education and Employment, Health Insurance and Law Enforcement, (1978) 68 American Economic Review (Am. Econ. Rev.) 20.

[42] *See*, e.g. *Steven Shavell*, Foundations of Economic Analysis of Law, 2004, pp. 578-591; *Steven Shavell*, The Optimal Strucuture of Law Enforcement, (1993) 36 Journal of Law and Economics (J. L. & Econ.) 255, 266-270; *Moremen*, (2006) 8 San Diego Int'l L.J. 5, 12-35; *Rose*, (2008) 108 Colum. L. Rev. 1301, 1325-1347.

[43] *Landes/Posner*, (1975) 4 J. Legal Stud. 1, 31 et seq.

[44] *Landes/Posner*, (1975) 4 J. Legal Stud. 1, 32.

violations of the law will be detected by some individual who has an incentive to enforce the law. Both systems have advantages and disadvantages.

A centralized public system is very costly as regards the collection of information. On the other hand, such system can achieve economies of scale, as for example in the case of a central registry for criminal offenders.[45] To be sure, any economies of scale achieved by a centralized system of public enforcement might be achieved by a monopolistic private enforcer as well.[46] However, assuming that a system of central information gathering is superior to a de-centralized system, it is highly doubtful whether society should entrust a private monopolist with this task. First, any centralized information collection system raises questions of data protection and accountability. Second, society runs the risk of becoming dependent on the monopolist, giving it an opportunity to overcharge for its service.

Many believe that the aggregate of private individuals usually has an informational advantage over a central agency, simply because the agency lacks resources to gather all the information that the dispersed public can collect.[47] In some areas of law, private individuals seem to have a "natural" informational advantage. In contract law, the contracting parties are the first to know whether a breach of contract has occurred or is likely to occur in the future.[48] The same is true for many torts – e.g. car accidents, nuisance cases, and neighbour disputes. In other situations, there is no such informational advantage for private enforcers, or even a "natural" informational disadvantage. Criminal law is an example. Most crimes are committed by people who intend to hide their identity. Moreover, in these situations a centralized system of information gathering can achieve great economies of scale, e.g. by setting up a database collecting data about repeat offenders.

---

[45] *Polinsky*, (1980) 9 J. Legal Stud. 105, 107. It should be noted that on the other side a system of central information gathering can suffer from specific diseconomies of scale due to multiple layers of decision and review within an administrative body; cf. *Stewart/Sunstein*, (1982) 95 Harv. L. Rev. 1193, 1298; *Stephenson*, (2005) 91 Va. L. Rev. 93, 108.

[46] *Polinsky*, (1980) 9 J. Legal Stud. 105, 107.

[47] *Steven Shavell*, Liability for Harm versus Regulation of Safety, (1984) 13 Journal of Legal Studies (J. Legal Stud.) 357, 360; *Cass Sunstein*, What's standing after Lujan? Of Citizen Suits, "Injuries", and Article III, (1992) 91 Michigan Law Review (Mich. L. Rev.) 163, 221; *Barton Thompson*, The Continuing Innovation of Citizen Enforcement, (2000) University of Illinois Law Review (U. Ill. L. Rev.) 185, 191 et seq.; *Stephenson*, (2005) 91 Va. L. Rev. 93, 107 et seq.

[48] *Steven Shavell*, Foundations of Economic Analysis of Law, 2004, pp. 587 et seq.

In some areas, optimal law enforcement may imply a division of labour: public authorities dedicate their scarce resources to detect and prosecute those types of violations where private enforcers lack information resources, or incentives.[49]

2. Enforcement incentives

Enforcement incentives are optimal when the incentives of the person enforcing the law are perfectly aligned with the socially desirable incentives to enforce the law, i.e. when the marginal social benefits from enforcing the law are equal to marginal social enforcement costs. A misalignment of incentives can occur under both private and public enforcement.

a) Public enforcement of laws

The central incentive-problem with public enforcement of laws is that the enforcer's personal interest in enforcing the law is usually lower than society's interest:[50] Public service employees usually receive a fixed salary and do not gain directly from enforcing the law. This poses an omnipresent threat of collusion between the violator of the law and the public enforcement agent. The former has an incentive to pay up to the expected fine (or the monetary equivalent of a non-monetary sanction) to evade punishment.[51] On the other hand, public servants can be overly eager to enforce the law. They might prosecute cases according to the public attention these cases promise to bring.[52] They might seek to maximize their budget as opposed to

---

[49] *John Coffee*, Rescuing the Private Attorney General: Why the Model of the Lawyer as Bounty Hunter Is Not Working, (1983) 42 Maryland Law Review (Md. L. Rev) 215, 224 et seq.; *Michael Selmi*, Pubilc vs. Private Enforcement of Civil Rights: The Case of Housing and Employment, (1998) 45 UCLA Law Review (UCLA L. Rev.) 1401, 1404; *Steven Shermer*, The Efficiency of Private Participation in Regulating and Enforcing the Federal Pollution Control Laws: A Model for Citizen Involvement, (1999) 14 Journal of Enviromental Law and Litigation (J. Envtl. L. & Litig.) 461, 469; *Stephenson*, (2005) 91 Va. L. Rev. 93, 109.

[50] This was the main concern of *Becker/Stigler*, (1974) 3 J. Legal Stud. 1.

[51] *Becker/Stigler*, (1974) 3 J. Legal Stud. 1, 2.

[52] On the choice of cases by agencies see *Richard Posner*, Economic Analysis of Law, 7th edition 2007, pp. 664 et seq.

optimally enforce the law.[53] And they might be "captured," i.e. discriminate against political enemies and favouring political friends when enforcing the law.[54] If there is the danger of capture, granting private enforcement rights discourages the regulated industry to lobby for a cut in the agency's budget or to otherwise weaken the agency's enforcement ability.[55] Granting private enforcement rights, however, does give the regulated industry an incentive to lobby for laxer regulation (a threat which might not be as severe, since it presumably is harder to lobby for different regulation, although this issue seems to be very case-specific).

b) Private enforcement of laws

Private incentives to enforce the law seem to be optimal when private parties are the victims of the violation of the law.[56] In this case, the probability of enforcement approaches unity, if the expected benefits from law enforcement exceed the expected costs. Those affected by the law violation often have a competitive advantage in weighing these costs and benefits, at least when the social interest in bringing suit is strongly correlated with the private interest of potential plaintiffs.[57] However, even when private enforcers are the victims of a violation of the law, their enforcement incentives might not be socially optimal for several reasons.

aa) Compensation problems

If the law makes use of only non-monetary sanctions such as imprisonment to deter wrongdoers, especially when the expected damage from break-

[53] Mark Cohen/Paul Rubin, Private Enforcement of Public Policy, (1985) 3 Yale Journal on Regulation (Yale J. on Reg.) 167, 169.
[54] See, e.g., Cohen/Rubin, (1985) 3 Yale J. on Reg. 167, 170-172; *Frank Cross*, Rethinking Environmental Citizen Suits, (1989) 8 Temple Environmental Law & Technology Journal (Temp. Envtl. L. & Tech. J.) 55, 67; *Bucy*, (2002) 76 S. Cal. L. Rev. 1, 32 et seq. (2002); *Moremen*, (2006) 8 San Diego Int'l L.J. 5, 19; *Stephenson*, (2005) 91 Va. L. Rev. 93, 110.
[55] *Stephenson*, (2005) 91 Va. L. Rev. 93, 112.
[56] *Roach/Trebilcock*, (1996) 34 Osgoode L.J. 461, 480.
[57] *Stephenson*, (2005) 91 Va. L. Rev. 93, 108 with reference to *Cohen/Rubin*, (1985) 3 Yale J. on Reg. 167, 188 et seq. and *Stewart/Sunstein*, (1982) 95 Harv. L. Rev. 1193, 1290.

ing the law is large, there will be under-enforcement by private enforcers because they will usually not be able to cover their enforcement costs.[58] As clear as this idea is, three qualifications seem to be necessary.

First, the incentives of private enforcers might be set at the right level if the state provides them with some monetary compensation.[59] This compensation would have to be as high as the costs of punishment for the perpetrator, because otherwise there would arise the opportunity of collusion between the perpetrator and enforcer to the detriment of the public.[60] If the compensation to private enforcers is increased to this level, however, the danger of under-enforcement would be replaced with the problem of over-enforcement as shown by *Landes* and *Posner* because private enforcers would try to increase p when regulators actually want to reduce p to minimize the total social loss from crime.[61] *Second*, setting compensation at the right level involves a valuation problem. Regulators would have to determine the money value of evading prison to the average perpetrator. While it is assumed that such value can be determined in economic models,[62] it is highly debatable whether such valuation is possible in the real world: What risk-preferences should we assume? Will the valuation depend on the average income of perpetrators, i.e. will rich people fear prison more than poor people? If so, which income and wealth level should we assume for different crimes? *Third*, the above mentioned argument assumes that private parties will be driven to enforce the law only for monetary rewards. Therefore, the problem of under-enforcement might not be as severe if we assume that people are driven by some desire for fairness, as is clearly the case in some areas of law such as environmental law.[63]

When the violation of the law causes negative externalities without directly affecting any person who could be defined as a victim ("victimless crimes" such as drug trafficking or insider trading), private parties may not have the right incentives to enforce the law. Since there is no compen-

---

[58] *Polinsky*, (1980) 9 J. Legal Stud. 105, 107; *Shavell*, (1984) 13 J. Legal Stud. 357, 360 et seq.; *Steven Shavell*, The Optimal Structure of Law Enforcement, (1993) 36 Journal of Law & Economics (J. L. & Econ.) 255, 278.
[59] *Landes/Posner*, (1975) 4 J. Legal Stud. 1, 32.
[60] *Landes/Posner*, (1975) 4 J. Legal Stud. 1, 32.
[61] *Supra* V.
[62] *Becker/Stigler*, (1974) 3 J. Legal Stud. 1, 2 n. 2.
[63] *Jeannette Austin*, The Rise of Citizen-Suit Enforcement in Environmental Law: Reconciling Private and Public Attorneys General, (1987) 81 Northwestern University Law Review (Nw. U. L. Rev.) 220, 257; *Rose*, (2008) 108 Colum. L. Rev. 1301, 1338 et seq.

sation to be gained from the suit (or since such consideration would not be identical to social harm), profit-driven private enforcers would require some additional compensation to be collected from the perpetrator, such as punitive damages, or through subsidies by the public. To set enforcement incentives at the right level, especially to avoid over-enforcement, regulators would be forced to solve complicated, almost impossible calculations such as measuring the external damage from drug use or the monetary value of a loss in faith in the integrity of capital markets.

bb) Collective action problems

In a system of competitive private enforcement[64] a collective action problem arises when several private plaintiffs engage in a wasteful "race to the courts".[65] Essentially, this is an incentive problem. If the expected reward is high enough, numerous private individuals may have an incentive to invest in preparing a suit even though enforcement by a single party may suffice, thus duplicating enforcement costs. Co-ordination could remedy the problem but might not be feasible due to individually rational strategic behaviour.

In other situations, under a system of profit-driven private enforcement parties will find it worthwhile to file suits even on unreasonable grounds, if the suit has a positive expected net value. They might bring "strike suits" just for their nuisance value, which depends on many considerations apart from the legal grounds of the claim, such as the danger of bad publicity or the expected litigation costs.[66] While this danger is present in public enforcement of laws as well, it does not seem as high[67] because public law enforcers do not profit monetarily from their enforcement[68], have a limited budget, and are held politically accountable for their actions.

---

[64] For a definition of this term *supra* III.5.
[65] *Cf.*, e.g. *Landes/Posner*, (1975) 4 J. Legal Stud. 1, 32 and 34.
[66] *Cf.*, e.g., *Stephenson*, (2005) 91 Va. L. Rev. 93, 116.
[67] *Cross*, (1989) 8 Temp. Evtl. L. & Tech. J. 55, 69 et seq.; *Stephenson*, (2005) 91 Va. L. Rev. 93, 116.
[68] *Howard Erichson*, Coattail Class Actions: Reflections on Microsoft, Tobacco and the Mixing of Public and Private Lawyering in Mass Litigation, (2000) 34 UC Davis Law Review (U.C. Davis L. Rev.) 1, 43.

cc) *Agency problems*

If private enforcement of laws involves an agency relationship, such as between plaintiffs and attorneys in a class action, there is the danger of perverse incentives for the agent. For example, the attorneys have an incentive to settle a lawsuit on terms unfavourable for the plaintiffs if the settlement involves generous attorney fees.[69]

3. Enforcement policy

a) Cooperation and self-regulation

Public and private enforcement differ in what might be called enforcement policy. Private enforcement renders it almost impossible to cooperate with regulated industries and to incentivize regulated industries to adopt self-regulation.[70] It is true that private litigation remedies the capture problem when an agency is inclined to collude with those regulated against society.[71] However, if there are alternative means to cope with the capture problem, private enforcement may engender an overemphasis on coercion and deterrence at the expense of negotiation and cooperation.[72] Also, it discourages companies to seek a cooperative solution when violations have occurred.[73]

---

[69] *Roach/Trebilcock*, (1996) 34 Osgoode L.J. 461, 488.
[70] *Stewart/Sunstein*, (192) 95 Harv. L. Rev. 1193, 1292 et seq.; *Austin*, (1987) 81 Nw. U. L. Rev. 220, 223; *Robert Blomquist*, Rethinking the Citizen as Prosecutor Model of Enviromental Enforcement under the Clean Water Act: Some Overlooked Problems of Outcome-Independent Values, (1989) 22 Georgia Law Review (Ga. L. Rev.) 337, 409 et seq.; *Matthew Zinn*, Policing Environmental Regulatory Enforcement: Cooperation, Capture, and Citizen Suits, (2002) 21 Standford Enviromental Law Journal (Stan. Envtl. L.J.) 81 , 84; *Bucy*, (2002) 76 S. Cal. L. Rev. 1, 64 et seq.; *Rose*, (2008) 108 Colum. L. Rev. 1301, 1336 et seq.
[71] *Supra* VI 2.a).
[72] *Stephenson*, (2005) 91 Va. L. Rev. 93, 118.
[73] *Cross*, (1989) 8 Temp. Envtl. L. & Tech. J. 55, 67; *Stephenson*, (2005) 91 Va. L. Rev. 93, 117; *Moremen*, (2006) 8 San Diego Int'l L.J. 5, 16; *Rose*, (2008) 108 Colum. L. Rev. 1301, 1336 et seq.

b) Discretion

Another disadvantage of private enforcement is that it renders it almost impossible to exercise discretion not to enforce the law when non-enforcement is beneficial to society. This point assumes that laws are usually overinclusive. Taken literally, they cover cases which the legislator would have chosen not to cover if it had known the particular case in advance. The economic explanation for overinclusion is that it is very costly to tailor a rule exactly to the conduct intended to be forbidden.[74] Such tailoring is left to ex-post adjudication of individual cases by the courts.

Private enforcers have no incentive to exercise discretion with regard to overinclusive laws. Profit-driven private enforcers will seize the opportunity to enforce the law any time a positive return on the investment of enforcement costs can be expected.[75] In contrast, a public enforcement agency can choose not to enforce the law in cases in which the social costs of enforcing the law exceed its benefits. This happens every day, e.g. when "the police overlook minor infractions of the traffic code; building inspectors ignore violations of building-code provisions that, if enforced, would prevent the construction of new buildings in urban areas; air traffic controllers permit the airlines to violate excessively stringent safety regulations involving the spacing of aircraft landing and taking off from airports".[76] Such discretionary non-enforcement can reduce the social costs of overinclusion without a corresponding increase in underinclusion.[77] Non-profit-driven private enforcers may be motivated to engage in socially beneficial discretionary non-enforcement, too. However, this holds only if such non-enforcement conforms to their moral or political convictions.

One might object that under a classic separation of powers, tailoring overinclusive rules is left to the courts and not to public agencies. This, by itself, however, is not an economic argument. From an economic standpoint, giving discretion to the court to tailor a rule ex post simply means that the power not to enforce overly inclusive law is shifted to another official body.[78] Often, agencies will have comparative advantages for such tailoring

---

[74] On the under- and overinclusiveness of rules from an economic standpoint *Louis Kaplow*, Rules Versus Standards, (1992) 42 Duke Law Journal (Duke L.J.) 557, 586-596.
[75] Landes/Posner, (1975) 4 J. Legal Stud. 1, 38.
[76] Landes/Posner, (1975) 4 J. Legal Stud. 1, 38.
[77] Landes/Posner, (1975) 4 J. Legal Stud. 1, 38; *Stephenson*, (2005) 91 Va. L. Rev. 93, 116.
[78] Landes/Posner, (1975) 4 J. Legal Stud. 1, 40.

because they are more familiar with the regulated activity and can act faster. Moreover, agencies can act before, and not after, the fact, thus preventing certain cases from ever going to court.

4. Enforcement and the legal process

When choosing between private and public enforcement of laws, we should finally consider the effects of both mechanisms on the legal process.

a) The case for private enforcement of laws ...

Assuming that private actors bring more suits to court than public agencies, the judiciary will have more opportunities to refine vague and general standards contained in the law. This can create a public good and might well be worth the litigation costs not internalized by the plaintiffs.[79] Of course, this is a consideration which can be taken into account by public enforcement agencies when exercising discretion not to enforce a law. However, some scholars argue that private parties are more likely than agencies to develop novel legal theories, creative approaches to dispute settlement and new techniques of investigation and proof.[80] For example, the prevailing view is that the most important U.S. antitrust law decisions by the Supreme Court were initiated by private litigation.[81]

b) ...and the case against it

On the other hand, it has been argued that an "incompetent, overworked, or inexperienced private counsel, whose interest may diverge from the public interest, may be generating case precedent that restricts government

---

[79] See, in general, George Priest/Benjamin Klein, The Selection of Disputes for Litigation, (1984) 13 Journal of Legal Studies (J. Legal Stud.) 1; in the context of the public versus private law enforcement debate: Roach/Trebilcock, (1996) 34 Osgoode L.J. 461, 481.

[80] Thompson, 2000 U. Ill. L. Rev. 185, 188, 206; Stephenson, (2005) 91 Va. L. Rev. 93, 112.

[81] Harry First, Antitrust Enforcement in Japan, (1995) 64 Antritrust Law Journal (Antitrust L.J.) 137, 179 et seq.; Roach/Trebilcock, (1996) 34 Osgoode L.J. 461, 481.

regulators".[82] Moreover, assuming that private enforcement entails costs not borne by private plaintiffs (especially litigation costs in a system of publicly subsidized courts), private plaintiffs have an incentive for excessive litigation.[83] This danger is especially severe if private parties derive benefits from litigation which, from a social perspective, do not justify additional enforcement costs. Under profit-driven private enforcement of laws, these benefits may include not only the monetary recovery from the suit but also any benefits derived from harassing and damaging the reputation of private competitors and the like.[84] Under non-profit-driven private enforcement, such benefits might include "the notoriety and increased membership that a public interest group may gain from a large number of high-profile cases"[85]. While this danger exists in a system of public enforcement of laws as well, it does not seem as severe because public agencies have a limited budget and can be held accountable for excessive litigation. Finally, in a system of private litigation the risk of erroneous decisions may increase because courts must decide sometimes difficult issues without the benefit of another public body reviewing the case first.[86]

---

[82] *Bucy*, (2002) 76 S. Cal. L. Rev. 1, 66; *see also Stephenson*, (2005) 91 Va. L. Rev. 93, 119.

[83] *Shavell*, (1997) 26 J. Legal Stud. 575, 577 et seq.; *Stephenson*, (2005) 91 Va. L. Rev. 93, 114; *see also Bucy*, (2002) 76 S. Cal. L. Rev. 1, 67 (stating that nonmeritous private actions can consume scarce judicial resources).

[84] *Joseph Brodley*, Antitrust Standing in Private Merger Cases: Reconciling Private Incentives and Public Enforcement Goals, (1995) 94 Michigan Law Review (Mich. L. Rev.) 1, 45; *Stephenson*, (2005) 91 Va. L. Rev. 93, 115 et seq.

[85] *Stephenson*, (2005) 91 Va. L. Rev. 93, 115 citing *Jonathan Adler*, Stand or Deliver: Citizen Suits, Standing and Enviromental Protection, (2001) 12 Duke Environmental Law & Policy Forum (Duke Envtl. L & Pol'y F.) 39, 50; *Zinn*, (2002) 21 Stan. Envtl. L.J. 81, 133, 138; *Mark Seidenfeld*, Empowering Stakeholders: Limits on Collaboration as the Basis for Flexible Regulation, (2000) 41 William and Mary Law Review (Wm. & Mary L. Rev.) 411, 432, 436-439.

[86] *Stephenson*, (2005) 91 Va. L. Rev. 93, 116.

VII. The Framework applied

1. Contract Law

If we apply the framework developed above to contract law, we can easily see why in virtually any legal environment contracts are almost exclusively enforced by the contracting parties. These parties are in the best position to know when a violation of the contract has occurred or is about to occur.[87] Proving that a party is liable for breach of contract might be costly, but this problem is mitigated by the law of evidence, which shifts the burden of proof usually to the least cost information seeker.[88] Also, the contracting parties have the socially optimal incentives to enforce a contract. Contracts rarely create a public good. That is why the contracting parties are in the best position to decide whether to enforce a contract or exercise discretion not to enforce (e.g. to overlook minor breaches of contract to preserve a valuable long-term relationship). There is no threat of disrupting some public enforcement policy because such policy does not exist. On the other hand, public enforcement of contractual obligations might very well disrupt a private enforcement strategy, e.g. not enforcing the contract to preserve the long-term relationship. Also, in contracts, the problem of a party being judgment proof rarely exists because the parties know each other and can negotiate ex ante.[89] Finally, because of their informational advantage and better incentives, the parties to a contract are in the best position to litigate contractual matters and decide about settlement and so on.

2. Criminal law

The paradigm of public enforcement of laws is the prosecution of crimes. In the area of criminal law, public enforcers usually have an informational advantage because crimes are typically committed with an intent to hide the identity of the perpetrator.[90] As there are numerous repeat offenders, public

---

[87] Steven Shavell, Foundations of Economic Analysis of Law, 2004, p. 587.
[88] Cf. Richard Posner, Economic Analysis of Law, 7th edition 2007, pp. 646 et seq.
[89] Steven Shavell, Foundations of Economic Analysis of Law, 2004, p. 586.
[90] Shavell, (1993) 36 J. L. & Econ. 255, 278; Katarina Svatikova, Economic Criteria for Criminalization: Why Do We Need the Criminal Law? (March 2009), RILE Working Paper No. 2008/12, http://ssrn.com/abstract=1150689 sub. 3.2.

enforcers can achieve economies of scale.[91] While it is true that specialized private firms might be able to achieve the same efficiency gains,[92] those firms will rarely have optimal incentives to enforce the law. As profit-driven firms they would have an incentive to prosecute crimes only if the monetary reward is high enough. This would pose the problem of over-enforcement, as shown by *Landes* and *Posner*,[93] and might as well lead to under-enforcement when perpetrators – as is often the case – are judgment proof.[94] If parties know who harmed them and have an incentive to enforce the law, e.g. to satisfy some retributive urge, reserving criminal law enforcement to public authority still has the benefit of preventing further harm and disruption of the public order (especially since criminal procedure law can – and usually does – provide for remedies to satisfy the desire for retribution even if not completely).[95] Finally, as mentioned above, public authority is also in the best position to discretionally not enforce the law when the overall costs of enforcement exceed its benefits.[96]

---

[91] *Katarina Svatikova*, Economic Criteria for Criminalization: Why Do We Need the Criminal Law? (March 2009), RILE Working Paper No. 2008/12, http://ssrn.com/abstract=1150689 sub. 3.2.
[92] *Becker/Stigler*, (1974) 3 J. Legal Stud. 1, 15.
[93] *Supra* V.
[94] *Supra* VI.2.b)aa).
[95] *Cf. Steven Shavell*, Foundations of Economic Analysis of Law, 2004, p. 589.
[96] *Supra* VI.3.

Part IV
Interaction with Neighbouring Fields

Rechtsvergleichende Beobachtungen zum Ineinandergreifen von Vertrags- und Deliktsrecht in Europa

Christian von Bar

I. Binnenmarktrelevanz von Systemfragen?

Das Ineinandergreifen von Vertrags- und Deliktsrecht wirft in allen Staaten der Europäischen Union Schwierigkeiten von beträchtlichem Ausmaß auf. Wir sind ihnen vor einiger Zeit in einem internationalen Juristenteam in einer für die Europäische Kommission verfassten Studie nachgegangen.[1] Die Untersuchung sollte vor dem Hintergrund der seinerzeit noch intensiv geführten Debatte, ob ein dereinstiger „politischer" Common Frame of Reference auch das Deliktsrecht umfassen solle, eine ganz eigenartige Frage beantworten: Ob nämlich „competition imbalances, or real or likely obstacles to the smooth running of the internal market might arise as a result of areas of interference, problems in enumerating of facts, or even differences in terminology or concepts ... between non-contractual liability law and contract law". Es ging also nicht um die Frage, ob unterschiedliche Vertrags- und/oder unterschiedliche Deliktsrechte ein Problem für den Binnenmarkt darstellen, sondern es ging allein um „problems and obstacles resulting from differences in systems of law", um die „identification of real or likely obstacles in contract and commercial practice to the smooth running of the internal market ... resulting from the interaction of ... non-contractual liability law ... with contract law."[2]

Aber können verschiedene Formen der Organisation des Ineinandergreifens von Vertrags- und Deliktsrecht als solche überhaupt die Ursache von Binnenmarkthindernissen sein? Ich gestehe, ich tat mich schwer mit dieser Frage. Das hatte seinen Grund darin, dass unterschiedliches Koordinierungsrecht im Einzelfall genauso gut und genauso oft *gleiche* Endergebnisse produziert, wie es vorkommt, dass gleiches Koordinierungsrecht

---

[1] Christian von Bar und Ulrich Drobnig (eds.), The Interaction of Contract Law and Tort and Property Law in Europe. A Comparative Study (München 2004).
[2] AaO S. 1, Rdnr. 1.

verschiedene Endergebnisse konserviert. Man denke nur an die in Deutschland mit den Stichworten „Linoleumrolle"[3] und „Bananenschale"[4] belegten Klassiker aus der Welt der sogen. *culpa in contrahendo* und des Vertrages mit Schutzwirkungen zugunsten Dritter. In Deutschland wanderten sie bekanntlich in das Recht der vertraglichen Haftung aus, um die problematischen Regeln der deliktischen Geschäftsherrenhaftung zu umgehen; man bezahlte dafür bis 2002 freilich noch den Preis, kein Schmerzensgeld gewähren zu können. In Frankreich dagegen wäre es außerordentlich unklug gewesen, die Vertragshaftung um solche unspezifischen Schutzpflichten zu erweitern. Denn hier gilt – mit dem Prinzip des *non-cumul des responsabilités* – eine andere Konkurrenzregel als in Deutschland: Die Haftung ist immer nur entweder vertraglich oder deliktisch, aber niemals beides zugleich.[5] Hätte man das Vertragsrecht in tatbestandlich auch vom Deliktsrecht erfasste Felder hinein erweitert, dann hätte das also notwendig zur Folge gehabt, dass das französische Deliktsrecht in diesem vertragsrechtlichen Erweiterungsbereich unanwendbar geworden wäre, und damit auch die wesentlich opferfreundlichere *Gardien*haftung aus Art. 1384 Abs. 1 CC. Ganz konsequent hat deshalb das französische Vertragsrecht Schutz- und Nebenpflichten in weit geringerem Umfang ausgebildet als das deutsche. Wenn z.B. ein Patient in der Praxis seines Arztes auf einem dort unzureichend gesicherten Teppich ausrutscht und zu Schaden kommt, dann hält erst die Nichtanwendung des Vertragsrechts den Weg zu Art. 1384 Abs. 1 CC offen. Folglich sagt man, dass der Arzt seinem Patienten vertraglich gerade nicht die sichere Begehbarkeit der Praxisräume schulde.[6] Man sieht also: Der Umstand allein, dass zwei benachbarte Rechtssysteme zwei jeweils unterschiedliche Vertrags- und Deliktsrechte mit einem ebenfalls unterschiedlichen Konkurrenzrecht kombinieren, kann demselben Endzweck und demselben Endergebnis dienen, dass nämlich die Rechtsstellung des an seinem Körper oder seiner Gesundheit verletzten Opfers gestärkt wird. Heute gilt das, wegen § 253 Abs. 2 BGB, sogar auch für den Ersatz des Nichtvermögensschadens. Hätten demgegenüber Frankreich und Deutschland ein identisches Konkurrenzrecht, so müssten die Gerichte beider Länder den Fall unterschiedlich lösen, und zwar ganz gleich, ob sie sich für die

---

[3] RG 17.7.1911, RGZ 78 S. 239.
[4] BGH 26.9.1961, NJW 1962 S. 31. S. ferner BGH 28.1.1976, BGHZ 66 S. 51 (Gemüseblatt).
[5] Einzelnachweise bei *Christian von Bar*, Gemeineuropäisches Deliktsrecht I (1996) Rdnr. 431-435, S. 429-433.
[6] Z.B. Cass. civ. 28.4.1981, D. 1981 I.R. 438 und Cass. civ. 10.1.1990, bei *Jourdain*, Rev. trim. dr. civ. 88 (1990) S. 481.

deutsche Lehre von der Anspruchs- oder die französische Lehre von der Gesetzeskonkurrenz entschieden. Denn die Haftung aus Art. 1384 Abs. 1 CC ist immer noch schärfer als die aus § 280 BGB.

Zwischen den nationalen Antworten auf die Frage, wie das Zusammenwirken von Vertrags- und Deliktsrecht zu organisieren sei, und dem reibungslosen Funktionieren des Binnenmarktes gibt es also keinen linearen Zusammenhang; ob sich die von den einzelnen Rechtsordnungen erzielten Ergebnisse gleichen oder nicht, hängt von einer so großen Zahl von Variablen ab, dass es willkürlich erscheinen muss, unter ihnen ausgerechnet die „Systemfrage" herauszugreifen. Binnenmarktrelevanz hat sie aus meiner Sicht gleichwohl, wenngleich unter einem anderen Aspekt. Denn auch die Kompliziertheit von Recht kann Menschen und Unternehmen daran hindern, die Möglichkeiten des Binnenmarktes auszuschöpfen. Für einen normalen Marktteilnehmer, ja selbst für einen auf diesem Gebiet nicht besonders geschulten Juristen, ist es bis heute oft schier unmöglich, das überall in Europa feingliedrig verästelte Geflecht der Interaktionen zwischen Vertrags- und Deliktsrecht länderweise zu durchdringen, zu den übrigen Rechtsordnungen Parallelen zu ziehen und aus der dann gewonnenen Informationsflut Handlungsanweisungen herauszudestillieren. Die Erwartung einer angemessenen rechtlichen Risikoabschätzung erweist sich in diesem Feld als reine Illusion. Und als Illusion kann sich schnell auch die Hoffnung auf eine das Marktgeschehen erleichternde Rechtsharmonisierung (bis hinein in die Form des Optionalen Instruments) erweisen, wenn sie sich den Interferenzfragen nicht stellt.

II. Rechtsangleichung

Wer dem Binnenmarkt ein Vertragsrecht geben, ihm aber ein Deliktsrecht vorenthalten will, produziert jenseits eines engen, seinerseits nur sehr schwer sinnvoll abzusteckenden Kernbereichs schnell eine Vielzahl von einander unkoordiniert überlagernden Rechtsschichten. Man denke nur an die Haftung des Vertreters ohne Vertretungsmacht, an die Auskunftshaftung und an all die sonstigen Materien, die man (nur) in den Ländern, die ihr Deliktsrecht auf das Konzept der Rechtswidrigkeit gegründet haben, auf das Bild von der Vertrauenshaftung zu projizieren versucht[7], während man in

---

[7] Siehe dazu jetzt die eindrucksvolle Tartuer Dissertation (2011) von *Urmas Volens*, Saldusvastutus kui iseseisev vastutussüteem saksamaa, šveitsi ja eesti tsiviil õiguses ning euroopa tsiviil õiguse ühtlustamispüüdlustes (Vertrauenshaftung als

praktisch allen anderen Ländern ganz unbefangen zum außervertraglichen Haftungsrecht greift. Schön und gut, wenn ein dem Vertragsrecht gewidmetes Optionales Instrument hier einheitliche Antworten geben könnte – nur was und wem nützten sie, wenn dann in einem Teil der Mitgliedstaaten weiterhin auch das dortige – nationale – Deliktsrecht anwendbar bliebe? Schon wieder stößt Rechtsangleichung hier an scharf bewachte nationale Grenzen. Wir kommen nicht von der Stelle, wenn wir nicht endlich auch die Grundsatzfragen anpacken. Wäre es also nicht doch besser, wir würden in Europa mit dem Willen zur Verständigung diskutieren, ob und wozu die Rechtswidrigkeitslehre des Deliktsrechts heute eigentlich noch benötigt wird, statt es bei einer Behandlung ihrer Symptome in (angeblich oder wirklich) vertragsnahem Kontext zu belassen? Man übersieht allzu leicht, dass eine Überprüfung unserer Deliktsrechtskonzepte gerade auch für das *Vertrags*recht von eminenter Wichtigkeit ist. Aber natürlich lässt sich dieser Satz auch umkehren. Denn es ist nicht nur so, dass ein deliktsrechtliches Rechtswidrigkeitskonzept ein bestimmtes Vertragsrecht hervorbringt, sondern auch so, dass zahlreiche vertragsrechtliche Lehren, z.B. *cause* und *consideration*, eine herausragende Bedeutung auch für das *Delikts*recht entfalten. Je enger das eine Rechtsgebiet, desto weiter das andere, und *vice versa*. Das lässt sich in der Auskunftshaftung leicht demonstrieren.[8]

III. Zweispurigkeit; Konkurrenzen

Es ist eine unerhörte Herausforderung an die Rechtsvergleichung, das Zusammenwirken und Ineinandergreifen von Vertrags- und Deliktsrecht in

---

selbständiges Haftungssystem in der deutschen, schweizerischen und estnischen Zivilrechtsordnung und in den Vereinheitlichungsbestrebungen des europäischen Zivilrechts; im Erscheinen).

[8] Man denke nur an die mit *Hedley Byrne v. Heller* [1964] AC 465 (HL) einsetzende englische Rechtsprechung zur Haftung für reine Vermögensschäden unter dem *tort of negligence*. Alle neueren Vertragsrechtsentwürfe internationaler Arbeitsgruppen (PECL, DCFR, PICC) verzichten auf das Erfordernis einer Gegenleistung *(consideration)*. Hätte dem House of Lords im Jahre 1964 dieselbe Möglichkeit zur Verfügung gestanden, so wäre es nicht undenkbar gewesen, manche Fälle der Auskunftshaftung auch dort vertragsrechtlich anzugehen. Allerdings schlägt auch Art. VI.-2:207 DCFR eine außervertragliche Lösung dieser Fallgruppe vor. Ihr korrekter systematischer Standort wird vermutlich solange streitig bleiben, wie es an einer gesamteuropäischen gesetzlichen Regelung für sie fehlt.

den Ländern der Europäischen Union aufzuhellen. Niemand wird von einem kurzen Konferenzbeitrag erwarten, dieser Herausforderung gerecht werden zu können. Gewiss lässt sich heute für alle mitgliedstaatlichen Rechtsordnungen eine „Zweispurigkeit" in dem Sinne feststellen, dass man überall sowohl ein Vertrags- wie auch ein Deliktsrecht „hat" und deshalb auch zwischen ihnen unterscheidet bzw. unterscheiden muss. Probleme, die aus dem Recht der ungerechtfertigten Bereicherung und dem Recht der auftragslosen Fremdgeschäftsführung bekannt sind – wie man nämlich rechtsvergleichend auf Gebieten des Rechts vorgehen muss, die nicht einmal überall wenigstens in dieselben dogmatischen Grundstrukturen gekleidet sind –, stellen sich in den Welten des Vertrags- und des Deliktsrechts nicht. Aber schon die (uralte und ewig junge) Frage, warum man eigentlich in dieser Weise differenziert, statt die Systeme zusammenzuführen, ja warum man nicht einfach jede Vertragsverletzung als Delikt qualifiziert, ist viel schwieriger beantwortet, als es auf den ersten Blick scheint. Auf einer „philosophischen" Ebene mag man sich vielleicht mit der Aussage begnügen, dass es im Vertragsrecht grundsätzlich um etwas „Gutes", im Deliktsrecht um etwas „Schlechtes" gehe. Aber im Konkreten liegen die Dinge doch komplizierter. Im französischen Recht hätte man zumindest in der Mehrzahl der Fälle kaum Mühe, die Verletzung eines Vertrages als *faute* zu qualifizieren. Dass es dazu nicht kommt und so die Selbständigkeit des Vertragsrechts gewahrt bleibt, ist am Ende wohl nur das Verdienst der Lehre vom *non-cumul des responsabilités*. Und in Deutschland? Hier scheint sich die Frage erst gar nicht zu stellen, weil die verspätete Lieferung oder die Lieferung einer mangelhaften Sache für sich genommen noch keine Eigentumsverletzung darstellen. Die Enge des Tatbestandes von § 823 Abs. 1 BGB entschärft das Problem. Indes verschiebt es sich auf diese Weise nur auf § 823 Abs. 2 BGB. Die gesetzlichen Regeln des Vertragsrechts, welche den Schuldner zu verpflichtungskonformer Erfüllung anhalten, ließen sich mühelos als Schutzgesetze im Sinne des Deliktsrechts deuten. Das geschieht jedoch gerade nicht; Schutz"gesetze" sind nur solche Gesetze, die von Pflichten handeln, welche die Politik aufgestellt hat, nicht die Parteien selber.[9] Das Ergebnis überrascht: Auch Deutschland hat, so betrachtet, sein *non-cumul*, nur hat dieses seinen Sitz nicht in einer Konkurrenzregel, sondern in der Definition des Schutzgesetzes i. S. v. § 823 Abs. 2 BGB! Wir halten uns folglich an die Lehre von der Anspruchskonkurrenz. Die Rechtsprechung akzeptiert nur ganz wenige Ausnahmen von ihr – zu wenige, scheint mir. Das Konzept der deliktsrechtsbasierten Haftung für die sogen. Weiterfresserschäden ist aus meiner Sicht rein innerdeliktsrechtlich

---

[9] Näher *von Bar* aaO (n. 5) Rdnr. 419 S. 415-416.

zwar nicht zu beanstanden, aber es bleibt konkurrenzrechtlich anfechtbar.[10] Denn es droht die Unterscheidung zwischen Vertrags- und Deliktsrecht einzuebnen, und es hat gerade aus diesem Grunde in den übrigen Ländern der Europäischen Union kaum Gefolgschaft gefunden.[11]

IV. Vertragsverletzungen als Tatbestandsvoraussetzungen eines Delikts und Delikte als Tatbestandsvoraussetzungen einer Vertragsverletzung

Die Zweispurigkeit von Vertrags- und Deliktsrecht schließt nicht aus, dass man es in einer Reihe von Fällen nur deshalb mit deliktischem Unrecht zu tun hat, weil der Beklagte eine Vertragspflicht verletzt hat. Genauso oft kommt es auch umgekehrt vor, dass die Begehung eines Deliktes eine Vertragsverletzung konstituiert. Man denke nur an den Bankkassierer, der Geld unterschlägt, sei es das Geld seiner Bank oder das Geld von deren Kunden.

Hauchdünn werden die Grenzlinien zwischen Vertrags- und Deliktsrecht aber vor allem in der ersten Fallgruppe. Wiederum stößt man auf einander manchmal verblüffend ähnliche dogmatische Konstruktionen. Viele Deliktsrechtssysteme tun sich bis heute mit der Haftung für Unterlassungen schwer. Gern ergreifen sie deshalb die Möglichkeit, an eine vertraglich begründete Aufsichts- oder sonstige Sicherungspflicht des Beklagten anzuknüpfen. Das betrifft sowohl die Kontrolle von Sachen als auch die Kontrolle von Personen. Überzeugend wirkt das zwar keineswegs immer. Denn der Vertrag, um dessen Verletzung es in solchen Fällen geht, ist typischerweise ja gerade nicht mit dem Geschädigten, sondern mit einer dritten Person geschlossen, und es erscheint schon deshalb zweifelhaft, dass seine Verletzung zur Haftungsbegründung dem Geschädigten gegenüber taugen könnte.[12] Aus dogmatischer Sicht bemerkenswert erscheint daran aber,

---

[10] Näher *Christian von Bar*, Probleme der Haftpflicht für deliktsrechtliche Eigentumsverletzungen (Mannheimer Vorträge zur Versicherungswissenschaft Bd. 55; Karlsruhe 1992).

[11] Einzelnachweise bei *von Bar und Drobnig* aaO (n. 1) Rdnr. 305-315, S. 206-210.

[12] Besonders dramatisch wird es, wenn Arbeitnehmer (wie in Deutschland, nicht aber in Frankreich) keinen haftungsrechtlichen Außenschutz genießen, ihnen aber infolge der Verletzung ihres Arbeitsvertrages (man denke an den Hausmeister, der bei Schnee und Glatteis nicht rechtzeitig räumt und streut) gleichwohl eine auch deliktsrechtlich relevante Verletzung einer eigenen (!) Verkehrssicherungspflicht vorgeworfen wird.

dass das Deliktsrecht in seinem *eigenen* Arsenal offenbar schon immer den Vertrag zugunsten Dritter kannte. Er war dort auch stets wesentlich breiter angelegt als sein vertragsrechtliches Pendant, denn im deliktsrechtlichen Ausgangspunkt ging und geht es stets um Jedermannpflichten. Sieht man die Dinge so, dann verliert vielleicht selbst die französische Lehre von der *opposabilité du contrat* einen Teil ihrer Schrecken. Ursprünglich entwickelt, um das Problem in den Griff zu bekommen, dass Verträge unter dem Code civil einerseits nur relative Rechte begründen (Art. 1165 CC), andererseits aber Eigentum übertragen (was unmöglich zusammenpasst), hat man ihr später auch eine haftungsrechtliche Facette gegeben: Ein vertragsfremder Dritter kann in einer nicht geringen Zahl von Fällen den Nachweis einer *faute* seines Schädigers allein schon dadurch führen, dass er zeigt, dass dieser Schädiger durch sein Verhalten seine Pflichten aus einem Vertrag mit einem Dritten verletzt hat.[13] Keine andere Rechtsordnung Europas arbeitet, so scheint es, so völlig ungezwungen (oder skrupellos) mit der Lehre vom Vertrag mit Schutzwirkungen zugunsten Dritter wie die französische – aber sie bemüht dazu nicht das Vertrags- sondern das Deliktsrecht!

V. Begrenzung vertraglicher Informationspflichten durch Deliktsrecht

Gelegentlich kann es allerdings auch umgekehrt vorkommen, dass sich die inhaltliche Konkretisierung bestimmter vertraglicher Nebenpflichten aus einer im Hintergrund drohenden Deliktshaftung gegenüber Dritten ableitet; man hat es dann, wenn das Wortspiel erlaubt ist, mit einer *opposabilité*

---

[13] Siehe aus einer umfangreichen Rechtsprechung u.a. Cass. soc. 21.3.1972, JCP 1972, II, 17236, Anm. *Saint-Jours*; RTD civ. 1973 S. 128, Anm. *Durry* („Toute faute contractuelle est délictuelle au regard des tiers étrangers au contrat"); Cass. com. 16.1.1973, Bull. civ. 1973, IV, Nr. 28, S. 22 ("un même fait susceptible de constituer un manquement à une obligation existant entre deux parties liées à un contrat, peut être, au regard des tiers étrangers au contrat, une faute quasi délictuelle engageant la responsabilité de son auteur"); Cass. civ. 15.12.1998, Défrénois 1999 S. 745, Anm. *Denis Mazeaud*; RTD civ. 1999 S. 625, Anm. *Mestre*; Cass. civ. 18.7.2000, Bull. civ. 2000, I, Nr. 221 ; JCP 2000, II, 10415, Anm. *Sargos*; JCP 2001, I, 338 Nr. 9, Anm. *Viney*; RTD civ. 2001 S. 146, Anm. *Jourdain*; Cass. civ. 13.2.2001, Bull. civ. 2001, I, Nr. 35; Défrénois 2001 S. 712, Anm. *Savaux*; JCP 2002, II, 10099, Anm. *Lisanti-Kalczynski*. Siehe andererseits aber auch Cass. civ. 5.4.2005, RDC 2005 S. 687, Anm. *Denis Mazeaud*.

du délit zu tun. Das Common Law z.B. operiert mit einem sehr strikten *law of defamation*. Deshalb kann das Weiterleiten eines Verdachts über einen vertragsfremden Dritten, das man zwischen einander vertrauenden und eng kooperierenden Vertragspartnern „an sich" erwarten würde, unterbleiben müssen, und es ist natürlich nicht zu erwarten, dass das Vertragsrecht Informationspflichten aufstellt, die das Deliktsrecht im Falle ihrer Erfüllung mit Schadensersatz bewehren würde. Ähnlich verhält es sich in den Rechtsordnungen, die in ihrem Deliktsrecht mit dem Tatbestand der Kreditgefährdung operieren. Da sich niemand vertraglich zur Begehung eines Delikts verpflichten kann, setzen solche Tatbestände auch der Vertragshaftung Grenzen.

VI. Anstiftung zum Vertragsbruch

Man kann sich freilich nicht nur nicht vertraglich wirksam einer Person gegenüber verpflichten, zum Nachteil einer dritten Person ein Delikt zu begehen („Auftragsdiebstahl"), sondern es kann auch ein Delikt konstituieren, jemanden dazu zu überreden, seinen Vertrag mit einem Dritten nicht zu erfüllen. Es ist also nicht nur die Anstiftung zur Begehung eines Delikts ihrerseits ein Delikt, sondern es ist auch die Anstiftung zur Nichterfüllung einer Vertragsschuld eine unerlaubte Handlung. Das scheinen inzwischen alle Rechtsordnungen der Europäischen Union zu akzeptieren.[14] Der persönliche Schutzbereich dieses Delikts umfasst allerdings nur den Gläubiger der verletzten Forderung, nicht auch ihren Schuldner. Letzterer kann m.a.W. seine eigene Schadensersatzpflicht nicht an den Anstifter „weiterreichen" und ihn in Regress nehmen. Denn der Schuldner „must resist" des Anstifters „efforts by strength of will".[15] Das Delikt der Anstiftung zum Vertragsbruch verwandelt die (gestörte) Forderung des Gläubigers gegen seinen Schuldner auch nicht etwa in ein dingliches Recht. Dabei ist es ganz einerlei, was man unter einer „Sache" i.S.d. Sachenrechts verstehen will. Auch wo bzw. wenn Forderungen zu den Sachen gezählt werden, ändert

---

[14] Einzelnachweise bei *Christian von Bar*, Principles of European Law. Study Group on a European Civil Code. Non-contractual Liability Arising out of Damage Caused to Another (München 2009), Anmerkungen unter Art. 2:211 (Loss upon inducement of non-performance of obligation) sowie *dems.* aaO (n. 5) Rdnr. 310, S. 319-320.

[15] *Boulting and Another v. Association of Cinematograph, Television and Allied Technicians* [1963] 2 Q.B. 606 (CA, per Upjohn LJ).

sich an dem Ergebnis nichts. Denn zwar mag man die Regeln über die Haftung aus Anstiftung zum Vertragsbruch (die, genau genommen, nicht einmal wirklich Forderungsverletzungen „durch" Dritte, sondern bloße Forderungsverletzungen auf „Veranlassung" eines Dritten betreffen) dahin deuten wollen, dass sie Forderungen mit einem gewissen Drittschutz ausstatten[16]; immerhin können sich diese Regeln ihrer Natur nach nur in einer Dreipersonenbeziehung entfalten. Der Anspruch des Verletzten gegen den Anstifter setzt in der Person des Letzteren jedoch mindestens Verschulden, typischerweise sogar Vorsatz voraus.[17] Der von dem Vertragsbruch seines Schuldners betroffene Vertragsgläubiger hat deshalb gegen den Dritten dann keinen Anspruch, wenn dieser die „eigentlich" dem Gläubiger geschuldete Leistung arglos von dessen vertragsuntreuem Schuldner annimmt. Sofern sich Letzterer aus eigenem Antrieb und ohne Veranlassung durch den Dritten mit diesem einigt, bleibt der Gläubiger auf die Rechte gegen seinen Schuldner beschränkt. Hätte sich Richard Wagner's Nichte Johanna von sich aus von ihrem Vertragspartner, dem Royal Opera House, abgewandt, um ihre Künste der Royal Italian Opera anzubieten, wäre es nicht zu dem Prinzip aus *Lumley v. Gye*[18] gekommen.

VII. Unterschiede

Das Hauptaugenmerk der meisten Untersuchungen zum Verhältnis von Vertrags- und Deliktsrecht liegt (mit Recht) auf der Frage, in welchen Bereichen sich die beiden Regime eigentlich inhaltlich unterscheiden. Auch diese Frage kann hier nicht vollständig beantwortet werden. Differenzierungen finden sich überall. Sie betreffen den Haftungsgrund ebenso wie

---

[16] Für ein neueres Beispiel siehe aus der niederländischen Rechtsprechung HR 8.1.2010, RvdW 2010 Nr. 125, NedJur 2010 Nr. 187 m. Anm. *Mok* (Verletzung eines kartellrechtlich zulässigen geschlossenen Vertriebssystems von Fiat für Alfa Romeos durch einen angeschlossenen, aber unerkannt gebliebenen Händler; Weiterveräußerung der Wagen durch einen Zwischenhändler an den beklagten niederländischen Parallelimporteur, der von der Vertragsverletzung zumindest wissen musste; Unterlassungsanspruch von Fiat gegen den niederländischen Beklagten unter Hinweis auf dessen deliktsrechtlich relevantes Verhalten bejaht).

[17] Wie Fn. 14. Die Haftung aus Anstiftung zum Vertragsbruch gehört seit jeher zum Anwendungsbereich der *actio de dolo*. Für England siehe *OBG Ltd. v. Allan* [2008] 1 AC 1 (HL).

[18] [1853] 2 El.&Bl. 216; 118 E.R. 749.

den Kreis der geschützten Interessen und die den Betroffenen zur Verfügung gestellten Rechtsbehelfe. Es kommt vor, dass nur das Vertrags-, nicht aber auch das Deliktsrecht Erfüllungsansprüche kennt, weil Letzteres den vorbeugenden Rechtsschutz vernachlässigt; es kommt aber auch vor, dass *specific performance* bzw. *specific relief* grundsätzlich weder dem einen noch dem anderen bekannt sind. Unkörperliche Persönlichkeitsrechte sind typischerweise ein Schutzgut des außervertraglichen, reine Vermögensinteressen dagegen ein Schutzgut des innervertraglichen Haftungsrechts – aber auf solche statistischen Aussagen kann man sich nicht verlassen. *Pure economic losses* spielen auch im modernen Deliktsrecht eine herausragende Rolle, und es gibt eine ganze Reihe von Deliktsrechtssystemen, die im Grunde mit der ganzen Kategorie nichts anzufangen wissen. Einem französischen Juristen sagt der Begriff des *dommage purement économique* rein gar nichts; Art. 1382 CC gibt keinerlei Veranlassung dazu, diese Schadenskategorie zu vereinzeln. Das gilt im Übrigen auch für die Nichtvermögensschäden. Auch Deutschland hat insoweit die Unterscheidung zwischen Vertrags- und Deliktsrecht inzwischen beseitigt, hinkt aber dennoch in beiden Bereichen weiterhin spürbar hinter dem französischen Recht hinterher. In anderen Ländern der Europäischen Union aber ist die Ersatzfähigkeit von Nichtvermögensschäden bis heute eine Eigenart des außervertraglichen Haftungsrechts geblieben.[19]

Delikts- und vertragsrechtliche Schadensersatzhaftung lassen sich nur in einigen Ländern zu der Unterscheidung zwischen verschuldensgebundener und verschuldensunabhängiger Haftung in Beziehung setzen; bei Einbeziehung weiterer Rechtsordnungen kann es zu aus deutscher Sicht ganz unerwarteten Überkreuzstellungen kommen. In Frankreich hat die *Gardien*haftung unter Art. 1384 der Haftung für *faute* unter den Artt. 1382 und 1383 CC wohl lange schon auch statistisch den Rang abgelaufen. Ein in ganz Europa heftig umstrittenes Konzept ist das der Haftung für den Verlust einer Chance. Im Vereinigten Königreich wird eine entsprechende Haftung sowohl vertrags- als auch deliktsrechtlich abgelehnt[20], in Frankreich und Belgien prinzipiell in beiden Bereichen bejaht[21], in Portugal ist sie vertragsrechtlich akzeptiert worden[22] und in Deutschland soll sie nach der Untersuchung eines Münsteraner Kollegen sogar nur vertrags-, nicht

---

[19] So verhalten sich die Dinge z.B. in Griechenland und in Italien.
[20] Umfangreiche Einzelnachweise bei *von Bar und Drobnig* aaO (Fn. 1) Rdnr. 119, S. 86-88.
[21] AaO Rdnr. 114 S. 84.
[22] Tribunal Supremo 2.12.1976, BolMinJus 262 (1977) 142.

aber deliktsrechtlich möglich sein.[23] Ein erhöhter Schadensersatz im Falle schweren Verschuldens (sogen *aggravated damages*) ist bislang, soweit es ihn überhaupt gibt, allem Anschein nach eine Besonderheit des außervertraglichen Haftungsrechts geblieben. In manchen Ländern folgt die Haftung für Gehilfen gleich in mehrfacher Beziehung je nachdem unterschiedlichen Regeln, ob die jeweilige Anspruchsgrundlage ihren Sitz im Vertrags- oder im Deliktsrecht hat. Dann geht es nicht nur darum, dass nur das Delikts-, nicht aber das Vertragsrecht eine Exculpationsmöglichkeit für den Geschäftsherren vorsieht, sondern auch darum, dass der Kreis der Personen, für die man haftet, deliktsrechtlich enger geschnitten sein kann als vertragsrechtlich. Vor einem gesamteuropäischen Horizont ist indes auch insoweit keine einheitliche Linie auszumachen. Die Haftung für Gehilfen ist meistens auch deliktsrechtlich strikt, Frankreich kennt eine deliktische Geschäftsherrenhaftung auch für Gelegenheitsgehilfen[24], die Niederlande eine solche Haftung auch für selbständige Unternehmer (Artt. 6:171 und 172 BW). Es ist denkbar, aber wiederum keineswegs überall der Fall, dass haftungsrechtliche Freizeichnungsklauseln je nachdem anderen Regeln unterliegen, ob sie sich auf die vertragliche oder die außervertragliche Haftung beziehen. Länder, deren Kodifikation die Kategorie des allgemeinen Schuldrechts kennt, neigen dazu, im Recht des Mitverschuldens nicht grundsätzlich zwischen Vertrags- und Deliktshaftung zu unterscheiden, in Italien verweist eine spezielle Deliktsrechtsnorm (Art. 2056 CC) auf die entsprechende vertragsrechtliche Vorschrift (Art. 1227 CC), im Vereinigten Königreich werden dagegen mitverschuldensrechtliche Fragestellungen je nachdem unterschiedlich beurteilt, ob sie sich im Zuge der Vertrags- oder der Deliktshaftung stellen, und im Übrigen wird selbst innerhalb der Letzteren noch zwischen verschiedenen *torts* unterschieden.[25] Ähnlich komplex liegen die Dinge endlich auch im Verjährungsrecht. Während das neuere deutsche Recht viel daran gesetzt hat, die vertrags- und die außervertragliche Verjährung anzugleichen, gibt es immer noch eine Reihe von Ländern, die mit enormen Unterschieden dieser beiden Regime leben.[26]

---

[23] Gerald Mäsch, Chance und Schaden. Zur Dienstleisterhaftung bei unaufklärbaren Kausalverläufen (Tübingen 2004).

[24] Z.B. Cass. civ. 27.11.1991, Resp. civ. et assur. 1992 Nr. 143 (Jäger hilft Jagdherren beim Aufbrechen von Wildbret; Verrichtungsgehilfeneigenschaft bejaht).

[25] Näher *von Bar und Drobnig* aaO (Fn. 1) Rdnr. 250 und 256, S. 171-174 und 176-178.

[26] Besonders dramatisch ist die Lage in Spanien mit seiner (jeweils allerdings von zahlreichen Ausnahmen durchbrochenen) fünfzehnjährigen vertragli-

VIII. Schluss

Wenn man die Beziehungen zwischen Vertrags- und Deliktsrecht nicht „nur" für seine eigene, sondern gleich für mehrere Rechtsordnungen beschreiben will, dann nötigt das unvermeidlich auch noch dazu, in einer Art Querschnittsanalyse die wichtigsten Fallgruppen zu einander in Beziehung zu setzen, welche in Europa zwischen den verschiedenen Hauptkategorien hin und her wandern, ja in einigen Ländern von manchen Autoren sogar zum Gegenstand einer eigenen Systemkategorie erhoben werden. Von der sogen. Vertrauenshaftung war schon die Rede. Mit ihren Vor- und Nachteilen können wir uns hier indes nicht im Einzelnen auseinandersetzen. Wir können weder die verschlungenen Wege nachzeichnen, welche die *culpa in contrahendo* in den europäischen Schuldrechtssytemen gewählt hat, noch auf das Recht der Haftung für Gewinnzusagen eingehen. Gewaltige Anschauungsfelder für europäische Klassifikationsunterschiede zwischen Vertrag und Delikt liefern desweiteren die Produzentenhaftung, die Haftung für fehlerhafte Dienstleistungen, die Haftung für fehlerhaften Rat und Auskunft und die Haftung für mangelnde Grundstücks- und Gebäudesicherheit. Auch in terminologischer Hinsicht wäre noch viel zu beleuchten, etwa der unterschiedliche Gebrauch eines so zentralen Begriffes wie der des Schadens je nachdem, ob man sich in einem vertrags- oder einem deliktsrechtlichen Zusammenhang ausdrückt. Wir müssen uns vielmehr mit der eher ernüchternden These begnügen, dass es de *lege lata* kaum eine Möglichkeit gibt, für alle Jurisdiktionen der Europäischen Union zutreffende, allgemeingültige Aussagen über die Interaktionen zwischen Vertrags- und Deliktsrecht zu machen. Vertrags- und Deliktsrecht werden zwar überall voneinander geschieden, aber die Kriterien, nach denen sich diese Unterscheidung haftungsrechtlich vollzieht, weichen bis heute von Land zu Land voneinander ab. Mit ein wenig gutem Willen müsste es allerdings möglich sein, gemeinsam etwas mehr Ordnung in dieses Chaos zu bringen.

---

chen (Art. 1964 CC) und seiner einjährigen deliktsrechtlichen Verjährungsfrist (Art. 1968 CC).

Liability Insurance

Helmut Heiss

I. Liability and Insurance in European Private Law

1. Introduction

Liability and liability insurance traditionally pursue the so-called "principle of separation", according to which the (insured) tortfeasor's relationship to the victim in tort is strictly distinct from the contractual relationship of the (insured) tortfeasor to his liability insurer.[1] Despite this dogmatic distinction, it is clear that insurance fulfils a complementary task with regard to liability: It protects the person liable, but also the victim of a tort from the insolvency of the tortfeasor. In contrast, alternative models, in particular the replacement of tort law and thus also of liability insurance with the so-called no-fault systems, have hitherto not achieved acceptance in European law.[2]

Nevertheless, there has been a significant erosion of the principle of separation, in particular in the area of compulsory insurance law, with the pioneering law on motor vehicle liability insurance. First and foremost, the victim's direct right of action against the tortfeasor's liability insurer should be mentioned. This is further reinforced when the insurer is liable to the victim, despite an insufficient insurance relationship, ie where the insurer is released from the obligation to perform as against the tortfeasor ("no defence *vis-à-vis* third parties"). A right of direct action and the exclusion of defences result in the liability insurer being liable to the victim even though the latter is not party to the insurance contract and the contract may not even give rise to liability.

---

[1] Cf *Christian von Bar*, Das „Trennungsprinzip" und die Geschichte des Wandels der Haftpflichtversicherung, Archiv für die civilistische Praxis 181 (1981) 289.
[2] They are commonly rejected in legal literature; cf, for example, *Gerhard Wagner*, Grundstrukturen des Europäischen Deliktsrechts, in: Reinhard Zimmermann (ed), Grundstrukturen des Europäischen Deliktsrechts (2003) 189 (324ff).

Such erosion of the principle of separation has been communitarised using the five Motor Vehicle Liability Insurance Directives,[3] which have recently been subsumed into the Consolidated Directive.[4] In other areas, the first signs of similar developments can also be observed: Thus, using the instrument of compulsory insurance in order to protect victims has, for example, also been implemented in the Insurance Mediation Directive[5] and the Regulation concerning Road Transport Operators.[6] While some other legal instruments adopted by the EU do not require compulsory insurance, they do allow Member States to impose their national requirements for insurance on foreign service providers.[7] For this purpose, the host country in which the service is provided must recognise the validity of the liability

---

[3] First Council Directive 72/166/EEC of 24 April 1972 on the approximation of the laws of Member States relating to insurance against civil liability in respect of the use of motor vehicles, and to the enforcement of the obligation to insure against such liability [1972] OJ L103/1; Second Council Directive 84/5/EEC of 30 December 1983 on the approximation of the laws of the Member States relating to insurance against civil liability in respect of the use of motor vehicles [1984] OJ L8/17; Third Council Directive 90/232/EEC of 14 May 1990 on the approximation of the laws of the Member States relating to insurance against civil liability in respect of the use of motor vehicles [1990] OJ L129/33; Fourth Directive 2000/26/EC of the European Parliament and of the Council of 16 May 2000 on the approximation of the laws of the Member States relating to insurance against civil liability in respect of the use of motor vehicles and amending Council Directives 73/239/EEC and 88/357/EEC [2000] OJ L181/65; Fifth Directive 2005/14/EC of the European Parliament and of the Council of 11 May 2005 amending Council Directives 72/166/EEC, 84/5/EEC, 88/357/EEC and 90/232/EEC and Directive 2000/26/EC of the European Parliament and of the Council relating to insurance against civil liability in respect of the use of motor vehicles [2005] OJ L149/14.

[4] Directive 2009/103/EC of the European Parliament and of the Council of 16 September 2009 relating to insurance against civil liability in respect of the use of motor vehicles, and the enforcement of the obligation to insure against such liability [2009] OJ L263/11.

[5] See Art. 4(3) of Directive 2002/92/EC of the European Parliament and of the Council of 9 December 2002 on insurance mediation [2003] OJ L9/3.

[6] Art. 7(2) of Regulation (EC) 1071/2009 of the European Parliament and of the Council of 21 October 2009 establishing common rules concerning the conditions to be complied with to pursue the occupation of road transport operator and repealing Council Directive 96/26/EC [2009] OJ L300/51.

[7] See Art. 6(3) of Directive 98/5/EC of the European Parliament and of the Council of 16 February 1998 to facilitate practice of the profession of lawyer on a permanent

insurance taken out in the service provider's home country, if equivalent.[8] Moreover, in the Environmental Liability Directive, the European legislature obliges the Member States to create incentives to obtain cover for the persons concerned.[9] This illustrates that, in creating liability, the legislature always has regard to its insurability.

In the field of motor vehicle liability insurance, the European regime of compulsory insurance has come into direct interplay with the law of torts in cases of road traffic accidents, which has hitherto largely been dominated by national legislation. This interplay constitutes the basis of a whole row of decisions by the ECJ as well as the EFTA Court, out of which the general principles, outlined below, underlying the relationship between the law on European compulsory insurance and national tort law can be extracted.

2. Starting point for case law: The purpose of the Motor Vehicle Liability Insurance Directive(s)

The EFTA Court[10] and the ECJ[11] have time and again stressed the fundamental importance of the Motor Vehicle Liability Directive to the mobility

---

   basis in a Member State other than that in which the qualification was obtained [1998] OJ L77/36.

[8] Art. 1(6) of Council Directive 89/48/EEC of 21 December 1988 on a general system for the recognition of higher-education diplomas awarded on completion of professional education and training of at least three years' duration [1989] OJ L19/16 (as amended); Art. 10(6) of Council Directive 92/51/EEC of 18 June 1992 on a second general system for the recognition of professional education and training to supplement Directive 89/48/EEC [1992] OJ L209/25 (as amended).

[9] Art. 14 of Directive 2004/35/EC of the European Parliament and of the Council of 21 April 2004 on environmental liability with regard to the prevention and remedying of environmental damage [2004] OJ L143/64.

[10] Case E-8/07 *Celina Nguyen v Staten v/Justis- og politidepartementet* [2008] EFTA Ct Rep 224, para 23; Case E-1/99 *Storebrand Skadeforsikring AS v Veronika Finanger* [1999] EFTA Ct Rep 119, paras 25ff; Case E-7/00 *Halla Helgadóttir v Daníel Hjaltason and Iceland Insurance Company* [2000-2001] EFTA Ct Rep 246, para 28.

[11] Case C-129/94 Criminal proceedings against *Ruiz Bernáldez* [1996] ECR I-1829, paras 13ff; Case C-348/98 *Ferreira v Companhia de Seguros Mundial Confiança SA* [2000] ECR I-6711, para 24; Case C-537/03 *Katja Candolin and others v Vahinkovakuutusosakeyhtiö Pohjola, Jarno Ruokoranta* [2005] ECR I-5745, para 17; Case C-484/09 *Manuel Carvalho Ferreira Santos v Companhia Europeia de Seguros, SA*

Helmut Heiss

of motor vehicles within the European Economic Area and of safeguarding "equivalent" compensation for the victims of road traffic accidents, irrespective of the EU/EEA Member State in which an accident takes place. This was by no means stated merely *obiter*. Instead, the purposes mentioned open the doors to a broad and dynamic interpretation of the provisions in the directive. This dynamic interpretation has led to the development of three basic principles in European motor vehicle liability insurance law, which will be discussed below.

3. Insurance follows liability

First, European case law affirms the principle that insurance follows liability as a result of the principle of separation.[12] The directives are thus only intended to harmonise the law of motor vehicle liability insurance.[13] It is not the purpose of the directives to harmonise the tort laws of the signatory states.[14]

In general, this means no more than that the insured's right of recourse, originating out of the liability insurance contract, only exists if and to the extent that he has become liable. Of course, this does not apply to the right to legal protection, which is also regularly included under liability insurance cover and which naturally serves the purpose of defending the insured against *unjustified* claims.[15] A right of *recourse* can, however, only be exercised by the insured *vis-à-vis* his liability insurer for liability which has actually arisen. Subsequently, the third party victim also has no right to sue the insurer where there is no claim for damages, even if he is granted the right to bring a direct action against the liability insurer by liability insur-

---

para. 79; Case C-409/09 *José Maria Ambrósio Lavrador v Companhia de Seguros Fideliodade-Mundial SA*, para. 23.

[12] ECJ: For example Case C-348/98 *Ferreira* [2000] ECR I-6711, para 23; Case C-356/06 *Elaine Farrell v Alan Whitty* [2007] ECR I-3067, paras 32f; Case C-484/09 *Manuel Carvalho Ferreira Santos v Companhia Europeia de Seguros, SA* para. 31; Case C-409/09 *José Maria Ambrósio Lavrador v Companhia de Seguros Fideliodade-Mundial SA*, para. 25.; EFTA Court: Case E-8/07 *Celina Nguyen v Staten v/ Justis- og politidepartementet* [2008] EFTA Ct Rep 224, para 23.

[13] Especially clear in Case E-7/00 *Helgadóttir* [2000-2001] EFTA Ct Rep 246, para 30.

[14] Case E-8/07 *Celina Nguyen v Staten v/Justis- og politidepartementet* [2008] EFTA Ct Rep 224, para 24; likewise the E Case C-356/06 *Elaine Farrell v Alan Whitty* [2007] ECR I-3067, para 33.

[15] Cf with regard to German law § 100 VVG.

ance law, for example Art. 18 of the (consolidated) Motor Vehicle Liability Insurance Directive.[16]

4. Liability requires insurance

A second, considerably broader principle is also embodied in European case law: Any liability for road traffic accidents prescribed by a national law within the EU/EEA must be accompanied by compulsory insurance cover. The national legislatures thus must ensure that insurance contracts which are subject to their system of compulsory insurance for motor vehicles completely cover the liability arising from the national laws of torts.[17] In doing so, the national legislatures may not confine themselves to their own tort laws, because – under Art. 14 of the (consolidated) Motor Vehicle Liability Insurance Directive[18] and based on the principle of single premium – the insurance contract also has to cover liability for use of the vehicle in other EU/EEA Member States. Insurance cover must, therefore, always suffice for the most stringent form of liability which may arise in accordance with national tort law within the EU/EEA. In this way, the liability

---

[16] Art. 18 of the Motor Vehicle Liability Insurance Directive (2009/103/EC) reads: *"Member States shall ensure that any party injured as a result of an accident caused by a vehicle covered by insurance as referred to in Article 3 enjoys a direct right of action against the insurance undertaking covering the person responsible against civil liability."*

[17] See, in particular, Case E-8/07 *Celina Nguyen v Staten v/Justis- og politidepartementet* [2008] EFTA Ct Rep 224, para 25; cf also the ECJ in Case C-166/02 *Daniel Fernando Messejana Viegas v Companhia de Seguros Zurich SA and Mitsubishi Motors de Portugal SA* [2003] ECR I-7871, para 21; Case C-484/09 *Manuel Carvalho Ferreira Santos v Companhia Europeia de Seguros, SA* para. 26; Case C-409/09 *José Maria Ambrósio Lavrador v Companhia de Seguros Fideliodade-Mundial SA*, para. 24 and 27.

[18] Art. 14 of the Motor Vehicle Liability Insurance Directive (2009/103/EC) reads: *"Member States shall take the necessary steps to ensure that all compulsory policies of insurance against civil liability arising out of the use of vehicles:*
(a) cover, on the basis of a single premium and during the whole term of the contract, the entire territory of the Community, including for any period in which the vehicle remains in other Member States during the term of the contract; and
(b) guarantee, on the basis of that single premium, in each Member State, the cover required by its law or the cover required by the law of the Member State where the vehicle is normally based, when that cover is higher."

laws of all of the EU/EEA Member States cumulatively determine the extent of compulsory insurance cover. This was inferred by the EFTA Court in the *Nguyen* case from the wording of the directives. For example, Art. 1(2) of the First Motor Vehicle Liability Insurance Directive[19] refers to "any" loss or injury.[20] Art. 1(1) of the Second Motor Vehicle Liability Insurance Directive[21] addresses "personal injuries". This term includes all types of loss which result from bodily injuries.[22] If one considers that the claim made by the bereaved in *Nguyen* did not, under Norwegian law, depend on the bodily injury being suffered personally,[23] then the term "personal injuries" used in the directives also includes third party damage resulting from personal injury suffered by another. The EFTA Court, however, also justified this broad understanding by referring to the purpose of the directives, which is as much to guarantee the free movement of motor vehicles in Europe as it is to protect the victims of road traffic accidents.[24]

When this broad approach is used consistently, it is immaterial whether the liability arises out of strict or general tortious liability[25] or whether it is for economic loss or non-economic injury.[26] It is likewise irrelevant that a judge is accorded a degree of discretion when awarding damages for non-economic injury. According to the EFTA Court, it is only of relevance that a right to compensation is awarded and that a civil liability claim exists. It should be noted that "civil liability" represents an autonomous concept in

---

[19] See now Art. 1(2) of the Motor Vehicle Liability Insurance Directive (2009/103/EC): "'*injured party' means any person entitled to compensation in respect of any loss or injury caused by vehicles.*"

[20] Case E-8/07 *Celina Nguyen v Staten v/Justis- og politidepartementet* [2008] EFTA Ct Rep 224, para 26.

[21] See now Art. 3 of the Motor Vehicle Liability Insurance Directive (2009/103/EC): "*[...] The insurance referred to in the first paragraph shall cover compulsorily both damage to property and personal injuries.*"

[22] Case E-8/07 *Celina Nguyen v Staten v/Justis- og politidepartementet* [2008] EFTA Ct Rep 224, para 26.

[23] Case E-8/07 *Celina Nguyen v Staten v/Justis- og politidepartementet* [2008] EFTA Ct Rep 224, para 12.

[24] Case E-8/07 *Celina Nguyen v Staten v/Justis- og politidepartementet* [2008] EFTA Ct Rep 224, para 27.

[25] See, for example, the ECJ in Case C-166/02 *Messejana Viegas* [2003] ECR I-7871, para 21.

[26] Case E-8/07 *Celina Nguyen v Staten v/Justis- og politidepartementet* [2008] EFTA Ct Rep 224, para 27.

the directives,[27] such that it is not substantively commensurate with the national definitions of the term.

The EFTA Court also interprets the concept of civil liability broadly in order to ensure that the protective purposes of the directives are achieved. For instance, it is inconsequential that the existence of liability is determined in the course of criminal, rather than civil proceedings. The Court is only concerned with whether the payment has a compensatory function. In the *Nguyen* case, the Court stated that the right to claim for non-pecuniary damages was a *"right to obtain compensation from another person"* and therefore a case of civil liability.[28] It therefore did not matter whether or not, in accordance with national definitions, compensation for non-pecuniary damages had a punitive function and whether this purpose of the compensation was of greater or less importance.[29] The EFTA Court thus demonstrated that it was in principle open towards punitive damages as defined in national laws. In doing so, it positioned itself similarly to the ECJ, which not only did not reject the award of punitive damages under national competition law, but in fact demanded its application in order to enforce European competition law in accordance with the "principle of equivalence" as stated by it.[30] According to this principle, "it must be possible to award [...] punitive damages, pursuant to actions founded on the Community competition rules, if such damages may be awarded pursuant to similar actions founded on domestic law".[31] Consequently, the question arises as to whether the national legislatures are also required to include purely punitive damages, ie those which do not have any compensatory function, in the cover of motor vehicle liability insurance. Considering the interest of victims to be able to effectively enforce claims for damages and the interest of insureds to also enjoy full insurance cover abroad, this view would be welcome. The other side of the coin not only, and by no means primarily, entails burdening the community of the insured with extra costs, but also leads to the question of whether the cover of punitive damages as required by the EFTA Court

---

[27] Case E-8/07 *Celina Nguyen v Staten v/Justis- og politidepartementet* [2008] EFTA Ct Rep 224, para 21.

[28] Case E-8/07 *Celina Nguyen v Staten v/Justis- og politidepartementet* [2008] EFTA Ct Rep 224, para 28.

[29] See Case E-8/07 *Celina Nguyen v Staten v/Justis- og politidepartementet* [2008] EFTA Ct Rep 224, para 28.

[30] See the ECJ, Joined cases C-295/04 to C-298/04 [2006] ECR I-6619, para 93 with further references.

[31] ECJ, Joined cases C-295/04 to C-298/04 [2006] ECR I-6619, para 93 with further references to older case law.

violates the national concepts of *ordre public*. This question is relevant for countries which do not recognise punitive damages, the award of which is viewed as a violation of public policy. These countries should of course be cautious when transposing the judgment on *ordre public* to liability insurance, as they are not able to prevent potential tortfeasors abroad from effectively being subjected to liability for punitive damages; these potential wrongdoers therefore have a need for insurance. The question is even more relevant for countries which recognise punitive damages. In some circumstances, they want to enhance the preventative effect of the instrument by using the American example and declaring insurance of punitive damages to be a violation of *ordre public*. A broad interpretation of the EFTA Court's reasoning would prevent them from doing so.

However, the *Nguyen* case is not suited to answering this question. One reason for this is because the EFTA Court only stated that a national interpretation of damages for non-economic injury as "punitive" does not provide any information about whether a case concerns "civil liability" according to the European terminology used in the Motor Vehicle Liability Insurance Directive(s). Thus, the EFTA Court autonomously examines whether civil liability should be imposed and does not bother itself with the intricacies of theoretical arguments at national level. At the same time, the EFTA Court emphasised the real compensatory function of the damages awarded in the case at hand. Consequently, the case could not, from the outset, serve as a precedent for the question of whether the Motor Vehicle Liability Insurance Directive also requires purely punitive damages to be covered by insurance.

5. Insurance requires liability

Contrary to the principle which states that insurance follows liability, existing liability insurance cover has the effect of creating and reinforcing liability in reality.[32] This stimulus produced by liability insurance has been endowed with a legal imperative at European level by European case law. It has been stressed in case law time and again that national liability laws are not affected by the Motor Vehicle Liability Insurance Directive, ie it remains within the autonomy of the national legislatures to create or to distance

---

[32] For examples of the impact on liability claims of liability insurance under German law, cf *Werner Lücke*, in: Erich Prölss and Anton Martin (eds), Versicherungsvertragsgesetz (28th edn, 2010) § 100 paras 77 ff.

themselves from a certain type of liability.[33] The national legislatures have broad discretion in this respect.[34] At the same time, however, the Court obliges the national legislatures not to create any regulations in tortious matters which would undermine the purpose of the Motor Vehicle Liability Insurance Directives and thus their effectiveness.[35] Of further reaching impact, the EFTA Court considered in the *Helgadóttir* case that if an EEA signatory restricted liability in such a way so as to significantly deviate from the general standards of liability within the EEA, this could also conflict with the purpose of the directives.[36] In this way, the protection provided to victims of road traffic accidents under the Motor Vehicle Liability Insurance Directives, to a certain extent, leads to the EEA Member States being compelled to harmonise tort law.

Two main areas of application have developed out of this: First, the directives offer the victims of accidents protection by setting a *minimum amount insured*, which is also available in cases of strict liability. The amounts which may be awarded for strict liability, which does not require fault, are however often limited themselves. It would, according to the ECJ's opinion, run contrary to the purposes of the directives and curb their effectiveness in regard to protecting victims of road traffic accidents if the minimum amount insured could not be exhausted merely because a national legislature had capped the maximum liability of motor vehicle owners to an amount below the minimum amount of cover.[37] The minimum amount insured therefore forms the minimum level of liability of motor vehicle owners in the EEA.

Second, under the directives, motor vehicle liability insurance must also cover claims for damages made by *passengers*,[38] even in cases where a pas-

---

[33] Case E-8/07 *Celina Nguyen v Staten v/Justis- og politidepartementet* [2008] EFTA Ct Rep 224, para 24.
[34] See Case E-7/00 *Helgadóttir* [2000-2001] EFTA Ct Rep 246, para 31.
[35] See ECJ in Case C-356/06 *Elaine Farrell v Alan Whitty* [2007] ECR I-3067, para 34; as well as Case C-537/03 *Candolin* [2005] ECR I-5745, para 28; Case C-484/09 *Manuel Carvalho Ferreira Santos v Companhia Europeia de Seguros, SA* para. 35 and 36; Case C-409/09 *José Maria Ambrósio Lavrador v Companhia de Seguros Fideliodade-Mundial SA*, para. 28.
[36] Case E-7/00 *Helgadóttir* [2000-2001] EFTA Ct Rep 246, para 31.
[37] Case C-348/98 *Ferreira* [2000] ECR I-6711, paras 36ff (esp para 41); Case C-166/02 *Messejana Viegas* [2003] ECR I-7871.
[38] In contrast, protection granted to passengers under the former Second Motor Vehicle Liability Insurance Directive had been limited, cf the ECJ in Case C-158/01 *Withers* [2002] ECR I-8301.

senger is the owner of the vehicle.[39] It would run contrary to the protective function if a national law of liability were able to exclude a claim for damages, for example because a passenger had got into a car with a drunken driver.[40] Furthermore, such an exclusion of liability would also considerably undermine the general standards of liability in the EEA.[41] In effect, compulsory liability and liability in favour of passengers ensue from the Motor Vehicle Liability Insurance Directives. In cases where, for example, the driver is under the influence of alcohol, the only possibility available to the insurer is to provide for a right of recourse against the driver in the contract.[42] The same applies to the liability of passengers "travelling in a part of a motor vehicle which has not been designed and constructed with seating accommodation for passengers".[43] In contrast, it is possible from the perspective of the directives, to award a lump sum for the loss of future income when setting the level of compensation.[44]

In the case law discussed, it has at times been expressed that a general reduction of compensation as a consequence of contributory negligence is only possible under "exceptional circumstances".[45] Such a narrow view was recently countered by two decisions of the ECJ.[46] In the preliminary ruling concerned, the case dealt with strict liability resulting from the operational hazards inherent in the vehicles involved; here two vehicles were involved in the accident, such that the question regarding the allocation of loss arose in the same way as it does in cases of contributory negligence. The applicable Portuguese law provides that in case of doubt the costs of

---

[39] See the ECJ, Case C-537/03 *Candolin* [2005] ECR I-5745, para 31.

[40] Case E-1/99 *Finanger* [1999] EFTA Ct Rep 119, para 32; in contrast, in Case C-129/94 *Ruiz Bernáldez* [1996] ECR I-1829, the ECJ had to decide on the converse case in which the drunken driver was liable, but where this liability was excluded from the insurance cover.

[41] Case E-1/99 *Finanger* [1999] EFTA Ct Rep 119, para 32.

[42] See the ECJ in Case C-129/94 *Ruiz Bernáldez* [1996] ECR I-1829, para 22.

[43] Case C-356/06 *Elaine Farrell v Alan Whitty* [2007] ECR I-3067, para 36 together with para 35.

[44] Case E-7/00 *Helgadóttir* [2000-2001] EFTA Ct Rep 246, paras 32ff (esp para 35).

[45] Case E-1/99 *Finanger* [1999] EFTA Ct Rep 119, para 34; cf also the ECJ in Case C-537/03 *Candolin* [2005] ECR I-5745, paras 29f.

[46] Case C-484/09 *Manuel Carvalho Ferreira Santos v Companhia Europeia de Seguros, SA*; Case C-409/09 *José Maria Ambrósio Lavrador v Companhia de Seguros Fideliodade-Mundial SA*, para. 23.

the damage are to be shared equally.[47] The Court correctly came to the result that reducing compensation for damages according to the inherent operational hazards and, in cases of doubt, allocating it in equal shares was compatible with the First, Second and Third Motor Vehicle Liability Insurance Directives.[48] The ECJ stated that the supposedly contradicting statements of the ECJ in *Candolin*[49] and *Farrell*[50] had concerned an area of law which fell within the scope and therefore the harmonising effect of the directives, ie those concerning motor vehicle liability insurance law.[51] In the footnotes, AG Trstenjak also cited the judgments of the EFTA Court so that these decisions should also fall within the scope of the restrictive interpretation. Whether this restrictive interpretation of the preliminary ruling is correct in every respect is however doubtful. Its correctness would require the tortfeasor to have been subject to civil liability in all of the cases decided hitherto and only the right of the victim to sue the liability insurer directly to have been restricted. Otherwise, limiting the judgments to the law of motor vehicle insurance would lead to the liability insurer not only having to cover the liability of the driver and/or owner, but also cover certain non-recoverable tortious damage to the victim. Such a result has however been expressly excluded by AG Trstenjak in her opinion.[52] In the *Candolin* and *Farrel* judgments it was provisions of compulsory insurance law that were actually concerned. It is, however, likely that in these cases not only a duty on the part of the insurer to cover, but also civil liability of the tortfeasor were missing. In any case, the provisions in dispute cannot be attributed unequivocally to either tort or insurance law. Furthermore, the only sensible conclusion from the statements of the ECJ made in both judgments which assert that the national provisions regarding the compensation of road traffic accidents may not deprive the directives' provisions

---

[47] For the applicable Portuguese law, see Case C-484/09 *Manuel Carvalho Ferreira Santos v Companhia Europeia de Seguros, SA*, para 8 et
[48] Case C-484/09 *Manuel Carvalho Ferreira Santos v Companhia Europeia de Seguros, SA*; Case C-409/09 *José Maria Ambrósio Lavrador v Companhia de Seguros Fideliodade-Mundial SA*, para. 23.
[49] Case C-537/03 *Candolin* [2005] ECR I-5745.
[50] Case C-356/06 *Elaine Farrell v Alan Whitty* [2007] ECR I-3067.
[51] Case C-484/09 *Manuel Carvalho Ferreira Santos v Companhia Europeia de Seguros, SA*, para. 79; Case C-409/09 *José Maria Ambrósio Lavrador v Companhia de Seguros Fideliodade-Mundial SA*, para. 39.
[52] See Case C-484/09 *Manuel Carvalho Ferreira Santos v Companhia Europeia de Seguros, SA*, Opinion of AG Verica Trstenjak (7 December 2010), paras 67 ff.

of their practical effectiveness[53] is that they also relate to tort law, since the law of compulsory insurance in the narrow sense must without question comply completely with the requirements set out in the directives. Moreover, since the judgments in *Ferreira*[54] und *Messejena Viegas*[55], there are decisions which deal directly with the provisions of Portuguese tort law.[56] It is therefore not possible to deny that the regime of compulsory insurance provided in the directives has an impact on national tort laws. Irrespective of this, however, the ECJ is to be supported in its view that the provisions of the directives do not prevent damages from being allocated in proportion to the respective degree of the operational hazard of the multiple vehicles involved in an accident under national law.

6. Conclusion

The Motor Vehicle Liability Insurance Directives do not lead to a harmonisation of the national laws on road accident liability ("insurance follows the liability"). They do however ensure that any type of liability provided for by the national laws in the EEA will be accompanied by mandatory insurance cover ("liability requires insurance"). The purpose of the Motor Vehicle Liability Insurance Directives, moreover, has an impact on the national laws of tort. In the interests of the road accident victims, the tort laws of the EEA Member States may not undermine the protection provided in the directives or significantly deviate from the general standards of protection in the EEA ("insurance requires liability").

---

[53] Case C-537/03 *Candolin* [2005] ECR I-5745, para 28; Case C-356/06 *Elaine Farell v Alan Whitty* [2007] ECR I-3067, para 34.
[54] Case C-348/98 *Ferreira* [2000] ECR I-6711, paras 36ff (esp para 41).
[55] Case C-166/02 *Messejana Viegas* [2003] ECR I-7871.
[56] The decisions were concerned with the maximum amount of liability which can be imposed for strict liability in cases of road traffic accidents under Art. 508(1) of the Portuguese *Código Cívil*.

II. Liability Insurance in European Conflict of Laws

1. Jurisdiction

Liability insurance is governed comprehensively by European conflict of laws and some aspects are dealt with specifically. Thus, international jurisdiction in liability insurance matters is determined in accordance with Chapter II, Section 3 of Brussels I,[57] which applies to matters relating to insurance. This section contains special provisions for liability insurance. As with other types of insurance, the insurer can be sued at the place where it is domiciled[58] and in case of co-insurance at the place of the leading insurer's domicile.[59] Alternatively, the policyholder and the insured of liability insurance are granted home jurisdiction.[60] Art. 10 of Brussels I also alternatively gives the court at the place where the harmful event occurred jurisdiction for an action against the liability insurer. Especially as this jurisdiction is also open for a claim in tort against the tortfeasor,[61] both the tortfeasor and the liability insurer can be sued in this forum. Further, Art. 11(1) of Brussels I permits an action for breach of warranty and/or an action in opposition to execution of a judgment against the insurer to be brought before the court at which the victim's action against the insured tortfeasor is pending.

The rule in Art. 11(2) of Brussels I is of significantly greater practical importance for the right of the victim to sue the liability insurer directly. Following the groundbreaking ECJ decision in the *Odenbreit*[62] case, the reference in Art. 11(2) of Brussels I to (*inter alia*) Art. 9(1)(b) of Brussels I is to be understood in such a way that the victim is awarded jurisdiction at his own place of domicile, irrespective of whether the case shows any connection to this forum – other than the domicile of the victim itself. To briefly recap the case: The *Odenbreit* case was concerned with damage suffered by a victim resident in Germany, while all of the other elements of the case (place of the occurrence of the loss, domicile of the tortfeasor, country of registration of the damaged vehicle, registered office of the liability insurer, applicable tort law, applicable insurance contract law) had

---

[57] Council Regulation (EC) 44/2001 of 22 December 2000 on jurisdiction and the recognition and enforcement of judgments in civil and commercial matters [2001] OJ L12/1.
[58] Art. 9(1)(a) of Brussels I.
[59] Art. 9(1)(c) of Brussels I.
[60] Art. 9(1)(b) of Brussels I.
[61] Art. 5 no 3 of Brussels I.
[62] ECJ, Case C-463/06 *Odenbreit* [2007] ECR I-11321.

no connection to Germany, but instead to the Netherlands. The practical scope of this ECJ decision, which is dogmatically questionable,[63] has probably not been sufficiently regarded up until now. This is because, although the *Odenbreit* case was concerned with motor vehicle liability insurance, the decision dealt with Art. 11(2) of Brussels I and every type of liability insurance, including general liability insurance. This means that the home jurisdiction of the victim is made available if the applicable law[64] provides a right of direct action. It should be borne in mind that a right of direct action is provided for all types of liability insurance in some EU Member States. The consequences of the decision in *Odenbreit* for general liability insurance, for example, but also for commercial liability insurance as well as D&O insurance are thus evident.

2. Applicable law

As far as the applicable law is concerned, liability insurance covering risks located in Member States are subject to the rule in Art. 7 of Rome I. There is a special rule for compulsory liability insurance in Art. 7(4).[65] According to Art. 7(4)(a), the policyholder has only fulfilled his duty to obtain insurance if his insurance contract corresponds substantively to the special provisions of the Member States which prescribe the duty to insure. If there are any discrepancies, the law of the Member State which prescribes the duty to insure will prevail. Art. 7(4)(b) permits Member States to subject liability insurance to the law of the Member State which prescribes the duty to insure in its entirety.

The rule dealing with direct claims in Rome II is however more important than the rule governing mandatory liability insurance in Art. 7(4) of Rome I. Where there is a right of direct action in favour of the victim, Art. 18 of Rome II provides an alternative connection to the tort law ap-

---

[63] Criticised, for example by *Helmut Heiss,* Die Direktklage vor dem EuGH: 6 Antithesen zu BGH 29.9.2006 (VI ZR 200/05), Versicherungsrecht 2007, 327; similarly, *Angelika Fuchs,* Internationale Zuständigkeit für Direktklagen, Praxis des internationalen Privat- und Verfahrensrechts 2008, 104.

[64] See Art. 18 of Regulation (EC) 864/2007 of the European Parliament and of the Council of 11 July 2007 on the law applicable to non-contractual obligations (Rome II); in this regard, see below.

[65] As to this provision for instance *Anton K Schnyder,* Versicherungsverträge, in: Christoph Reithmann and Dieter Martiny (eds), Internationales Vertragsrecht (2010) paras 4755 f.

plicable under Rome II and to the insurance contract law applicable under Rome I. Should one of the two laws grant a right of direct action, this right is valid. Two restrictive aspects should of course be highlighted: Art. 18 of Rome II does not apply in Member States which are signatories to the Hague Convention on The Law Applicable to Traffic Accidents. Thus, the similar rule in Art. 9 of the Convention, in effect, applies.[66] Of more significance is the fact that the rule in Art. 18 of Rome II ends up being too narrow. It namely only refers to a right of direct action of a victim in tort against the liability insurer. Such rights of direct action, however, often also exist for claims to damages arising from a contract. Thus, for example, it is possible for a victim suffering loss ensuing from a defective product to directly sue the vendor's liability insurer covering this risk for contractual compensation, which stems from the law concerning guarantees on purchase. Since Rome I does not contain a rule dealing with the right of direct action, there is a gap here which will probably be closed by analogy to Art. 18 of Rome II.

III. Single Market of Liability Insurance

1. Need of policyholders for "euro policies"

In the recent past, the need of policyholders for so-called "euro policies" has been discussed over and again.[67] The discussion concerns either policies which uniformly cover multiple risks situated in different Member States or policies which policyholders can take with them without having to adapt it to the local legal environment when they move their domicile or establishment to a different EU Member State.[68]

There is no doubt that this need of policyholders exists in the area of liability insurance. There is, for example, a commercial need to uniformly insure multiple group companies with their subsidiaries in various EU/

---

[66] As to the relationship of Rome I and The Hague Convention on the law applicable to traffic accidents (1971) see *Helmut Heiss* and *Leander Loacker*, Die Vergemeinschaftung des Kollisionsrechts der außervertraglichen Schuldverhältnisse durch Rom II, Juristische Blätter 2007, 613 (617).

[67] *Jürgen Basedow*, in: Fritz Reichert-Facilides and Anton K Schnyder (eds), Versicherungsrecht in Europa – Kernperspektiven am Ende des 20. Jahrhunderts (2000).

[68] With regard to the problem of a policyholder changing his domicile, see *Helmut Heiss*, Mobilität und Versicherung, Versicherungsrecht 2006, 448.

EEA Member States against liability for commercial risks. The need became visible in the ECJ decision of 12 May 2005 *(Peloux)*.[69] In this decision, the question regarding international jurisdiction in a matter relating to insurance was raised. Looking at the facts of the case on which the decision is based, it becomes clear that a Belgian parent company had concluded an insurance contract covering liability for commercial risks to which both it and its various subsidiaries based in other European Member States were exposed. This was undertaken due to the wish to purchase uniform insurance cover for the entire group.

There are often similar interests in D&O insurance. Group parent companies prefer to conclude uniform contracts for all of the directors and officers in both the parent company and the individual subsidiaries. The same applies to product liability insurance if it is clear to a producer that his products will be brought into circulation on the markets of other EU/EEA Member States.[70] The same need also naturally appears for motor vehicle liability insurance, especially as only corresponding European-wide cover can guarantee the freedom of movement in Europe.[71] For motor vehicle liability insurance, this not only applies to private, but also – if the example of a car rental company is taken – to commercial risks. Especially for car rental companies, there is an interest in uniformly covering the liability risks of the hire cars registered in various EU Member States under one policy.

The creation of such European policies does not pose any supervisory hurdles within Europe, since the home country control principle[72] allows any insurer registered in Europe to carry on its insurance business throughout the whole EU. From the perspective of supervisory law, there is one considerable restriction, which is that the application of the home country control principle is restricted to the EU/EEA Single Market. Yet, companies which are part of a group often require uniform policies far beyond the boundaries of the EU Single Market. In third countries, however, the assumption of cover by an EU liability insurer may encounter supervisory constraints. In particular, a foreign supervisory body may view providing cover to risks located in the third country concerned as an unlawful business activity ("non-admitted problem"). EU law is clearly not in a position

---

[69] Case C-112/03 *Société financière et industrielle du Peloux v Axa Belgium* [2005] ECR I-3727.
[70] Cf Art. 5(1)(c) of Rome II.
[71] See Recital 2 of the consolidated Motor Vehicle Liability Insurance Directive.
[72] See now Title I, Chapter VIII of Directive 2009/138/EC of the European Parliament and of the Council of 25 November 2009 on the taking-up and pursuit of the business of Insurance and Reinsurance (Solvency II) [2009] OJ L335/1.

to solve this problem. The insurance market has, however, developed forms of insurance with which it is hoped that the non-admitted problem can be avoided. In this regard, the magic words are "financial interest cover". To achieve this, a parent company, for example, concludes an insurance contract with an insurance undertaking in its country of establishment. The risk undertaken by the insurer is the balance sheet loss, which arises when the parent company has to internally settle claims for liability *vis-à-vis* subsidiaries domiciled in third countries, ie the parent refunds the subsidiary its liability costs. When the balance sheet loss incurred is assumed by the insurer, the risk is located within the EU/EEA so that a "non-admitted problem" *prima facie* does not arise; functionally however this form of insurance is in effect liability insurance in favour of a subsidiary in third country outside of the EU.

With regard to the insurance contract, it should of course be pointed out that euro policies are only useful if they are recognised by the national insurance contract law of every Member State in which an insured risk is located. To the extent, however, that these laws have an impact on the contract, be it through mandatory provisions to the benefit of the policyholder or be it through mandatory provisions to the benefit of the third party victim, the contents of the euro liability policies will be changed in each of the EU/EEA Member States concerned. This makes the creation of euro policies more difficult.

2. Interest of the insurer in European policies

Insurers, at least those of a certain size, have a clear interest in being able to offer their liability insurance products cross-border and not just merely on domestic markets. Yet, cross-border business activity, at least when dealing with mass risks, leads to the problem that insurers under Art. 7(3) of Rome I must observe mandatory provisions for the protection of policyholders or for the protection of the victim in the country in which the risk is located. Insurers must therefore adapt their liability insurance policies to the mandatory law of each of the countries in which they carry on business.[73] It should of course be highlighted that the problem is less dramatic for the cover of so-called large risks because for such cases the parties are given a free choice of law under Art. 7(2) together with Art. 3 of Rome I. Yet,

---

[73] As to the scope of choice of law see *Anton K. Schnyder,* Versicherungsverträge, in: Christoph Reithmann and Dieter Martiny (eds), Internationales Vertragsrecht (2010) paras 4738 f.

even large risk liability is curbed by the limits of compulsory insurance law, which prevails over any such choice of law under Art. 7(4) of Rome I.

But there is even more: Due to the alternative conflict-of-laws connection of a right of direct action to the benefit of the victim pursuant to Art. 18 of Rome II, insurers must, as far as the direct action is concerned, in addition to the applicable insurance contract law also take into consideration the applicable tort law, which might be more beneficial, but is impossible to predict. This problem of the alternative connection naturally also arises for liability insurers in purely domestic transactions, especially as a policyholder may be exposed to claims for damages in the insurer's country of establishment, which may be subject to a foreign law of torts. In addition, with regard to the insurer's interest in being a provider, the mandatory provisions in liability insurance law, irrespective of whether they serve to protect the policyholder or whether they serve to protect the victim, hinder cross-border activity.

3. Principles of European Insurance Contract Law: A Model Law

a) The PEICL

The Principles of European Insurance Contract Law have been designed as an optional instrument of insurance contract law, which would require their implementation by means of an EU regulation.[74] This instrument wishes to enable insurers to develop their products on the basis of a single legal system, ie that of the PEICL, and to sell them in all of the EU Member States. Demand for such an optional instrument exists in particular for mass risk transactions, where the extensive mandatory connection provided in Art. 7 of Rome I leads to the application of the (mandatory) provisions of the respective country in which the business is being carried on. For the most part, the PEICL are therefore confined to creating mandatory provisions of insurance contract law, which take the place of the national mandatory provisions when the contracting parties choose to exercise this option.[75] The version of the PEICL published in 2009 did not contain any rules for liability insurance; these have however since been drafted. The following,

---

[74] See *Helmut Heiss*, Introduction, in: Jürgen Basedow, John Birds, Malcolm A Clarke, Herman Cousy and Helmut Heiss (eds), Principles of European Insurance Contract Law (PEICL) (2009) I 45 f.
[75] See Article 1:103 PEICL.

cursory remarks are based on the current status of the work on the PEICL, although this is of course subject to change.

b) Liability insurance related definitions in the PEICL

First, liability insurance is defined in the PEICL. It is, however, not defined as an assumption of risk, but rather more broadly as cover of an insured's risk of being exposed to liability claims. The intention behind this broad definition was to ensure that claims made by an insured to defend himself against unjustified liability claims fall within the definition. Liability insurance as defined in the PEICL under Draft Article 14:101 includes defence costs by treating them as expenditure for the mitigation of loss.

In addition to the definition of liability insurance, the PEICL also contain a definition of the term "victim" in Article 1:202 para 4. According to this, "'Victim', in liability insurance, means the person for whose death, injury or loss the insured is liable".

c) Provisions for the protection of the policyholder

The intention of the PEICL is to increase the degree of protection offered to policyholders in liability insurance. Thus, they contain rules which state that prohibitions on recognising a claim (Draft Article 14:104 PEICL) and on assignments (Draft Article 14:105 PEICL) in liability insurance contracts are void. The ineffectiveness of a prohibition on assignments in particular leads to the insured tortfeasor, by assigning his right of recourse to the victim, being in a position to enable the victim to sue the liability insurer directly, even when Draft Article 15:101 PEICL does not provide for such a right of direct action.

To so-called *euromobile* policyholders, the right to be issued written confirmation of any past insurance cases (Draft Article 14:106 para 1 PEICL) is of no less importance. Should an insured move abroad and change to another liability insurer there, the presentation of such written confirmation enables allowance to be made in the new country of residence of any no-claims bonus in his former country of residence. Furthermore, the insurer is obliged to do so according to the PEICL (Draft Article 14:106 para 2).

d) Provisions for the protection of the victim

Protecting the victim is achieved by the PEICL in particular by providing a relatively comprehensive right of direct action (Draft Article 15:101 PEICL): Such a right always exists where compulsory insurance is involved, when the policyholder or the insured goes into insolvency, the policyholder or the insured – where a company is concerned – is put into liquidation, or the victim suffers physical injury.

The direct action exists in accordance with the liability insurance contract and only within its bounds. Generally, an insurer is therefore able to use any defences stipulated in the insurance contract against the victim. Draft Article 15:101 para 2 PEICL, however, subjects compulsory insurance to special provisions.

The victim is especially protected from any detrimental behaviour by the policyholder or the insured following the event of damage or loss. Defences raised by the insurer out of the insurance relationship are always excluded by the second sentence of Draft Article 15:101 para 2 PEICL if they are based on the behaviour of the policyholder or the insured following the event of damage or loss. Similarly, Article 2:303 para 2(c) PEICL excludes the provision of a general right to the policyholder to avoid a liability insurance contract. The reason for this is that liability loss could already have occurred between the contract conclusion and the declaration of revocation, and the policyholder should be prevented from removing insurance cover retrospectively and to the detriment of the victim by exercising the right of revocation.

The policyholder's duty to inform the victim should also be highlighted (Draft Article 15:102 PEICL). The duty relates to any information the victim requires in order to be able to make a direct claim against the insurer. The duty to inform must be fulfilled by the policyholder at the request of the victim.

Likewise, the victim is protected from any collusion between the policyholder and the insurer. Agreements, waivers, payments or equivalent actions which take place following the occurrence of the insured event are ineffective *vis-à-vis* the victim (Draft Article 14:102 PEICL). This rule applies in general; it is not restricted to situations where the victim has a direct claim.

Especially with regard to the right of direct action, the optional instrument of the PEICL of course has inherent limits. In Draft Article 15:101 para 1, the PEICL grant such a right of direct action under certain circumstances. As Draft Article 15:101 para 1(e) PEICL correctly emphasises, the right to a direct claim ensuing from the alternative connection under Art

18 of Rome II not only exists when it is granted by the European regime of the PEICL (the "applicable insurance contract law"), but also whenever the national law of torts so provides. The problem for insurers of always having to take a national law into consideration cannot be eliminated because the PEICL are applied on the basis of an agreement between the policyholder and insurer, to which the third party is normally not a party. Exceptionally, it is however possible to conceive situations in which the victim is involved from the outset in the choice in favour of the PEICL. This is true for D&O insurance, for example, where there is the special feature of the policyholder and the potential victim often being identical. The company by which the directors and officers are employed is the party concerned here. Thus, the potential victim could agree to the application of the PEICL.

4. Conclusion

In addition to the unification of private international law of liability insurance, the Single Market – in the interests of the policyholder and the insurer – requires a uniform liability insurance law. Yet, European conflict of laws considerably hinders the sale of euro policies of liability insurance throughout the EU/EEA. This restrictive effect of the conflict of laws on the Single Market could largely be eliminated using an optional instrument following the template of the PEICL. An optional instrument, however, has its own limitations. The alternative reference to national tort law in Art. 18 of Rome II, for example, cannot be withdrawn.

Part V
Panel Discussion

Statements on the question:
"Are there General Concepts and Principles of Compensation in EU Law?"

Developing General Concepts and Common Principles of EU Tort Law[*]

Wolfgang Wurmnest

I think it is indispensable to develop general concepts and common principles of Union tort law for interpretative purposes and the coherence of Union law. Such principles will provide guidance to national courts. National courts need more guidance as the current body of EU tort law is of a rather fragmentary nature. So how may such principles be developed?

The EU legislator could assist in creating such principles. It could first draft tort law provisions more coherently. But the existing body of tort law legislation has not been drafted in such a manner. For instance, the concept of damage is inconsistently defined in the different directives in the field of tort law.

Second, the EU legislator could – in addition to a more thorough drafting – enact a Community instrument on general principles of tort law – be it binding or non-binding. But the current political discussion on the (academic) Draft Common Frame of Reference indicates that a (political) Common Frame of Reference *including* the field of tort law will not be adopted in the foreseeable future.

Against this background, the formulation of general principles lies – for the time being – in the hands of the European Court of Justice ("the Court"). "Judge-made" principles of EU law will of course never become as coherent and complete as a general body of tort law. The reasons for this are simple: As the EU thus far has only adopted a market-oriented *Sonderdeliktsrecht* (and not a general law of tort), one has to be careful to infer common rules from bases which are quite limited in nature. Moreover, the Court has to decide on the basis of the legislation as it stands and can only in part correct the various technical deficiencies of legislative drafting. Broader principles pronounced by the Court may however help to overcome certain ambiguities.

---

[*] Opening statement of the panel discussion: "Are there General Concepts and Principles of Compensation in EU Law?" The panel discussion was held in Münster on 25th November 2010 as part of the round table discussion on 25th and 26th November 2010, organised by the Centre for European Private Law.

It is important to note that the Court has already begun to develop such common concepts. To give some examples: The calculation of pecuniary damages must include not only actual losses but also loss of future profits, as far as those losses will occur with a reasonable degree of certainty. The compensation to be paid must further usually comprise interest. Victims are also to be compensated for non-pecuniary losses, i.e. damages that cannot be directly measured in money. Moreover, in comparison to certain national jurisdictions, EU law compensates non-pecuniary rather generously.

Even though the Court has begun to develop more general lines of tort law over the years, more guidance would be given to national courts if the Court could set aside its reluctance to analyse cases from a broader private law perspective. Although a judge obviously has to apply the law to the question submitted, there is inevitable leeway to include some reflection on broader principles of law in a judgment.

The example already used in my talk this afternoon shall demonstrate this point. In EU Anti-discrimination law the Court has ruled that the practical effect of the anti-discrimination rules would be weakened considerably if the liability of an employer were made subject to proof of a fault attributable to him. Does this principle also apply to the enforcement of the EU competition rules? The Court – although seized with claims for damages for breach of EU competition law – has declined to rule on this issue. This reluctance does little to enhance legal clarity. Thus, more courage is needed to develop tort law principles that will sufficiently guide national courts when applying Union law.

Why Should One Size Fit All? A Call for a Differentiated Look on the Renewed European Approach Towards Private Enforcement[*]

Konrad Ost
Peter Gussone

I. Introduction

Private enforcement has been prominently on the agenda of Commissioner Almunia's predecessor Neelie Kroes. And it is well known that the new Commission will continue to summon support for a coherent EU framework in this regard.

The public is well aware that Germany, including the Bundeskartellamt, did not agree with some of the proposals that were outlined in the 2008 White Paper and the following proposal for a directive last year. The arguments will be presented below. The Bundeskartellamt therefore welcomes the apparently more cautious approach by Commissioner Almunia, who stated in March this year:

> "Regarding private enforcement, I will consider very carefully all the opinions on the table since our first draft and the report of the Parliament, before putting forward proposals."[1]

Firstly, the paper will review the status quo – where do we stand with private enforcement today? Secondly the paper will briefly comment on the most controversial issues in the debate. It will concludes with some expectations for any new proposal at European level.

---

[*] All views are personal to the authors.
[1] Speech by Commissioner Almunia at the International Forum on EU Competition Law Tuesday 9 March 2010, Brussels.

II. The state of private enforcement in Germany

There is the widespread impression that private enforcement is completely underdeveloped in Europe. In the same way, Germany is sometimes viewed as a jurisdiction where private enforcement plays second – or third – fiddle to public enforcement. The picture, however, is a lot more complex and it is important to notice that private enforcement is gaining more and more ground in Germany.

This is all too clear from the case numbers, with more than 400 damages actions between 2004 and 2008. This information is well known and the Bundeskartellamt certainly had its share in communicating to others the success story of German private damages actions.

More important is what one hears from lawyers and the business world: nowadays they strive to have private actions filed in either the United Kingdom or Germany. Apparently the German system has gained attractiveness. The improvements to the legal conditions brought about by the 7th Amendment of the Act against Restraints of Competition have certainly contributed to this development.

The most important changes with regard to private enforcement are as follows:

- clarification that competitors as well as customers are entitled to claim damages; no more need for the violation of competition law to be directed at the plaintiff
- defendant has burden of proof for passing-on defence; in any case, it is up to the courts to assess whether the set-off satisfies the purpose of compensation and does not unduly exonerate the tortfeasor (cf. the "adjustment of benefits" principle – Vorteilsausgleichung)
- rules on civil procedure allow for an estimate of the damage by the court
- the decisions on the merits of the BKartA, Commission and other EU NCAs are binding in any ensuing court damages proceedings
- limitation period suspended during administrative proceedings

The German courts and their decisions have also helped private enforcement on its way. The Higher Regional Court in Düsseldorf accepted the transfer of damages claims to a third party which was not affected but wanted to enforce these claims collectively.[2] The Federal Court of Justice rejected the non-admission complaint afterwards.[3] Business claimants, such

---

[2] *Oberlandesgericht Düsseldorf* (OLG Düsseldorf), WuW/E DE-R 2311-2317.
[3] *Bundesgerichtshof* (BGH), GRUR-RR 2009, 319.

as the well known Cartel Damages Claims S.A., have had legal certainty ever since. Business and private claimants increasingly sue undertakings that have infringed competition law.

Most of the decisions against hardcore-cartels worldwide are followed up with private actions. These concern cartels in the ready-mixed concrete, cement, paper, bleaching agent, vitamin, marine hose, airfreight and hydrogen peroxide industries – to name but a few prominent examples.

When assessing the outcome of private actions, different remedies have to be taken into account. The Commission has focused on damages actions in the past, neglecting other types of antitrust remedies available. Private enforcement, however, can also be an effective and reconciliatory tool. As a matter of fact, damages claims lead to expensive and lengthy proceedings. One could speculate that victims prefer, e.g., injunction to compensation in some cases as this promises more certain and more immediate relief. Also, small and medium-sized enterprises are sometimes neither in the position nor it is in their interest to sue their suppliers. Sound and reliable business relations and secured future supply channels seem to have priority in these cases.[4]

In Germany, claims for monetary compensation can be asserted by damages actions and unjust enrichment actions. Claims for injunctive relief, voidness, conclusion or continuation of a contract directly concern the bilateral relationship between plaintiff and defendant. A recent study on the development of private enforcement in Germany points out the inherent difficulties in analyzing the data available on private antitrust cases.[5] The author assumes:

> "... the observed amount of antitrust litigation in Germany seems to be rather the tip of the iceberg than the maximum number of antitrust disputes."[6]

It is the statistical data and empirical evidence for private enforcement that are obviously lagging behind and not the legal framework. This is also due to the fact that private enforcement claims are usually settled either pre-trial

---

[4] Cf. *Andreas Möhlenkamp*, Private Schadenersatz- und Sammelklagen im Kartellrecht – ein Blick aus dem Mittelstand, Österreichische Zeitschrift für Kartell- und Wettbewerbsrecht (ÖZK) 2010, 163 ff.

[5] *Sebastian Peyer*, Myths and Untold Stories – Private Antitrust Enforcement in Germany, CCP Working Paper 10-12, 2010.

[6] *Peyer*, CCP Working Paper 2010, 53.

or in court. In fact, according to practitioners, the majority of cases in this field are settled.

III. Some comments on the most controversial issues

The story has been told several times, but as long as the Commission has not published a new proposal, the points of contention remain. The paper briefly touches on the issues of collective redress, inter partes evidence disclosure, the passing-on defence, and the interaction between actions for damages and leniency and settlement programs.

1. Collective redress and opt-out

Shaping the instruments for collective redress is a delicate task. Abusive litigation leading to U.S.-style class actions has – as it is incompatible with European legal standards – to be avoided from the outset. Especially opt-out claims are missing the target. Where the injured party cannot be named, the claim ultimately entails skimming-off the proceeds from the cartel rather than compensating the individual damage occurred.

While tort law is based on the idea of individual compensation, the disgorgement of profits is better entrusted to independent and objective public enforcement authorities.

2. Inter partes evidence disclosure

Another critical point is access to evidence as there is an intrinsic information asymmetry between plaintiff and defendant. Again, the US with their discovery proceeding should not be a role-model for us. Such far-reaching disclosure rules facilitate mutual investigation by which access to competitors' business secrets is gained. There is the notion that discovery-like disclosure rules would encourage abuse of the instrument. Even without sufficient evidence against them, undertakings might agree to a settlement in order to avoid having their business secrets disclosed.

This creates a strong disincentive to cooperate with the cartel authority and apply for leniency. A first-mover disadvantage, one may call it, as the first undertaking in the proceeding is the first to be threatened by disclosure.

3. Passing-on defence

The passing-on defense is a controversial issue. The Commission did see the intrinsic problems that arise if the defendant is entitled to invoke the passing-on defence and, at the same time, the indirect purchaser can rely on the rebuttable presumption that the illegal overcharge was passed on to him in its entirety. But the Commission has yet failed to offer a practical solution to the dilemma. To quote from the Working Paper accompanying the White Paper:

> "In case of joint, parallel or consecutive actions brought by purchasers at different levels in the distribution chain, national courts are encouraged to use whatever mechanism under national or Community law at their disposal in order to avoid under- or over-compensation of the harm caused by a competition law infringement."[7]

As long as these mechanisms remain undefined (as is the case in Germany)[8] the risk of multiple damages remains as well. There is a need for more economic evidence that cartel-induced surcharges are generally passed on to the last market level before a statutory regulation of the passing-on defence can be introduced.

4. Interaction between actions for damages and leniency programs

The strengthening of private enforcement is a two-edged sword. While private actions are an important complement to public antitrust enforcement, the framework has to be designed cautiously, balancing the interests of both sides. Only recently, this approach has been recognized by the European Court of Justice in preliminary ruling in the "Pfleiderer" case.[9] The question had arisen whether the provisions of EU competition law must be interpreted as meaning that access to file can be restricted for parties adversely

---

[7] Commission staff working paper accompanying the White paper on damages actions for breach of the EC antitrust rules {COM(2008) 165 final} {SEC (2008) 405} {SEC (2008) 406}, ref. 225.

[8] *Kammergericht Berlin* (KG Berlin), WuW/E DE-R 2773-2788 accepting joint and several creditor vs. *Oberlandesgericht Karlsruhe* (OLG Karlsruhe), 11.6.2010, denying passing-on and allowing only the direct purchaser to sue.

[9] *Court of Justice*, C-360/09 Pfleiderer, judgment of 14 June 2011.

affected by a cartel. In the "Pfleiderer" case the Bundeskartellamt had, as laid down in its leniency program, denied access to the leniency applications and all documents voluntarily submitted with it. The Court found that EU competition law does not preclude full access to file for affected persons seeking damages. At the same time it is up to the national courts to weigh the "respective interests in favour of disclosure of the information and in favour of the protection of that information provided voluntarily by the applicant for leniency".[10] The Court thus underlined the need for a general and careful balancing of interests in this regard based on the respective national law. Far-fetching opt-out actions for instance are likely to threaten the effectiveness of leniency programs. With the threat of having to face claims for damages that may well exceed the fine, undertakings will think twice before exposing themselves to this risk by triggering proceedings.

Most of the success in fighting hard-core cartels in the past years stems from leniency programs. It is also in the interest of private enforcement not to undermine its attractiveness. The prospects of success in follow-on damages actions are much better than in stand-alone claims.

IV. Outlook

In the past weeks the discussion about an EU framework for private enforcement has erupted again. It has now become apparent that the European approach to collective redress is being reviewed. A public consultation is said to start in 2011. At the beginning of October 2010 the Commissioners Reding, Almunia and Dalli published a joint information note "Towards a Coherent European Approach to Collective Redress: Next Steps".[11]

The note identifies some overarching principles for the design of a coherent European framework for collective redress. The Commissioners reiterate their support for effective compensation for everyone having suffered damages. The right to compensation should be effectively and efficiently obtained, allowing for a single collective redress procedure in a mass claim situation. Thereby, the litigation costs for the parties are reduced and judicial and out-of-court schemes are more efficient. Another important principle is that any European approach should avoid abusive litigation from the outset. Also, means of alternative dispute resolutions should be taken into account and may become a legal requirement. The Commissioners further

---

[10] *Court of Justice*, C-360/09 Pfleiderer, ref. 30.
[11] SEC(2010) 1192.

require the ability to enforce collective judgements throughout the EU. This would need a minimum harmonization of civil and procedural law in order to make such judgements enforceable in the whole Union. Finally, the note underlines the need for adequate means of financing to allow citizens and businesses to have access to justice.

There are still some doubts whether the reasons for acting now are convincing. Empirical data and statistics on private enforcement in the EU seem to be, at least, insufficient. Why not evaluate and assess the experiences with existing national instruments of collective redress[12] first before defining common principles that might be alien to Member States' legal traditions and litigation culture? As the Commission envisages only minimum standards and not full harmonization the arguments based on the idea of a level playing field or the danger of forum shopping are not convincing.

In any case, previous mistakes have to be avoided taking into account the issues outlined above. Given the complex and diverse situation in 27 different Member States with different legal frameworks, principles, and traditions, a one-size-fits-all approach is quite ambitious.

---

[12] For instance, in Germany the Capital Investors Model Proceedings Act (Kapitalanleger-Musterverfahrensgesetz) tries to reconcile collective redress with fundamental German principles of procedural law. In Sweden, the "Lag om grupprättegång", law on class actions, provides for individuals, associations, and public institutions to seek redress with binding effect for all members of the class. The Netherlands have introduced a similar law, the "Wet collectieve afwikkeling massaschade" in 2005.